Contrastive Rhetoric

Contrastive Rhetoric
Issues, Insights, and Pedagogy

Edited by
Nagwa Kassabgy
Zeinab Ibrahim
Sabiha Aydelott

The American University in Cairo Press
Cairo   New York

Dar el Kutub No. 16138/03
ISBN 977 424 829 5

Designed by Hugh Hughes/AUC Press Design Center
Printed in Egypt

This edition is dedicated to our husbands

Raouf Elhamy

Hassan Mansour

John R. Aydelott

Contents

Cases in Writing/Translation

Diglossia

Studies in Second Language Acquisition

Pragmatics

About the Contributors

Nahwat A. El-Arousy is an associate professor of applied linguistics in the English Department, Faculty of Arts, Helwan University. She received her B.A. from Ain Shams University, Cairo, her M.A. TEFL from the American University in Cairo, and her Ph.D. in sociolinguistics and pragmatics from Cairo University. She has conducted research in the area of psycholinguistics and teaching methodologies.

Sabiha T. Aydelott is currently teaching English as a Foreign Language in the Academic Bridge Program at the Qatar Foundation in Doha. She has a doctorate in education, with specialization in reading and writing, from the University of Tennessee, Knoxville. She has taught in Pakistan, Iran, Turkey, Egypt, and the United States. Her research interests are in reading assessment, diagnosis and remediation, comparative studies, and reading and writing across the curriculum. She is the author and editor of several publications.

Reem Bassiouney graduated from Alexandria University, where she holds a teaching post in English language and linguistics. She has taught Arabic as a foreign language at both Alexandria and Oxford universities. She graduated from Oxford University with an M.Phil. in general linguistics and a D.Phil. in general linguistics. She has taught Arabic for eight years, and has taught linguistics at the University of Cambridge for one year. She currently teaches in the Foreign and Commonwealth Office and in Somerville College, Oxford.

Ulla Connor is professor of English, adjunct professor in Women's Studies and Philanthropic Studies, adjunct professor of Philanthropic Studies, and director of the Indiana Center for Intercultural Communications at Indiana University–Purdue University. Her fields of specialization and research include applied linguistics and second-language teaching, contrastive rhetoric, linguistic and rhetorical analysis of texts, intercultural communication, the language of fund-raising, and business English. She is the author and editor of several publications, and has presented papers at various national and international conferences.

Mohammed Farghal is professor of linguistics and translation at Kuwait University. He has published widely in such international research journals as the *Journal of Pragmatics, Multilingua,* and *Anthropological Linguistics.* He has supervised a large number of MA theses in linguistics and translation. Currently, his interests center on semantics and pragmatics, sociolinguistics, and translation theory.

Ola Hafez is an associate professor of linguistics at Cairo University. Her areas of research are teaching methodology and discourse analysis in English and Arabic. Her recent work is on integration of loanwords into Arabic, voice in novels about Egypt, and discourse analysis of drama dialogue, public speaking, and the press.

Martin Harfmann is currently a German Academic Exchange lecturer in German language and literature at the University of Jordan. He studied Arabic, applied linguistics, and history at the University of Hamburg, and obtained his M.A. in 2001. He did research at the Goethe Institute in Damascus in 1994, at the German Cultural Center in Gaza in 1996, and at the Goethe Institute in Ramallah in 1998–99. In 2000–01 he participated in a research project at the University of Hamburg that focused on translation analysis.

Mona Kamel Hassan holds a B.A. in English language and literature from Cairo University and an M.A. in TEFL from the American University in Cairo. She has been teaching at the Arabic Language Institute of the American University in Cairo since 1994. Her research interests are in the field of pragmatics.

Zeinab Ibrahim is a sociolinguist. She has been in the field of teaching Arabic as a foreign language since the 1980s. She received her Ph.D. from Georgetown University and has written several articles on language variation, attitudes, and culture. She served as the Arabic Language Institute (ALI) coordinator, then as executive director of the Center for Arabic Studies Abroad (CASA) while teaching at the American University in Cairo. She is currently president of the American Association of Teachers of Arabic (AATA).

Jülide İnözü is a graduate of Bosphorus University in Istanbul. She received her M.A. and Ph.D. in English Language Teaching from Çukurova University, Turkey. She is an instructor in the Department of English Language Teaching at Çukurova University and is interested in instructional materials evaluation and adaptation, critical reading, and cognitive development.

Georgette Ioup teaches applied linguistics and coordinates the ESL writing program at the University of New Orleans, USA. She is also president of the Louisiana Teachers of English to Speakers of Other Languages affiliate, LaTESOL. Her research focuses on psycholinguistic aspects of second language acquisition.

Nagwa Kassabgy is an instructor in the English Language Institute at the American University in Cairo (AUC). She obtained her M.A. in TEFL from the American University in Cairo. She is also involved in teacher training and has done research on English as a Foreign Language (EFL) reading, vocabulary acquisition, and teaching grammar. She is a founding member of the Board of EGYPTESOL, an affiliate of the international organization of Teachers of English to Speakers of Other Languages (TESOL) and is a published author and editor.

Miranda Y.P. Lee obtained her advanced degrees in translation and linguistics at the University of Hong Kong and University College London, England, and is currently teaching bilingual communication at the Hong Kong Polytechnic University. Her research interests include contrastive rhetoric of English and Chinese, bilingual writing performance, and L2 writing.

Zuhal Okan is assistant professor in the English Language Teaching Department, Faculty of Education, Çukurova University, Turkey.

Mona M. Osman teaches at the German University in Cairo. Her particular fields of interest are pragmatics and cross-cultural communication and miscommunication.

Andreas Papapavlou was assistant professor of psycholinguistics in the TEFL M.A. program at the American University in Cairo, Egypt, from 1978 to 1984, has taught in several other universities, and since 1991 has been associate professor of psycholinguistics at the University of Cyprus. He has published numerous articles in various international journals and his research interests are in language acquisition, language attitudes, language borrowing, and bilingualism.

Paul B. Stevens is an associate professor of linguistics in the TEFL M.A. program at the American University in Cairo. His fields of interest are sociolinguistics and pragmatics, with a particular interest in cross-cultural communication and miscommunication.

Hülya Yumru received her M.A. in TEFL from Bilkent University, her M.Sc. in TEFL from Aston University in Birmingham, and her Ph.D. in ELT from Çukurova University, Turkey. She is an instructor in the Department of English Language Teaching at Çukurova University and is interested in constructivist research on teacher thinking.

Izzedin al-Zou'bi is a lieutenant-colonel in the Jordan Armed Forces, occupying the position of chief of the English Department in the JFA's Language Institute. He received an M.A. in translation studies from Yarmouk University in Jordan in 2000. He has taught Arabic in the United Kingdom. His interests center on teaching and translation.

Preface

The field of contrastive rhetoric has greatly evolved and developed over the last few decades, which has led researchers, linguists, and academics to continue with their study and exploration of various issues related to it. In an effort to further augment understanding of this field, this volume presents the research and discussion of various scholars and researchers. The essays included in this volume are a collection of studies that we, the editors, feel will provide valuable insight into the field. This volume explores the field of contrastive rhetoric—the study of how a person's first language (L1) and culture influence his/her acquisition of another language. The field of contrastive rhetoric encourages inquiry into various levels of discourse and text. It focuses on the conventions and rhetorical structures of L1 and their influence on the usage of another language. This field also studies the cognitive dimensions of transfer in relation to both writing and speech. Ulla Connor, in her book *Contrastive Rhetoric: Cross-cultural Aspects of Second Language Writing*, defines contrastive rhetoric as "an area of research in second language acquisition that identifies problems in composition encountered by second language writers and, by referring to the rhetorical strategies of the first language, attempts to explain them."

Contrastive Rhetoric: Issues, Insights, and Pedagogy contains four sections. The first section focuses on contrastive rhetoric and cases in writing/translation, and opens with an article by Ulla Connor in which she discusses the role of contrastive rhetoric in examining differences and similarities in writing across cultures. She looks at contrastive rhetoric in the past and the direction toward which it is currently moving. She points out that although in its first twenty years it was mainly concerned with student essay writing, contrastive rhetoric today contributes to knowledge about preferred patterns of writing in many English-for-specific-purposes situations. Its goal continues to be that of helping teachers, students, and professionals around the world. She surveys some of the more recent developments in an effort to discern the shape of contrastive rhetoric's emerging research and teaching paradigms. Miranda Lee, whose article is also part of this section, provides pedagogic insights into contrastive rhetoric that aid the enhancement of English writing for advanced second-language (L2) learners. She compares the different rhetorical devices adopted by native speakers and Hong Kong students in the writing of English narratives. Mohammed Farghal and Izzeddin al-Zou'bi examine the definite article in translation with reference to the citation of animal names in the Holy Qur'an. They provide examples from three translations and evaluate them critically in terms of definitiveness. Martin Harfmann compares German written communication to Arabic written communication, provides evidence of similarities and differences between them, and attempts to explain them.

The second section focuses on issues related to diglossia. Andreas Papapavlou investigates the verbal fluency of speakers in a bi-dialectal setting who normally use two codes in their daily interactions. Specifically, he a) examines whether the verbal fluency of Greek Cypriots in using Standard Modern Greek is lagging behind that of mainland Greeks, and b) identifies those factors that are perceived to be affecting the verbal fluency of Cypriots. Mona K. Hassan investigates the speech acts of apology and thanking in both classical and colloquial Arabic as used by both native and non-native speakers of Arabic. She discusses the implications of the findings of her study for the pedagogy of teaching Arabic as a foreign language. Reem Bassiouney provides evidence that the mixing between Standard Arabic and Egyptian Arabic varieties by native speakers is not haphazard but is governed by syntactic and pragmatic rules. Her study implies that those rules should be incorporated into the teaching materials for students of colloquial Arabic.

The focus of the third section is second language acquisition. Georgette Ioup discusses the ongoing controversy in L2 writing, which is concerned with the value of overt grammatical correction, one side arguing that it is beneficial, the other claiming that it is useless. She provides examples of both sides, citing studies to support their respective positions. She uses cognitive arguments to argue that both positions are valid, and, therefore, grammar correction can be useful. Zuhal Okan discusses language-learning strategies as they relate to the principles of constructivist learning and shows how the framework helps raise students' awareness of their own L2 learning. Hülya Yumru and Jülide İnözü focus on how to initiate improvement in students' writing abilities through actively involving them in identifying and analyzing problems in their written products. They go on to discuss the changes in students' perceptions and how this is reflected in their written products.

The final section of the book focuses on pragmatics. Ola Hafez looks at hyperbolic expressions in Egyptian Arabic and British English. She states that hyperbolic expressions are idiomatic expressions that have a universal language, though the "specific formulaic expressions differ from one language to another." She presents a taxonomy of "equivalent" hyperbolic expressions from Arabic and English, discussing their functions and their linguistic and cultural differences and similarities, and points out implications for language teaching and translation. Mona Osman and Paul Stevens provide a report of a study conducted by them which examines the relationship between the degree of English-language proficiency of groups of native-speaking and non-native-speaking subjects, on the one hand, and the level of politeness and directness in expressing apologies, on the other. Their study also examines whether there is communication between L1 and L2 speakers. Nahwat El-Arousy investigates hedging as a speech act in Arabic, including the use of "vague" expressions and modality.

We believe this book provides a valuable contribution to the field of contrastive rhetoric and furthers our understanding of second language acquisition. It is also our hope that this volume will be valuable to language teachers, applied linguists, and those researching issues related to second-language acquisition and contrastive rhetoric.

We would like to thank Yehia El Ezabi, John Aydelott, Mahmoud Farag, and Neil Hewison for their continued support and encouragement, without which this volume would not have been published.

The phonological and phonetic transcriptions of Arabic and Greek in this book are given in the International Phonetic Alphabet.

Contrastive Rhetoric

Old and New Directions

Ulla Connor

Contrastive rhetoric examines differences and similarities in writing across cultures. It considers texts from several significant aspects, for example, as products and, sometimes, in their relationship to contexts. Although mainly concerned in its first thirty years with student essay writing, the discipline today contributes to knowledge about preferred patterns of writing in many other English-for-specific-purposes situations. Undeniably, it has had an appreciable impact on our understanding of cultural differences in writing; and it has had, and will have, an effect on teaching.

This essay will consider some of the possible future directions contrastive rhetoric may take, especially as it increasingly emphasizes the rhetorical aspects of texts (especially audience and authorship) as much as and perhaps even more than the linguistic. First, the goals, methods, and accomplishments of research in contrastive rhetoric during the past thirty years will be briefly reviewed. In a book on this subject (Connor 1996), I showed how the discipline expanded from its early beginnings as the study of paragraph organization in ESL student essay writing (Kaplan 1966) to an interdisciplinary domain of second language acquisition with rich theoretical underpinnings in both linguistics and rhetoric. The second section of the chapter will discuss how contrastive rhetoric has been pursued with varying aims and methods within different types of institutions in addition to composition studies. Examples will be given from research conducted in EFL situations in Europe. Finally, recent criticisms of contrastive rhetoric and their effects on changing currents in the field will be surveyed. The new currents involve innovative views of culture, literacy, and critical pedagogy and their influence on contrastive rhetoric. However, before

discussing the impact and possible future of the discipline, it may be helpful to look at some concrete examples of the many differences in writing
across cultures which contrastive rhetoric has actually examined.
The following examples represent two genres in professional writing,
job application letters and grant proposals. The first consists of a job application letter written in English for a simulated job by a Flemish-speaking
college student and a letter written by a U.S. college student in the same
simulated job application process. The letters come from a large computerized corpus collected at Indiana University in Indianapolis during the
last ten years (See Connor *et al.* 1995a; and Upton and Connor, 2001).

Flemish applicant:
Dear Dr. Davis
    In reply to your advertisement in which you offer a business
education Internship at your Indiana University, I would like to
apply for the job.
    I am doing my second year the Antwerp University of
Economics and you will find a full account of my qualifications
on the attached personal record sheet.
    If you feel that my qualifications meet with your require-
ments, I shall be pleased to be called for an interview.
    Sincerely yours

U.S. applicant:
Dear Sirs:
    Dr. Ken Davis, Professor of English W-331 at Indiana
University–Purdue University at Indianapolis, has provided me
with your job description for the position of Assistant to the
Tourist Information Manager for the City of Antwerp, Belgium.
This position greatly interests me because in [sic] encompasses
both my work experience and my interest in international culture, as indicated on the attached resume.
    I have had over twelve years experience in the public rela-
tions/marketing field. During that time, I have served as the
Marketing Director for a major Indianapolis chiropractic clinic
with responsibilities for developing marketing plans and public
relations venues for four clinics. I also assisted with, produced
and directed a local radio talk show for the clinic. My employment duties have included a variety of coordination duties for
clients and dignitaries, including travel and hotel accommoda-
tions. As an assistant to the Practice Development Director at
a major Indianapolis law firm, my duties included organization

of client receptions, travel arrangements for attorneys and clients, and intercommunication with attorneys and clients, some of whom have been in foreign countries.

I have a special personal interest in European culture, based upon my experience as a host parent for Youth for Understanding international youth exchange program. During my involvement with this group, I have hosted children from Denmark, Finland and Germany, as well as Chile and Japan.

I will be available for interviews at any time. I may be reached at my place of business at (317) XXX-XXXX from 8:00 a.m. (USA time) until 5:30 p.m., Monday through Friday, or at home at (317) XXX-XXXX at any time.

Thank you for your review of this application.

Sincerely,

The Flemish letter is shorter, more to the point. The first brief sentence performs the speech act of application, the next sentence mentions the student's university status and states that the applicant's credentials are listed on an attached résumé, and the last sentence expresses a desire for an interview. The U.S. letter, on the other hand, uses a large number of words to perform the same functions; the most noteworthy part is the lengthy discussion of the candidate's credentials applicable to the job even though a résumé is enclosed with this application as well. Furthermore, the applicant adds various types of information not seen in the Flemish letter. Thus, in the first paragraph the applicant describes how he or she is especially suited for the position and how his/her background would benefit the job; this line of reasoning is expanded in the third paragraph of the letter. Finally, the U.S. applicant includes information on how to be contacted for an interview. Also noteworthy is the polite expression of thanks at the end of the letter. Clearly, cultural differences in expectations about what a job application demands will affect generic form.

The second example of cross-cultural differences in writing comes from a set of European Union grant proposals written by European scientists. Instead of focusing on the scientific content of the proposals, this example highlights another section in the proposals, namely, the personal section, in which the competence of the researchers is emphasized. The first example is a short biographical statement written by a Finnish scientist. Here, the scientist lists his or her appointments as well as the number of theses and dissertations supervised and papers published. No evaluation of background and experience relative to the project is apparent.

In contrast, the second illustration is a biography of a Swedish researcher. The statement is not a mere list of qualifications; instead, two strong positive appraisals are included—"a very distinguished academic record," "the department has excellent facilities."

> Prof. N.N. joined the Department of . . . in 19xx. He has been involved in X in Finland and abroad since 19xx. During 19xx–19xx he acted as the head of . . . On joining U. University, N.N. initiated a research and teaching program focused mainly on the effects of E. on the quality of Y. He has recently been appointed Assisting Co-leader of the Unesco-sponsored project, which is aimed at . . . At present two Ph.D. theses and five M.Sc. thesis projects are being carried. A number of abstracts have been published, some of which are mentioned in the list of publications below and the manuscripts of some of these are being in different stages of preparation for publication in international journals.

> Professor N.N. has a very distinguished academic record with over 150 publications in scientific journals, books, and conference proceedings since 19xx including 80 publications in the last eight years. He has made over 65 presentations (oral and posters) at international meetings and over 20 at national scientific symposia, conferences and workshops, including several invited and plenary lectures since 19xx. He has led over 20 research grants and contracts as principal investigator and is a member of over 12 boards and scientific and technical committees. He has also undertaken consulting activities in relation to industrial problems of P. His teaching activities include courses in chemistry, processes in P and population control since 19xx. He has supervised 20 graduate students (Ph.D.) since 19xx. The Department has excellent facilities for experimental studies of environmental systems, presently focused on . . . 25 theses have been submitted in the last x years. Additional members of the proposer's team will include Dr. A.A., Professor B.B., Dr. C.C., and Polish and German Contacts.

Early History of Contrastive Rhetoric

Contrastive rhetoric has been defined as an area of research in second language acquisition that identifies problems in composition encountered by second-language writers. It attempts to explain these problems by referring to the rhetorical strategies of the first language (Connor 1996:5). Initiated thirty years ago in applied linguistics by Robert Kaplan, contrastive rhetoric maintains that, to the degree that language and writing are cultural phenomena, different cultures have different rhetorical tendencies. Furthermore, the linguistic patterns and rhetorical conventions of the first language often transfer to writing in ESL and thus cause interference. It is important to distinguish this concern from potential interference at the level of grammar. In contrastive rhetoric, the interference manifests itself—as we have seen in the examples cited above—by rhetorical strategies, including differences in content.

Kaplan's (1966) study was the first serious attempt by a U.S. applied linguist to explain the written styles of ESL students as opposed to patterns of L2 speech. Kaplan's pioneering study analyzed the organization of paragraphs in ESL student essays and identified five types of paragraph development. He claimed that Anglo-European expository essays follow a linear development, Semitic languages use parallel coordinate clauses, and that Oriental languages prefer an indirect approach and come to the point at the end, while in Romance languages and in Russian, essays employ a degree of digressiveness and extraneous material that would seem excessive to a writer of English.

As is well-known, Kaplan's early contrastive rhetoric has been criticized as being too ethnocentric and as privileging the writing of native English speakers, as well as for dismissing linguistic and cultural differences in writing among different languages, e.g., lumping Chinese, Thai, and Korean speakers in one Oriental group. Kaplan himself (Connor and Kaplan 1987) modified his earlier position, moving away from what could be described as a Whorfian interpretation, namely, that particular rhetorical patterns exclusively reflect patterns of thinking in L1. Instead, as compared to his 1966 position, he now holds that cross-cultural differences in writing can be explained by different conventions of writing, which are learned, rather than acquired.

However, Kaplan's earlier model, which was concerned with paragraph organization, was useful in accounting for cultural differences in essays written by college students for academic purposes. It also introduced the linguistic world to a real, if basic, insight: writing was culturally influenced in interesting and complex ways. Nevertheless, the model was not particularly successful in describing writing for academic and professional purposes. Nor was it successful in describing composing processes across cultures.

Research Methods

In its earlier years, contrastive rhetoric was heavily based in applied linguistics and text analysis. In the 1980s, contrastive rhetoricians included text analysis as a tool to describe the conventions of writing in English and to provide analytical techniques with which to compare writing in the students' first and second languages. Volumes edited in 1987 (Connor and Kaplan), 1988 (Purves), and 1990 (Connor and Johns) typically included several chapters with a text analytic emphasis, especially methods of analyzing cohesion, coherence, and the discourse superstructures of texts. A text analytic approach was also adopted in such large international projects of student writing as the International Education Achievement (IEA) study and the Nordtext project. The IEA study compared high school students' writing in their mother tongues at three different grade levels in fourteen different countries. The Nordtext project involved linguists in the Nordic countries whose interest was in EFL writing. Each project was designed to create useful models for instructional practice, and each was heavily text-based.

To sum up the research paradigm of the 1980s (reviewed in Connor 1996), it is fair to say that text analytic models with less and more of text boundedness characterized the field along with the attempt to develop measurable and teachable models. The efforts of contrastive rhetoric in the 1980s and 1990s were consistent with the TESOL practitioners' desire to develop the techniques and methods of teaching and research specifically designed for L2 learners as opposed to the replication of L1 models. The attempts of contrastive rhetoric to develop analytic, quantifiable methods paralleled other movements in the ESL/EFL language teaching profession.

Contrastive studies of academic and professional genres and the socialization into these genres of second-language writers were thus a natural development in L2 writing research. Following the lead of L1 writing research and pedagogy, where the 1970s were said to be the decade that discovered the composing process and the 1980s the decade that discovered the role of social construction in composing, empirical research on L2 writing in the 1990s became increasingly concerned with social processes in cross-cultural undergraduate writing groups (Carson and Nelson 1994, 1996; Connor and Asenavage 1994; Nelson and Carson 1998), about the initiation and socialization processes that graduate students go through to become literate professionals in their graduate and professional discourse communities (Belcher 1994; Casanave 1995; Connor and Kramer 1995; Connor and Mayberry 1995; Prior 1995; and Swales 1990), and, finally, about the processes and products of L2 academics and professionals writing in English as a second or foreign language for publication and other professional purposes (Belcher and Connor 2001; Braine 1998; Connor *et al.* 1995b; Connor and Mauranen 1999; Flowerdew 1999; and Gosden 1992).

Despite the reliance on the textual analysis of cohesion and coherence patterns in a great deal of contrastive rhetorical research, some researchers in contrastive rhetoric had early on questioned the adequacy of purely text-based analyses. For example, Hinds (1987) proposed a new analytic system: the distribution of responsibility between readers and writers; that is, the amount of effort expended by writers to make texts cohere through transitions and other uses of metatext. Thus, Hinds refers to Japanese texts as reader responsible as opposed to texts which are writer responsible. And in much of my own work on contrastive rhetoric in the 1980s, I was involved in building a comprehensive model of texts, one which integrated rhetorical analyses with linguistically-oriented discourse analyses. For example, in a cross-cultural study of writing, which compared argumentative writing in students' essays from three English-speaking countries, the rhetorician Janice Lauer and I developed a linguistic/rhetorical system that helped quantify both linguistic features in essays (such as cohesion, coherence, and discourse organization) and rhetorical features (including the three classical persuasive appeals—logos, pathos, ethos—and Toulmin's 1958 argument model of claim, data, and warrant (Connor and Lauer 1985, 1988).

One could conclude even from such studies as the above that the measures developed in the 1980s still largely focused on texts rather than on the processes by which they were produced. However, research in the 1990s that used a contrastive frame began to include the socialization processes of academic and professional genres (Connor and Kramer 1995; Connor and Mayberry 1995; Swales 1990, and Matsuda 1997). Matsuda was critical of the "static" theories of texts in contrastive rhetoric and proposed a "dynamic" model of L2 writing for examining how writers' and readers' linguistic, cultural, and educational backgrounds as well as conventions of discourse communities might be negotiated through interactions mediated by texts.

Major Accomplishments of the Past Thirty Years

Significant changes have taken place in contrastive rhetoric in the past thirty-plus years. In my 1996 book, I suggested that contrastive rhetoric had taken new directions in the following domains: 1. contrastive text linguistics, 2. the study of writing as a cultural–educational activity, 3. classroom-based studies of writing, and 4. contrastive genre-specific studies, including a variety of genres composed for a variety of purposes such as journal articles, business reports, letters of application, grant proposals, and editorials.

A sample study from each of the above listed subgenres of contrastive rhetoric illustrates the focus of each domain.

1. In text linguistics in the 1980s, perhaps the work with the most impact was by the late John Hinds, who compared patterns of coherence across Japanese texts and texts in English. Hinds found that many newspaper columns in Japan followed the ancient organizational pattern of ki-shoo-ten-ketsu, a four-step process that roughly translates to the following: begin your argument, develop it, turn to material with a connection but not direct association with the text, and conclude. In reading direct translations of Japanese writing in various genres, native English speakers found the introduction of the "ten" component of the ki-shoo-ten-ketsu pattern incoherent. Based on this research, Hinds (1987) suggested that Japanese writing is more "reader responsible," meaning that readers need to work harder to construct the meaning of a text than in "writer responsible" writing such as English expository prose. In numerous publications, Hinds also argued that native English speakers prefer a deductive type of argument. Although English speakers are familiar with induction, they are not used to reading prose organized in ways other than deduction.

2. Among studies investigating the development of academic literacy in L1 language and culture, the most comprehensive research was conducted by the late Alan Purves (1988) and others in the previously mentioned International Education Achievement (IEA) research group. Fourteen countries were included in an ambitious international study of writing achievement. The research yielded significant findings about the writing patterns of students at three age levels (12, 16, and 18) writing for three different purposes—narration, exposition, and argumentation. One major contribution was an increased understanding of the procedural importance of the tertium comparationis, or the common platform of comparison, which recognizes that contrastable texts are those which are comparable by virtue of some shared equivalence. For example, expectations about what an argumentative essay entails vary from culture to culture. Thus, in some cultures, a good argumentative essay is a story, and narration would constitute the primary comparability of such essays. Therefore, insisting on exactly the same prompts for research purposes—either in genre expectation (e.g., narration vs. argumentation) or in content—may not be appropriate in cross-cultural research; and texts should be chosen for contrastive research which share comparable prompts.

3. Classroom studies have been conducted to study patterns of collaboration found in writing groups in writing classes. The research of Carson and Nelson at Georgia State University is the most exten-

sive. Through text analyses and transcripts of collaborative writing sessions, they have found, among other things, that Chinese-speaking ESL writers are more concerned about maintaining harmonious group relations than providing critical input on others' drafts, while Spanish-speaking students in the groups in the U.S. used more or less an opposite approach.

4. Genre-specific contrastive studies have extended the framework of contrastive studies. Tirkkonen-Condit (1996), for example, has contrasted the discourse of newspaper editorials in Finland, England, and the U.S., and has found, using various textual analyses, that editorials in Finnish newspapers are typically written to build consensus while in the U.S. they argue for a particular point of view.

Other studies in the above four domains are as follows:

1. Contrastive text linguistic studies examine, compare, and contrast how texts are formed and interpreted in different languages and cultures using methods of written discourse analysis. See Clyne 1987; Connor and Kaplan 1987; Eggington 1987; Hinds 1983, 1987, 1990.

2. Studies of writing as cultural and educational activity investigate literacy development on L1 language and culture and examine effects on the development of L2 literacy. See Carson 1992; Purves 1988.

3. Classroom-based contrastive studies examine cross-cultural patterns in process writing, collaborative revisions, and student-teacher conferences. See Allaei and Connor 1990; Goldstein and Conrad, 1990; Hull, Rose, Fraser, and Castellano 1991; Nelson and Murphy 1992.

4. Genre-specific investigations are applied to academic and professional writing. See Bhatia 1993; Connor Davis and De Rycker 1995; Jenkins and Hinds 1987; Mauranen 1993; Swales 1990; Tirkkonen-Condit 1996; Ventola and Mauranen 1991.

What have we learned about the writing of ESL students in these thirty years of contrastive rhetoric research? We have found that all groups engage in a variety of types of writing, each with its own conventions and tendencies. Preferred patterns of writing depend on the genre. We have also found that what is perceived as straightforward writing depends on reader expectation. Thus, Kaplan's diagram of the linear line of argument preferred by native English speakers may represent what such speakers view as straightforward, but speakers of other languages do not necessarily interpret the features of English argumentative texts the same way.

At a TESOL colloquium in honor of Kaplan's work in 1996, I proposed new diagrams to supplement Kaplan's 1966 "doodles." These diagrams supposedly represented cultural patterns of coherence. The playfully drawn new "squiggles" in Figure 1 show that the writing of native English speakers, such as article introductions, does not follow a straight line—the supposed Anglo-American preference. Finally, the research by Ventola and Mauranen (1991) and Mauranen (1993) suggests that the writing of Finns, either in Finnish or English, follows a circular pattern of organization.

Figure 1. New diagrams

1. *English Article Introductions (Swales 1990)*

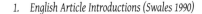

    1. Establish territory

    2. Summarize previous research

    3. Indicate a gap

    4. Introduce present research

2. *"Moves" in Letters of Job Application*

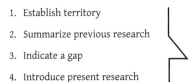

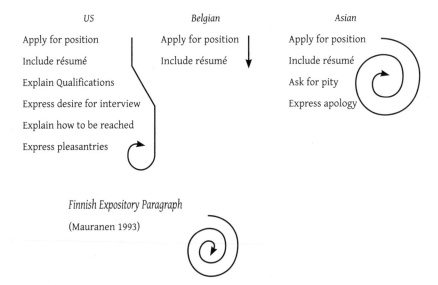

US	Belgian	Asian
Apply for position	Apply for position	Apply for position
Include résumé	Include résumé	Include résumé
Explain Qualifications		Ask for pity
Express desire for interview		Express apology
Explain how to be reached		
Express pleasantries		

Finnish Expository Paragraph

(Mauranen 1993)

These diagrams are meant to show that coherence lies in the culturally conditioned eye of the beholder and that one needs to exercise care in attaching identifying labels to others' writing.

Applications of Contrastive Rhetoric in English as a Foreign Language (EFL) Situations

According to Atkinson (2000), "The contrastive rhetoric hypothesis has held perhaps its greatest allure for those in non-native-English-speaking contexts abroad, forced as they are to look EFL writing in the eye to try to understand why it at least sometimes looks 'different'—often subtly out of sync with that one might expect from a 'native' perspective" (319). The text linguist Nils Erik Enkvist, in his 1997 article "Why we need contrastive rhetoric," suggests that contrastive rhetoric could be pursued with varying aims and methods rather than from a single perspective within different institutions at universities and even outside universities in EFL situations. He shows how contrastive rhetoric is of interest to many programs catering to training in foreign language skills at universities in the small country of Finland. First, Finnish universities, of course, have language departments which teach language, literature, linguistic and literary theory, and applied linguistics. Secondly, for the past twenty-five years, Finland has had language centers at universities which teach languages for specific purposes along with providing translation and editing services. Other types of educational institutions interested in contrastive rhetoric include the School of Economics at the Åbo Akademi University and the School of International Communication at the University of Helsinki. Figure 2 includes a diagram by Enkvist to show the applications of contrastive rhetoric in Europe.

Figure 2. Applications of Contrastive Rhetoric in Europe (from Enkvist (1997))

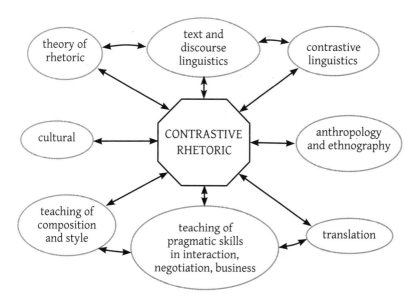

The following examples illustrate the use of the contrastive rhetoric framework in research relevant to academic and professional settings in Europe, including institutions mentioned by Enkvist.

Academic and Professional Writing in EFL

For their research on EFL writing in Finland, Ventola and Mauranen (1991) have convincingly shown the value of text analyses in a contrastive framework. Their research relates to cultural differences between Finnish and English-speaking research writers. Their contrastive text linguistic project investigated language revision practices by native English speakers in Finnish scientists' articles written in English and also compared those texts to articles by native English-speaking writers. A contrastive systemic linguistic study found that Finnish writers used connectors less frequently and in a less varied fashion than native English-speaking writers. The Finnish writers tended to use the article system inappropriately, and there were also differences in thematic progression. Other research by Mauranen (1993) found that, in addition, Finnish writers employed less text about text, or "metatext," and also preferred placing the statement of their main point later in the text than native English speakers.

In a project titled "Milking Brussels,"[1] which analyzed research grant proposals written by Finnish scientists for European Union research funds, it was discovered that Finnish writers had these same difficulties when writing grant proposals—such as not stating their theses at the beginning of the writing but preferring to delay the introduction of the purpose (Connor et al. 1995b). Other textual differences in the Finnish writers' proposals included a lack of transitions and other metatext to guide the reader, differences similar to the ones found in Ventola's and Mauranen's research on academic research articles discussed above.

These differences between American English and Finnish became apparent during the production of a Finnish-language guidebook for grant writers based on the above research. Writing the guidebook provided an illustrative experience in the sort of clashes in contrasting rhetorics that the discipline of contrastive rhetoric attempts to clarify. In an intense discussion one day, I made the point that the guidebook was supposed to describe how English writing differs from Finnish; therefore, it was important to state right at the start what the purpose of the book was and how important it is for Finns to learn to state their main points at the beginning, give examples, and provide transitions throughout the text and then to repeat the main point. The Finnish research assistant in the team wrote the first draft, which I found incoherent. I made suggestions in the margins such as "we need to state the main point at the beginning of the paragraph," and "we shouldn't jump around with ideas, and leave the most important thing as the very last in the book." My summary comments on the draft to the Finnish research assistant and the team read (translated from Finnish): "Perhaps I'm reading this text as an American. It's all fine text, but I find it incoherent in places, hard to follow. I expect the main point at the beginning of the paragraph. I expect a paragraph to contain examples about the main point—no jumping between several points. If others [the other researchers in the project] don't object to the current presentation, I must be completely Americanized."

With the globalization of business and professional communication, writing in such genres as letters, résumés, and job applications for readers with a different language and cultural background than one's own is becoming a reality for more and more people. It has been found that in these contexts, too, second-language writers transfer patterns and styles from the first language to the second. Predictably, differing reader expectations cause misunderstandings. For example, requests in letters can be interpreted as being too direct when directness is more valued in the first language than in the second.

The studies by Ventola and Mauranen and Connor et al. cited above, conducted in the contrastive framework in Europe and focusing on academic and professional writing, show how the contrastive rhetorical framework, originally developed for ESL settings in the U.S., can be helpful in analyzing and teaching writing in EFL in academic and professional contexts. However, researchers and teachers in other EFL situations in countries such as Lebanon, Egypt, Spain, and Mexico are also finding the contrastive rhetoric framework useful for a variety of second-language contexts. Two conferences in the past year in the Middle East have focused on the impact of contrastive rhetoric on the teaching of writing, namely, the Regional English Conference: Language and Change, at the American University of Beirut, Lebanon, November 17–18, 2000, and the Second International Conference on Contrastive Rhetoric, in Cairo, Egypt, March 23–25, 2001. The research of Ana Moreno on cross-cultural differences between Spanish and English research articles in Spain provides inspiration for researchers of academic writing (Moreno 1997). In Mexico, Virginia LaCastro (LaCastro and Santos 2001) is embarking on a new project on improving the writing skills of Mexican high-school students using a contrastive framework.

Criticisms of and Advances in Contrastive Rhetoric

Despite these new developments in contrastive rhetoric and their contributions to teaching in ESL and EFL settings, the discipline has become the target of criticisms by researchers with varied disciplinary affiliations.

In 1997, three papers criticized contrastive rhetoric for an alleged insensitivity to cultural differences. Spack and Zamel, who work with ESL students in the U.S., were concerned about the labeling of students by their L1 backgrounds and the tendency of contrastive rhetoric to view cultures as "discrete, discontinuous, and predictable" (Zamel 1997). Scollon, in the same issue of the *TESOL Quarterly*, criticized contrastive rhetoric research for being too concerned about texts and too neglectful of oral influences on literacy to consider EFL situations like the one in Hong Kong (Scollon 1997). In another issue of the *TESOL Quarterly* in 1999, Kubota was critical of the perception of a cultural dichotomy between the East and West (Kubota 1999). According to her, researchers tend to create cultural differences which promote the superiority of Western writing, its supposed linearity, clarity, and coherence, and ignore the dynamic, more fluid nature of Japanese writing.

One could view these criticisms as stemming from the different disciplinary backgrounds of the writers. Zamel and Spack could be described as being closely aligned to L1 writing traditions with an emphasis on process writing and individual expression (Ramanathan and Atkinson 1999). Scollon comes from anthropology, a discipline whose major focus is not a pedagogical application, unlike that of contrastive rhetoric. Kubota, on the other hand, takes a position stemming from critical pedagogy when she questions the teaching of Western norms of academic writing.

Instead of viewing their work from an adversarial perspective (Belcher 1997), I would like to use it to develop a more generous conception of the contrastive rhetoric framework, especially regarding changing definitions of culture. The following discussion tries to discover their research positions and inquiry practices, together with those of other like-minded critics. My goal is to suggest the outlines of an emerging research paradigm in contrastive rhetoric.

Both Spack and Zamel bring up changing definitions of culture in which forces of heterogeneity and homogeneity are juxtaposed and the latter seriously questioned. Their criticism is not surprising, for the concept of culture has received a great deal of discussion in applied linguistics with relevance to contrastive rhetoric in the last couple of years. Dwight Atkinson (1999) provides a comprehensive review of competing definitions of culture as they relate to TESOL. According to Atkinson, two competing views of culture in TESOL are the "received view" and alternative, nonstandard views. The received view refers to a notion of culture based largely on geographically and often nationally distinct entities, which are presented as relatively unchanging and homogenous (e.g., Japan,

Japanese). The alternative, nonstandard views stem from postmodernist-influenced concepts and have evolved from critiques of the traditional, received view of culture. In the latter camp, Atkinson discusses concepts such as those of "identity," "hybridity," "essentialism," and "power," all of which have been used to criticize traditional views of culture:

> These terms indicate the shared perspective that cultures are anything but homogenous, all-encompassing entities, and represent important concepts in the larger project: the unveiling of the fissures, discontinuities, disagreements, and cross-cutting influences that exist in and around all cultural scenes, in order to banish once and for all the idea that cultures are monolithic entities, or in some cases anything substantial at all. (627)

Following Atkinson (1999), it can be argued that contrastive rhetoric in the past largely adopted the notion of "received culture." For example, I once defined culture as "a set of patterns and rules shared by a particular community" (1996:101). A great deal of traditional contrastive rhetoric has similarly viewed ESL students as members of separate, identifiable cultural groups and, as discussed by Tannen (1985), can come under the criticisms currently directed at any research on cross-cultural communication. Thus, Tannen notes that, "some people object to any research documenting cross-cultural differences, which they see as buttressing stereotypes and hence exacerbating discrimination" (212). She goes on to argue, however, that ignoring cultural differences leads to misinterpretation and "hence discrimination of another sort" (212).

However, although the discipline has often defined national cultures in the "received" mode, researchers in contrastive rhetoric have certainly not interpreted all differences in writing as stemming from the first language or the national culture. Instead, they have tried to explain such differences in written communication as often stemming from multiple sources including L1 national culture, L1 educational background, disciplinary culture, genre characteristics, and mismatched expectations between readers and writers. In this respect, contrastive rhetoric is similar to intercultural research on spoken language or intercultural pragmatics analysis, as described by Sarangi (1994) who suggests the term "intercultural" to refer to migrants' fluid identities. He recommends that we consider reasons of language proficiency, native culture, and interlocutors' accommodation in explaining miscommunication between native and non-native speakers in immigrant language situations.[2]

Nevertheless, future contrastive rhetoric research needs to develop greater sensitivity to the view that sees writers as belonging not to separate, identifiable cultural groups but as individuals in social groups which are undergoing continuous change.

How helpful has contrastive rhetoric been? Some critics denigrate its educational effect. For example, Scollon (1997) discounts the influence of contrastive rhetoric on ESL and EFL by stating that "much of contrastive rhetorical thinking does not, of course, originate with Kaplan" (354). Instead, he continues, "One of the most significant antecedents was the essay by Panofsky (1951) on Gothic architecture," in which artistic traditions are conceived as contrastable "languages," and that if Kaplan had not read the book, he should have. Scollon argues, moreover, that contrastive rhetoric has "an excess focus of textual comparisons" and needs to focus on the oral-to-literate influences such as those seen in Hong Kong Chinese students through the popular culture media of music videos and film.

In my opinion, Scollon's assessment of contrastive rhetorical research may have missed the point that contrastive rhetoric has been an applied linguistics pursuit whose goal has been to help teachers of writing assist students struggling to learn L2 writing. Significant advances were made in text analysis under the contrastive rhetoric umbrella, and these have been instrumental in the construction of, for example, innovative ways to teach coherence. Granted, the oral-to-literate continuum is a worthwhile pursuit; but it should not be the only one.

Although I think that criticism of contrastive rhetoric may be partial, the discipline needs to consider new definitions of literacy. Literacy today is seen as a dynamic sociocognitive activity, as was pointed out in my 1996 review of the contrastive rhetoric field. Influential writers in this area in L1 have been Fairclough (1992) and Berkenkotter and Huckin (1993) among others. Fairclough presents a three-dimensional concept of discourse as consisting of text, discursive practice (production, distribution, and consumption), and social practice. In his model, he calls the part that deals with the analysis of texts "description," and the parts that deal with analysis of discourse practice and social practice "interpretation." Ideology and expression of the dynamics of power are located in the realm of social practice. On the other hand, Berkenkotter and Huckin's work has focused on the definitions of genre and has been especially helpful in locating specific genres in disciplinary and professional cultures where humans as "social actors" learn to write. For such writers, genre knowledge involves oral conversations in addition to writing and written comments on one's writing.

Finally, contrastive rhetoric work that considers literacy as a complex social interaction between writing and speech has examined different expectations concerning the role of spoken language in composing written work. For example, a Finnish graduate student studying in the United

States was not comfortable using his peers as content editors, nor did he seek his professor for advice while writing a term paper, which is a common practice in the States. In fact, the student tried to avoid all face-to-face and oral interaction regarding his writing (Connor and Mayberry 1995).

A major question in contrastive rhetoric deals with an ideological problem about whose norms and standards to teach and the danger of perpetuating established power roles. This has been raised as an issue in postmodern discussion about discourse and the teaching of writing (Kubota 1999; Ramanathan and Atkinson 1999). The discussion has, of course, been in the forefront in contrastive rhetoric; recent critics of contrastive rhetoric have blamed contrastive rhetoricians for teaching students to write for native speaker expectations instead of expressing their own native lingual and cultural identities.

Researchers working in the current contrastive rhetoric paradigm have maintained that cultural differences need to be explicitly taught in order to acculturate EFL writers to the target discourse community. Hence, they maintain that teachers of English and others such as consultants in grant proposal writing need to educate students or clients about the expectations of their readers. Thus, at workshops for Finnish scientists about how to write proposals in English, a western style of grant proposal writing was taught which used a set of rhetorical moves adopted from Swales (1990) (Connor *et al.* 1995b). The Finnish scientists were told that if they wished to get European Union (EU) research grants, they needed to follow EU norms and expectations, which, at the time, were based on an Anglo-American scientific and promotional discourse. When, on the other hand, Finnish scientists write grant applications in Finnish, it was suggested that they would do well to follow the expectations of the Finnish agencies. Although the decision about language choice seems straightforward in the case of grant proposals in the project described above, it may be more complex in case of student writers in undergraduate colleges. Encouraging the preservation of the first language and style may be perfectly acceptable in an effort to preserve the national identity of students.

In the EU project, we became aware of another issue facing contrastive rhetoric, namely, that there may not be an English-language norm for the writing of EU grant proposals. It seems clear that there may be changes in the norms and standards of English in grant proposals because the raters of grant proposals for the EU in Brussels are not solely native speakers of English but are scientists from all EU countries with many different first languages and many different rhetorical orientations. In fact, something like a "Eurorhetoric" has probably emerged. In this case, the blurring of standards and norms in written language is consistent with recent developments in spoken language. David Crystal (1997), for example, suggests that a new kind of English, World Standard Spoken English (WSSE), may be arising for use in situations when the need comes to communicate in English with people from other countries for purposes of business, industry, and diplomacy. Little, however, has yet been conjectured about the nature of this world English, and no theoretical model, as is the case with "Eurorhetoric," has been established.

Conclusions

Major changes are taking place in contrastive rhetoric in terms of its impact as well as its goals and methods. With regard to the former, there has been an expansion of the influence of contrastive rhetoric theories beyond the teaching of basic ESL and EFL writing, as the examples given in this study show. The influence of contrastive rhetoric in the teaching of areas such as business and technical writing is obvious not only in L2 situations overseas but also in the teaching of "mainstream writing" in the United States. A recent edited volume by Panetta (2001), for example, recommends the uses of contrastive rhetorical theory in the teaching of business and technical writing in non-ESL U.S. classrooms.

With regard to scope and goal, contrastive rhetoric is embracing new influences. While adhering to its now well tested premises (the cultural resonance of rhetorical patterns and the influence of L1 on L2 acquisition) and while retaining its traditional pedagogical applications, it will need to become even more responsive to new currents in critical approaches to culture, writing, and the internationalization of English. Consistent with postmodern indications, contrastive rhetoric needs to promote further research-situated reflexivity, to be more sensitive to the local situatedness and particularity of writing activity, and to become more conscious of the influences of power and ideology in any setting. The following four directions for future contrastive rhetoric research seem especially promising.

First, contrastive rhetoric needs to become sensitive to feminist and minority concerns. Too often, contrastive rhetoric proceeds as if differences in gender did not make any difference in text, as even in the monumental and valuable IEA project. In this regard, Panetta's book presents reflections about the usefulness of contrastive rhetorical theories for the research and teaching of writing to other "marginalized groups," such as African American and women writers (see also Fox 1994).

Second, contrastive rhetoric has typically examined texts synchronically, at one point in time. Studies should also be conducted to identify the evolution of patterns diachronically. For example, rather than comparing Belgian, Finnish, and U.S. letters of application written during one year, one could examine if and how the letters in the corpus have changed stylistically in a period of ten years. Preliminary results show interesting findings: letters in the earlier years of the corpus show greater differences between the cultural groups, while letters in the later years of the corpus show fewer differences. All letters in the corpus have changed toward a more "homogenized" style of application letter: U.S. letters have become shorter and less self-appraising while Belgian letters have become longer and include more appraisal of the candidacy. The authors have speculated that either the teachers and students taking part in this corpus building have begun using a common norm acceptable in this experiment or maybe there is a universal form of a letter of application in progress that is changing norms across countries. Contrastive rhetoric will provide a useful framework for answering these questions.

Third, the new contrastive rhetoric, because of its emphasis on context and audience, provides a welcome framework for analyzing new media such as websites cross-culturally. A study by Yli-Jokipii (2001) uses a contrastive frame to study the English and German websites of a company and documents variation in the hierarchical structure of the website as well as in the emphasis of topics. The work of Kress and Leeuwen (1996) on visual literacy has cultural connotations as well.

Fourth, and finally, contrastive rhetoric research continues to provide empirically testable models of cross-cultural texts and writing behaviors. It has been pointed out by Barton (2000), in the case of first language writing, that empirical discourse analysis is needed along with the current popular emphasis on theorizing about culture and cultural diversity. It is especially important for contrastive purposes. I would add that there is a continuing need, which has been stressed elsewhere (Connor 1996:163), to develop models that would ensure impartial comparisons.[3]

Notes

1. The European Union is based in Brussels.
2. The notion of "interculture" is suggested by Sarangi to describe the migrants' fluid identities of native and target cultures in immigrant situations, reminiscent of Selinker's (1972) concept of interlanguage, which refers to shared features of a speaker's native and target languages.
3. It has been pointed out to me by the linguist Ray Keller at IUPUI that there is a directly analogous procedure in computer science (Langley *et al.* 1987), which employs the interpolation of inclusive frames generalized from the significant features of comparable data sets. Because data sets can be mapped fairly well into such frames, their distinctive differentiating features can be distinguished and

thus contrasted from a necessarily neutral perspective (p. 53). This procedure, often called "curve fitting" might be developed into a model for comparisons/ contrasts in empirical contrastive rhetoric research such as the national or cultural differences in grant proposals noted above.

References

Allaei, S. K., and Connor, U.M. 1990. "Exploring the Dynamics of Cross-cultural Collaborations in Writing Classrooms." *The Writing Instructor* 10 (1), 19–28.

Atkinson, D. 1999. "Culture in TESOL." *TESOL Quarterly* 33 (4), 625–654.

———. 2000. "On Robert B. Kaplan's Response to Terry Santos *et al.'s* 'On the Future of Second Language Writing.'" *Journal of Second Language Writing* 9 (3), 317–320.

Barton, E. 2000. "More Methodological Matters: Against Negative Argumentation." *College Composition and Communication* 51 (3), 399–416.

Belcher, D. D. 1994. "The Apprenticeship Approach to Advanced Academic Literacy: Graduate Students and Their Mentors." *English for Specific Purposes* 13 (1), 23–34.

———. 1997. "An Argument for Nonadversial Argumentation: On the Relevance of the Feminist Critique of Academic Discourse to L2 Writing Pedagogy." *Journal of Second Language Writing* 6 (1), 1–21.

Belcher, D. D., and Connor, U. 2001. *Reflections on Multiliterate Lives.* Avon, England: Multilingual Matters.

Berkenkotter, C., and Huckin, T. N. 1993. "Rethinking Genre from a Sociocognitive Perspective." *Written Communication* 10 (4), 475–509.

Bhatia, V. K. 1993. *Analyzing Genre: Language Use in Professional Settings.* New York: Longman.

Braine, G. (ed.). 1998. *"Non-native Educators in English Language Teaching."* Mahwah, NJ: Lawrence Erlbaum.

Casanave, C. P. 1995. "Local Interactions: Constructing Contexts for Composing in a Graduate Sociology Program," in D. Belcher and G. Braine (eds.), *Academic Writing in a Second Language: Essays on Research and Pedagogy* (83–110). Norwood, NJ: Ablex.

Carson, J. G. 1992. "Becoming Biliterate: First Language Influences." *Journal of Second Language Writing* 1 (1), 37–60.

Carson, J. G., and Nelson, G. L. 1994. "Writing Groups: Cross-cultural Issues." *Journal of Second Language Writing* 3 (1), 17–30.

———. 1996. "Chinese Students' Perceptions of ESL Peer Response Group Interaction." *Journal of Second Language Writing* 5 (1), 1–19.

Clyne, M. G. 1987. "Cultural Differences in the Organization of Academic Texts: English and German." *Journal of Pragmatics* 11 (2), 211–247.

Connor, U. 1996. *Contrastive Rhetoric: Cross-cultural Aspects of Second Language Writing.* New York: Cambridge University Press.

Connor, U., and Asenavage, K. 1994. "Peer Response Groups in ESL Writing Classes: How Much Impact on Revision?" *Journal of Second Language Writing* 3 (3), 257–275.

Connor, U., Davis, K., and DeRycker, T. 1995a. "Correctness and Clarity in Applying for Overseas Jobs: A Cross-cultural Analysis of U.S. and Flemish Applications." *Text* 15 (4), 457–475.

Connor, U., Helle, T., Mauranen, A., Ringbom, H., Tirkkonen-Condit, S., and Yli-Antola, M. 1995b. *Tekokkaita EU-projektiehdotuksia*. Helsinki, Finland: TEKES.

Connor, U., and Johns, A. M. (eds.). 1990. *Coherence in Writing: Research and Pedagogical Perspectives*. Alexandria, VA: TESOL.

Connor, U., and Kaplan, R. B. 1987. *Writing across Languages: Analysis of L2 texts*. Reading, MA: Addison-Wesley.

Connor, U., and Kramer, M. 1995. "Writing from Sources: Case Studies of Graduate Students in Business Management," in D. Belcher and G. Braine (eds.), *Academic Writing in a Second Language: Essays on Research and Pedagogy* (155–182). Norwood, NJ: Ablex.

Connor, U., and Lauer, J. 1985. "Understanding Persuasive Essay Writing: Linguistic/Rhetorical Approach." *Text* 5 (4), 309–326.

———. 1988. "Cross-cultural Variation in Persuasive Student Writing," in A. C. Purves (ed.), *Writing across Languages and Cultures* (138–159). Newbury Park, CA: Sage.

Connor, U., and Mauranen, A. 1999. "Linguistic Analysis of Grant Proposals: European Union Research Grants." *English for Specific Purposes* 18 (1), 47–62.

Connor, U., and Mayberry, S. 1995. "Learning Discipline-specific Academic Writing: A Case Study of a Finnish Graduate Student in the United States," in E. Ventola and A. Mauranen (eds.), *Academic Writing: Intercultural and Textual Issues* (231–253). Amsterdam, PA: John Benjamins.

Crystal, D. 1997. *English as a Global Language*. Cambridge: Cambridge University Press.

Eggington, W.G. 1987. "Written Academic Discourse in Korean: Implications for Effective Communication," in U. Connor and R. B. Kaplan (eds.), *Writing across Languages: Analysis of L2 Text* (153–168). Reading, MA: Addison-Wesley.

Enkvist, N.E. 1997. "Why We Need Contrastive Rhetoric." *Alternation* 4 (1), 188–206.

Fairclough, N. 1992. *Discourse and Social Change*. Cambridge, England: Polity Press.

Flowerdew, J. 1999. "Writing for Scholarly Publication in English: The Case of Hong Kong." *Journal of Second Language Writing* 8 (2), 123–146.

Fox, H. 1994. *Listening to the World: Cultural Issues in Academic Writing*. Urbana, IL: National Council of Teachers of English.

Goldstein, L.M., and Conrad, S.M. 1990. "Student Input and Negotiation of Meaning in ESL Writing Conferences." *TESOL Quarterly* 24 (3), 443–460.

Gosden, H. 1992. "Research Writing and NNS: From the Editors." *Journal of Second Language Writing* 1 (2), 123–140.

Hinds, J. 1983. "Contrastive Rhetoric: Japanese and English." *Text* 3 (2), 183–195.

———. 1987. "Reader versus Writer Responsibility: A New Typology," in U. Connor and R. B. Kaplan (eds.), *Writing across Languages: Analysis of L2 Text* (141–152). Reading, MA: Addison-Wesley.

———. 1990. "Inductive, Deductive, Quasi-inductive: Expository Writing in Japanese, Korean, Chinese, and Thai," in U. Connor and A. M. Johns (eds.), *Coherence in Writing: Research and Pedagogical Perspectives* (87–110). Alexandria, VA: TESOL.

Hull, G., Rose, M., Fraser, K.L., and Castellano, M. 1991. "Remediation as a Social Construct: Perspectives from an Analysis of Classroom Discourse." *College Composition and Communication* 42 (3), 299–329.

Jenkins, S. and Hinds, J. 1987. "Business Letter Writing: English, French and Japanese." *TESOL Quarterly* 21 (2), 327–354.

Kaplan, R.B. 1966. "Cultural Thought Patterns in Intercultural Education." *Language Learning* 16 (1), 1–20.

Kress, G., and van Leeuwen, T. 1996. *Reading Images: The Grammar of Visual Design.* London, Rutledge.

Kubota, R. 1999. "Japanese Culture Constructed by Discourses: Implications for Applied Linguistics Research and ELT." *TESOL Quarterly* 33 (1), 9–64.

LaCastro, V., and Santos, S. 2001. "Contrastive Rhetorical Study of Spanish and English." Paper Presented at the Meeting of the Teachers of English to Speakers of Other Languages (TESOL), St. Louis, MO.

Langley, P., Simon, H.A., Bradshaw, G.L., and Zytow, J.M. 1987. *Scientific Discovery: Computational Explorations of the Creative Processes.* Cambridge, MA: MIT Press.

Matsuda, P. 1997. Contrastive Rhetoric in Context: A Dynamic of L2 Writing." *Journal of Second Language Writing* 6 (1), 45–60.

Mauranen, A. 1993. *Cultural Differences in Academic Rhetoric.* Frankfurt am Main: Peter Lang.

Moreno, A.I. 1997. "Genre Constraints across Languages: Casual Metatext in Spanish and English RAs." *English for Specific Purposes* 16 (3), 161–179.

Nelson, G. L., and Carson, J. G. 1998. "ESL Students' Perceptions of Effectiveness in Peer Response Groups." *Journal of Second Language Writing* 7 (2), 113–132.

Nelson, G. L., and Murphy, J. M. 1992. "An ESL Writing Group: Task and Social Dimensions." *Journal of Second Language Writing* 1 (3), 171–194.

Panetta, C. G. (ed.) 2001. *Contrastive Rhetoric Theory Revisited and Redefined.* Mahwah, NJ: Lawrence Erlbaum.

Panofsky, E. 1951. *Gothic Architecture and Scholasticism: An Inquiry into the Analogy of the Arts, Philosophy, and Religion in the Middle Ages.* New York: Meridian.

Prior, P. 1995. "Redefining the Task: An Ethnographic Examination of Writing and Response in Six Graduate Seminars," in D. Belcher and G. Braine (eds.), *Academic Writing in a Second Language: Essays on Research and Pedagogy* (47–82). Norwood, NJ: Ablex.

Purves, A. C. 1988. *Writing across Languages and Cultures: Issues in Contrastive Rhetoric.* Newbury Park, CA: Sage.

Ramanathan, V., and Atkinson, D. 1999. "Individualism, Academic Writing, and ESL Writers." *Journal of Second Language Writing* 8 (1), 45–75.

Sarangi, S. 1994. "Intercultural or Not? Beyond Celebration of Cultural Differences in Miscommunication Analysis." *Pragmatics* 4 (3), 409–427.

Scollon, R. 1997. "Contrastive Rhetoric, Contrastive Poetics, or Perhaps Something Else?" *TESOL Quarterly* 31 (2), 352–363.

Selinker, L. 1975. "Interlanguage." *International Review of Applied Linguistics,* 10, 209–231.

Spack, R. 1997. "The Rhetorical Construction of Multilingual Students." *TESOL Quarterly* 31 (4), 765–774.

Swales, J. M. 1990. *Genre Analysis: English in Academic and Research Settings.* New York: Cambridge University Press.

Tannen, D. 1985. "Cross-cultural Communication," in T. A. Van Dijk (ed.), *Handbook of Discourse Analysis* (203–216). New York: Academic Press.

Tirkkonen-Condit, S. 1996. "Explicitness vs. Implicitness in Argumentation: An Intercultural Comparison." *Multilingua,* 15 (3), 274–275.

Upton, T., and Connor, U. (2001). "Using Computerized Corpus Analysis to Investigate the Textlinguistic Discourse Moves of a Genre." *English for Specific Purposes: An International Journal,* 20, 313–329.

Ventola, E., and Mauranen, A. 1991. "Non-native Writing and Native Revisiting of Scientific Articles," in E. Ventola (ed.), *Functional and Systematic Linguistics* (p. 457–492). Berlin: Mouton de Gruyter.

Yli-Jokipii, H. (2001). "Cybermarketing in English and German: Observations on the Multi-lingual Web Site of a Finnish Company," in J. Eschenbach and T. Schwe (eds.), *Festschrift für Ingrid Neumann.* Halden, Norway.

Zamel, V. 1997. "Toward a Model of Transculturation." *TESOL Quarterly* 31 (2), 341–352.

Contrasting Arabic and German School Essays

Martin Harfmann

In this study it is presupposed that text knowledge which guides the production and the reception of texts is different from culture to culture. Knowledge about native and foreign text types is valuable since an intercultural comparison can elicit not only the "strangeness" of a foreign text type but also the characteristics of the native one (cf. Esser 1996:12). Moreover, it is possible to find a lot of similarities between the foreign and the native manner of writing.

In this study, written communication in German is compared to written communication in Arabic. On the one hand, I conducted this research to find out if the Arabic and German texts under study supply evidence of similarities and differences between the two corpora. On the other hand, I wanted to provide a detailed description of the similarities and differences that I found and to try to explain them.

The results of such a study could be of special interest for teachers and learners of German in Arabic-speaking countries. The differences of writing conventions regarding certain text types should be discussed in teaching lessons more often. Learners should be made aware of the fact that knowledge of text types in L1 does not always correspond to the knowledge they need to have to write a text in L2. The learning of writing conventions of the target language would enable learners to consciously choose between different writing norms in L1 and L2.

The purpose of this study was to verify the following hypotheses:

1. German essays have a stronger tendency toward I-orientation than Arabic essays, i.e., German students use the first person pronoun singular more often. Compared to Arabic-speaking students, German students prefer a rather personal approach to writing.

2. Arabic-speaking students refer more often directly to the reader or other participants of the discourse than German students.
3. Arabic-speaking students in contrast to German students make use of parallelisms. They also make use of repetition more often than German students in order to strengthen the "rhetorical effect" of the text or to produce a text which is linguistically appealing to the reader.
4. Arabic-speaking students include proverbial expressions and/or general statements about life in their essays. They refer to a greater extent to traditions to express an opinion or to give reasons for a statement they make.

Description of Corpora

For this contrastive study, I analyzed twenty Arabic and twenty German school essays. Fifteen of the Arabic essays were written by Palestinian students attending a private Evangelical school. Five of the Arabic essays were composed by Palestinian students in a state school for girls. The twenty German essays were written by students in a secondary school.

The topic of all the compositions was "How Do I Imagine My Future?" Every student was asked to write at least one page (A4–size paper) and to write his/her name on the paper. Seventeen Arabic-speaking and seventeen German students were in eleventh grade when the experiment was conducted; three Arabic-speaking students and three German students were in tenth grade. In both the German and Arabic corpora, eleven essays were written by boys and nine by girls.

The Palestinian students were given the task as a homework assignment. I attended one class of the tenth and one of the eleventh grade in the private school and explained the task in the presence of the teacher. The students had one week to write the essay. In the state school for girls I was not able to explain the task personally. Instead, the director of the school explained the homework to the class. This means that there is an important difference between the essays written by students of the private school and the essays written by the students of the state school for girls. In the state school the girls composed essays for their director in the first place, whereas it can be assumed that the boys and girls of the private school wrote essays for me. This is because, first of all, I personally asked them to do so, and, secondly, because the teacher of the class cannot read Arabic (she is German) and, accordingly, could not have been the addressee.

The state school essays were handed over to me nine days after the students were assigned the task. In the German school, I could explain the task to all the students in the presence of a teacher. Most of the German compositions (sixteen) were written in class. These students had ninety minutes to complete their writing. Most of them turned in their essays in sixty minutes. Four students of the eleventh grade were given the task as a homework assignment. The teacher of this class gave me their writing two days after I had explained the task to them.

The Analysis Model

In order to analyze the texts of the two corpora, I used a model that was originally developed to assess the quality of translations (Translation Quality Assessment, House: 1977, 1997). From House's model, I took the categories of register analysis. Register means functional language variation and refers to the relationship between the context of the situation in which language is used and the appropriate linguistic forms of expression in this situation (House 1997:105). The notion of register presupposes a close relationship between text and context. Linguistic means are the starting-point of the analysis and are related to the situation in which they are expressed (ibid.).

The register categories Field, Tenor, and Mode are defined and distinguished as follows:[1]

Field—the social action or 'what is actually happening':
Field refers to the topic and the content of the discourse. Additionally it captures the field of activity and the heart of the social action.

In order to clarify further the meaning of Field, I will describe in the following passage how House (1997) uses this category in her analysis of an excerpt from *Hitler's Willing Executioners: Ordinary Germans and the Holocaust* by Daniel Jonah Goldhagen.[2] House mentions in her analysis of the English original with regard to Field, that it is an academic text within the province of history.[3] She explains the hypothesis which the author is putting forward in his work and discusses the lexical, syntactic, and textual means he uses to make his hypothesis clear to the reader. She points out that Goldhagen frequently makes use of complex sentences featuring subordination, coordination, and apposition. House concludes that Goldhagen's text is characterized by strong cohesion, which is achieved through repetition of key words.

Tenor—the role structure or 'who is taking part':
Tenor refers to the participants, their roles and statuses, and the relationship between them concerning social power and social distance. Included

here is the degree of emotionality in the relationship between addresser and addressee. Tenor comprises the addresser's cognitive and affective stance toward the content he is portraying and the communicative act he is carrying out, as well as his or her temporal, geographical, and social provenance.

House (1997) points out in her analysis of the excerpt that the author is to a large degree personally involved in the matter he is discussing. The work is dedicated to his father who is a Holocaust survivor. According to House, the author's extensive use of intensifying linguistic devices (e.g., superlatives), which emphasize the propositional meaning of a statement, provide evidence of his involvement.[4] The use of highly emotive language leads to a reduction of social distance for the reader.

House also emphasizes that the author has a professional interest in his subject and that the text contains features that are typical of scientific discourse. The scientific character of the writing is indicated by the absence of personal pronouns. Furthermore, the writer shows that he is an expert in the field he is engaged in. He achieves a high degree of authority by quoting extensively from primary sources to prove his thesis.

Mode—medium and participation: or 'what role language is playing':
Mode refers, on the one hand, to the spoken and the written medium. House (1997) differentiates between simple and complex media. The medium is simple if one remains within one category, e.g., a text is written to be read. The medium is complex if one switches from one category to the other, e.g., a text is written to be spoken. On the other hand, Mode captures participation in its simple and complex manifestations. A monologue with no addressee participation in the text is simple. A monologue which contains some addressee-involving elements is complex.

In her analysis of the medium, House (1997) makes use of the empirically established oral-literate dimensions hypothesized by Biber (1988). These are as follows:

1. involved versus informational text production
2. situation-dependent versus explicit reference
3. abstract versus non-abstract presentation of information

On dimension (1), the spoken Mode tends to be involved, whereas the written Mode tends to be informational. However, personal letters are clearly marked by an involved text production and prepared speeches and broadcasts are strongly marked by an informational text production. Along dimension (2), the written Mode is characterized by a high degree of explicitness. The spoken mode is marked by situation-dependent reference. But public speeches and interviews capture the characteristics of the written Mode, whereas fiction genres are closer to the spoken Mode.

Concerning dimension (3), the written Mode contains much abstract information, whereas the spoken Mode tends to lack it. Yet fiction genres and personal letters are closer to the spoken Mode in this regard.

Biber (1988) shows that a written text is not necessarily marked by the typical characteristics of the spoken Mode (that is, the characteristics of an informational, explicit, and abstract text production). This is the case if a writer consciously makes use of stylistic means which enable him/her to produce a written text which is marked by the typical characteristics of the spoken Mode (that is, an involved, situation-dependent, and non-abstract text production). Also, it is possible to produce a spoken text which is closer to literacy than to orality because the text is quite informational, explicit, and full of abstract information.

In her analysis of Goldhagen's work, House (1997) concludes that the text production is explicit and abstract but also highly involved.[5] She considers the medium as simple (written to be read). There are no features of orality in the text such as, for example, interjections, anacolutha, or elliptic clauses. The text is determined through text-immanent criteria; for example, there is no pronominal reference to the author and the readers. Because there is no reader participation, the text is a simple monologue. According to House, the text production is involved due to the frequent use of emotive lexical items which are repeated.

Adapting the Model for My Analysis

Field

In this category, I did not consider the text type and the task since all texts belong to the same genre (school essay) and the task was the same for all the students participating in the experiment, i.e., to write an essay on "How I Imagine My Future." In Field, I elicited what the main points that a student was trying to make clear to the reader in his/her text were. The aspects of the future the writer was considering are stated (e.g., Is the student writing about the profession s/he wants to pursue? Does his/her family life play a role? Are political topics emphasized?). I also discuss the linguistic means that a student uses to convey the message to the reader on the lexical, syntactic, and textual levels.

Tenor

I adopted the category Tenor in an unchanged form from the model. In this category, I examined the personal viewpoint of the writer. His/her cognitive and emotional stance was analyzed (e.g., Do the utterances in the text tend to the emotional or the rational? Does the writer view his/her future prospects as positive or negative?) The social relationship between addresser and addressee are in the focus of the analysis (e.g., Did the writer present the content with an air of authority or did s/he signal insecurity toward the reader? Did the writer try to convince the reader of his/her views?). Furthermore, I attempted to answer the question whether the writer produced an I-orientated text or preferred an impersonal way of writing. As in Field, I analyzed the linguistic means that the writer employed to convey meaning on the lexical, syntactic, and textual levels.

Mode

For the category Mode, I adopted Biber's oral-literate dimensions in a modified form. It has to be pointed out that Biber's text analysis has been developed for English and therefore, cannot be used in its original form for the analysis of Arabic and German texts. My adoption of Biber's oral-literate dimensions is based on the assumption that these parameters will be reflected by linguistic choices in Arabic and German texts also. But it is assumed that the linguistic forms which are used to realize these dimensions are partly different from the ones used in English texts.

The poles of dimensions are defined as follows:

a) Involved versus Non-involved Text Production

The dimension involved versus informational will be renamed involved versus non-involved. Looking over the essays it became clear to me that none of the texts was characterized by an informational text production. This is due to the task, in which the students were requested to write about how they personally imagine their future. The pupils were asked to activate their imagination rather than to convey information. Following Biber (1988:105) an involved text production is due to an interactive and affective purpose and/or to highly constrained production circumstances. The involved text production is reflected by linguistic forms with an affective or fragmentary character.

Cognitive and cognitive-affective verbs (e.g., think, feel) which express thoughts and feelings can be counted as a linguistic means with an affective function (ibid.). Verbs in the present tense which refer to actions that take place in the immediate context of the situation serve this function too. Also, intensifying linguistic devices (e.g., exclamatory expressions, certain adverbs, and superlatives) belong to this category. Linguistic forms with a fragmentary character are, for example, anacolutha, elliptical structures, and colloquial expressions. First and second person pronouns are features of interactive text production (ibid.).

That is why I will treat addressee participation on the involved–non-involved parameter. Also, according to House, addressee participation belongs to Mode, but she does not intermingle it with the involved versus informational dimension.

Since in the Arabic language personal pronouns are included in the verb, verbs in the first and second person will be counted as an indication of affective and interactive text production.

b) Situation-dependent versus Situation-independent

The dimension situation–dependant versus explicit I have renamed situation–dependant versus situation–independent. According to Biber (1988:110), a text is situation-dependent if there is a preponderance of references which point to the physical and local situation outside of the text. To understand this text the addressee has to infer which local and temporal circumstances the author is referring to. In situation-dependent texts text-immanent criteria prevail. To understand the text the addressee has to recognize which referents in the text the author is referring to.

I use the term situation-independent since the texts I examined are all more or less situation-dependent and none of them is explicit. This is due to the task in which the students were asked to comment personally on the matter, i.e., to use the first person. The use of first person pronouns (I, we) is taken as an indication of a situation-dependent text production because by using I or we the writer refers to his role in the context of the situation (Halliday and Hasan 1976:48). In addition, time adverbials and place adverbials which are not pointing to text-immanent criteria but refer to the physical context of the discourse are seen as an indication for a situation-dependent text production.

c) Abstract versus Non-abstract

Utterances are considered to be abstract if they contain propositions with reduced emphasis on the agent, or if the agent is elided altogether (Biber 1988:112). This can be achieved through the use of passive constructions which give prominence to the verb or the patient of the verb which is typically a non-animate referent and often an abstract concept. Also, impersonal expressions, which in German are formed by using impersonal pronouns (i.e., es, man), are taken as an indication of abstractness. Furthermore, an utterance is called abstract if the agent of that statement is an abstract concept, i.e., if it represents a non-animate referent.

The analysis of the school essays based on the register dimensions can elicit how the students understood and solved the task. In the analysis, it is important to take into account the students' personal differences in text organization, because every student had the possibility—within the framework of the task—to write the text according to his/her personal conception.[6] Therefore, it is assumed that the students' manner of writing is to a great extent influenced by their own decisions.

The question as to whether the Arabic and German school essays provide evidence of similarities and differences between the two corpora is answered based on the following questions:

1. What are the main concerns of the student writing the text? (Field)
2. Who is the student including in his/her writing? What kind of social relationship is the student establishing with the addressee and others who are included in the portrayal? What kind of attitude (on the cognitive and emotional level) is the student displaying toward the topics s/he is dealing with? (Tenor)
3. What kind of text production is the student choosing? Is the text production involved or non-involved, situation-dependent or situation-independent, abstract or non-abstract? (Mode)

The decisions relating to the categories Field, Tenor, and Mode are based on analyzing the linguistic means on the lexical, syntactic, and textual levels. For each of the texts, a text profile was established in which the linguistic features of an essay were correlated with the register categories.

Application of the Model

In order to compare twenty Arabic with twenty German essays, it was necessary as a first step to conduct an exemplary analysis of four Arabic and four German texts. Then it was determined whether the linguistic features found in the exemplary analysis could also be discovered in the remaining Arabic and German writings.

For the exemplary analysis, I selected representative texts. From the Arabic corpus, I chose essays which seemed to confirm my hypotheses (i.e., essays characterized by a low degree of I-orientation, by reader participation, and by the use of parallelisms and proverbial expressions) and essays which contradicted them (i.e., essays not, or are only partly, characterized by these features). This way it was guaranteed that those essays that do not contain the proposed characteristic features were taken into consideration. For the same reason, those German essays were included in the exemplary analysis that seemed to be characterized by a low degree of I-orientation and, therefore, contradicted one of my hypotheses.

Results of the Study

In the presentation of the results, I will restrict myself to the discussion of the linguistic means that I found in the texts under study. There is not enough room to summarize all of the results along the dimensions Field, Tenor, and Mode. This is the case because the decisions that the individual Arabic and German students made along the register dimensions are too diverse to be shown in this article. It is impossible, for example, to sum up here the main points (in Field) that either the Arabic or the German students considered to be important in their writing, or to give an overview of the many different viewpoints (in Tenor) expressed in the Arabic and the German essays respectively.

For the discussion of linguistic phenomena it is necessary to give examples taken from the school essays. These quotations are presented in the following manner. First, the English translation of an Arabic or a German word, sentence, or paragraph is stated. This is followed by the original Arabic or German utterance. The Arabic quotations are presented in phonological transcription. The German citations are given in standard German.

How many males versus females made use of a certain linguistic means will only be stated if the proportion is largely dissimilar. If this is not the case, only the total number of texts which feature a certain linguistic means will be stated.

Results of the Analysis of Twenty Arabic Texts
Field: Textual Means
Sagacious Utterances: Proverbs, Parables, Universal Statements
On the textual level of Field, eight of the texts under study contain sagacious utterances (Arabic: /ħikam/). Some of these utterances are proverbs, whereas others are universal statements formulated by the students themselves. In proverbs, an element of the utterance is repeated. Through repetition, a rhyme or a rhythmic balance emerges. The following statement taken from an essay is a proverb: "Sound means grant sound results" /fa-l-asbaːb as-saliːma tuʕṭi: binataːʔiʒ saliːma/. A rhyme emerges because two constituents of a sentence exhibit the same structure: in both constituents the respective substantives /fa-l-asbaːb/ and /binataːʔiʒ/ are succeeded by the same attributive adjective, though in the first constituent it is determined /as-saliːma/ and in the second one it is not /saliːma/. The rhythmic balance emerges because the elements before and after the verb /tuʕṭi:/ which is between the two constituents of the sentence contain the same number of syllables, i.e., seven. That this utterance has the character of a proverb is also made visible by the quotation marks through which its verbal character is emphasized.

Sagacious utterances can also be considered parables (Arabic: /maθal/). A male student ends his essay in the following manner (Example 2): "Winds do not go as ships desire" /tasiːr ar-rijaːħ bima: la: taʃtahi: assufun/. Also, universal statements that were formulated by the student himself are to be categorized as sagacious statements. One male student writes in the beginning of his text (Example 3): "The future is the thing that cannot be passed by [i.e., the future is the thing that cannot be left out of consideration]. It is the result of the past and the present" /almustaqbal aʃ-ʃajʔ allaði: la: jumkin taʒa:wazuhu, wa huwa nita:ʒ alma:di: wa-l-ħa:dir/.

Repetition and Parallelism
Fourteen of the texts are characterized by repetition and parallelism: ten of these texts are written by males and four by females. An example of a parallel structure I quote is two paragraphs written by a girl. The first paragraph contains general reflections about human beings and their relation to the future. In the second paragraph these thoughts are linked to the personal situation of the student (Example 4):

> So he [the human being] thinks about what he will do in the coming days, but the human being faces some difficulties and obstacles, which he must overcome because they determine what will happen after that /fa huwa jufakkir bima: sajafʕaluhu fi:-l-ʔajja:m al-qa:dima, la:kin tuwa:ʒih al-marʔ baʕd aş-şuʕu:ba:t wa-l-ʕaqaba:t allati: jaʒib ʕalajhi taʒa:wuzuha: liʔannaha: tuħaddid ma: sajaħduθ baʕdaha:/.
> I as a human being have to think about my future and about what I will do and about approaching a phase or a big obstacle in my life. I have to think well about what has to be done to overcome this obstacle. . . . The coming obstacle will determine what will happen to me after that /wa ʔana: ka ʔinsa:n jataħattam ʕalajja at-tafki:r bimustaqbali: wa ma: sawfa ʔafʕaluhu wa bima: ʔannani: muqbila ʕala: marħala ʔaw ʕaqaba kubra: fi: ħaja:ti: fa jaʒib ʕalajja at-tafki:r ʒajjidan bima: jaʒib fiʕluhu liʒtija:z ha:ðihi-l-ʕaqaba . . . . fa-l-ʕaqaba al-qadi:ma satuħaddid ma: sawfa jaħduθ li: baʕdaha:/.

It is significant that the topics in both paragraphs (in the first paragraph the human being and the future, in the second paragraph myself [the writer refers to herself] and my future) are organized parallel to each other:

1. In both paragraphs thinking about the future is at the beginning. In the first paragraph the verb "think about" /jufakkir bi/ is used. In the second paragraph the nominalization "the thinking about" /at-tafki:r bi/ occurs, which appears in my translation as a verb for

clarity. Here parallelism is created by repeating the Arabic root [f-k-r]. Furthermore the root [f-k-r] appears both times in Form II of the morphological system, the first time as a verb, the second time as a nominalization.

2. In both paragraphs the act now follows, i.e., what one has to think about. In the first and the second paragraph the root [f-ʕ-l] occurs. The general meaning of this root is doing. Both times a verb in the future tense is used. The personal suffix of the third person /-hu/ is attached to both verbs; it does not appear in the translation. In the first paragraph the verb refers to the human being and is therefore in the third person singular, /sajaf̣ʕaluhu/ (which means literally, "he will do it"). In the second paragraph the verb refers to the girl herself and is therefore in the first person singular, /sawfa ʔaf̣ʕaluhu/ (which means literally, "I will do it").

3. The third parallel element is the mentioning of difficulties that stand in one's way when someone wants to cope with the future. The student uses in the first paragraph the word "obstacles" /ʕaqaba:t/ and states the word again in its singular form in the second paragraph, "obstacle" /ʕaqaba/.

4. The fourth element that is repeated is the necessity of overcoming the obstacles (or an obstacle). On the one hand, the student uses the verb /waʒaba/, which has the basic meaning of "to be necessary." On the other hand, she repeats the root [ʒ-w-z] in the first paragraph, where it appears in Form VI as a nominalization (/taʒa:wuzuha:/), meaning literally "their overcoming," and in the second paragraph in Form VIII as a nominalization (/liʒtija:z/, meaning literally, "for overcoming."

5. The last parallel element is the reason that the student gives for the necessity of overcoming the obstacles. In the first paragraph the reason that the student gives is explicitly expressed since she uses the causal conjunction /liʔanna/ ("because"): ". . . because they determine what will happen after that . . . ." /liʔannaha: tuħaddid ma: sajaħduθ baʕdaha:/. In the second paragraph the reason is implicitly stated: "The coming obstacle will determine what will happen to me after that" /fa-l-ʕaqaba al-qadi:ma satuħaddid ma: sawfa jaħduθ li: baʕdaha:/. The student repeats the verb "to determine" in the third person singular /juħaddid/ and the verb "to happen" in the third person singular in the future tense (in the first paragraph: /sajaħduθ/; in the second paragraph: /sawfa jaħduθ/), as well as the preposition with an attached personal suffix in the third person singular feminine /baʕdaha:/ "after that".

The analysis of the two paragraphs shows that through repetition a high degree of cohesion between parts of a text can be achieved. This example can be seen as a very complex parallel structure which, therefore, cannot be considered as typical of the Arabic corpus. In the two paragraphs a train of thought is repeated that contains several steps.

The analysis of the two passages can bring to light many different kinds of repetition that can also be found in the other thirteen texts which contain parallel structures:

1. lexical repetition (of a verb, a noun, or a preposition).
2. repetition of a root in the same morphological pattern (e.g., [f-k-r] in Form II).
3. repetition of a root in different morphological patterns [ȝ-w-z] (in Forms II and VI).
4. repetition of a morpheme (e.g., the suffix of the third person singular feminine /-ha:/, attached to the preposition /baʕda/).

In the other Arabic essays several parallel structures which feature only one or two kinds of repetition can be found. Very often the students make use of lexical repetition.

Tenor: Syntactic Means
The Use of the First Person Plural
It was found that in ten Arabic texts, verbs and personal suffixes in the first person plural were used often, or at least several times. Seven of these texts were written by males and three by females. Many students state explicitly that they see themselves as members of the Palestinian community and they emphasize what they have in common with their fellow citizens. In the following quotation a student points out the Palestinians' disappointment over the lack of support for them from outside (Example 5): "Regarding us, us Palestinians, we do not see anyone who tries to help us in building our future and increasing our abilities and fulfilling our hopes" /ʔamma: bin-nisba lana: naḥnu al-filasṭini:ju:n fala: nara: man juḥa:wil ʔan jusa:ʕidana: libina:ʔ mustaqbalina: wa tanmijat qudra:tina: wa ʔa:ma:lina:/.

But "we" does not always refer to the Palestinians. One female student uses the first person plural to include the reader in her writing. First, she describes in her essay the character of a "diligent and assiduous" person and then concludes (Example 6): "We find that he [the diligent person] impatiently awaits this future" /naȝiduhu jantaẓir ha:ða:-l-mustaqbal bifa:riɣ aṣ-ṣabr/. The student, by using "we," presupposes that the reader shares her conclusion.

In another essay a girl uses the first person plural to refer to herself and her future husband (Example 6): "Concerning my life with my husband I want us to be like friends" /ʔamma: bin-nisba liħaja:ti: maʕa zawʒi: faʔuri:d ʔan naku:n kal-ʔaṣdiqa:ʔ/.

The Collective, the Personal, and the Impersonal Style of Writing
Even though many students express a collective way of thinking and feeling, eight texts are characterized by a personal style of writing which is indicated by the frequent use of verbs and personal suffixes in the first person singular in parts of the text. Seven texts contain paragraphs that are marked by an impersonal style of writing which lacks the I-form and the we-form. It must be emphasized that the collective, the personal, and the impersonal styles of writing can be found in the same text, because often a student changes from one manner of writing to another. For example, a student writes at the beginning of a text in an impersonal manner and describes his thoughts and feelings only at the end of the text in a personal way.

The following quotations were written by a female student. The first example represents the collective style of writing: "we" in this case refers to all human beings. The second example starts out with a personal approach: a wish is being expressed that is of an aggressive, anti-Israeli character. Then the student turns to a description of Jerusalem which is expressed in an impersonal (and at the same time emphatic) manner:

(Example 8) "The past: we lived it; the present: we live in it; the future: how will it be? We lived the past and were satisfied with part of it." /alma:ḍi: ʕiʃ.ia:hu; alħa:ḍir naʕi:ʃ bihi; al-mustaqbal kajfa sajaku:n?! ʕiʃna: alma:ḍi: wa ʔiqtanaʕna: biʒuzʔ minhu/.

(Example 9) "I imagine Jerusalem resistant, cleansed of the dirt of the usurpers. Her gates receive her Muslim visitors. Her wall is high and proud and it directs Islamic greetings to the visitors of Jerusalem and the honored sanctuary [al-Haram ash-Shariif], crying out in its victory joyfully and saying, 'God is great, God is great.'" /ʔataxajjal al-quds ṣa:mida muṭahhara min danas al-ɣa:ṣibi:na, wa ʔabwa:buha: fa:tiħa lizuwwa:riha: al-muslimi:na, wasu:ruha: ʕa:lin ʃa:mixun julqi: taħijjat al-ʔisla:m ʕala zuwwa:r al-quds wal-ħaram aʃ-ʃari:f, jaṣrux farħan bintiṣa:rihi wajaqu:l ʔallahu akbar, ʔallahu akbar/.

Mode

a) Involved versus Non-involved

In Mode, the analysis made clear that all of the Arabic texts under study are involved. In the first place, this is due to the lexical, syntactic, and textual means that emphasize the meaning of an utterance. On the lexical level, thirteen students used words that indicate an identification with their homeland. Eight students included vocabulary with positive connotations in their writings to express their wishes for the future. Seven students made use of words with negative, partly aggressive, connotations which show their negative stance toward the Israeli presence in the West Bank and the Gaza Strip.

The Arabic-speaking students often used syntactic means to emphasize a statement. In eleven essays, for example, certain utterances are stressed through adversative structures. A male student, for example, stresses the Palestinians' negative future prospects (Example 10): "So we do not go with the future, on the contrary we go from the present into the past, far away from the future" /fa naḥnu la: naṣi:r maʕa-l-mustaqbal waʔinnama: naḥnu naṣi:r min al-ḥa:ḏir ila:-l-ma:ḏi: baʕi:dan ʕan al-mustaqbal/. In this sentence there are two oppositions. The negative statement is succeeded by a positive one which is emphasized by "on the contrary" /ʔinnama:/, which consists of the particle /ʔinna/ and the suffix /ma:/. Then the adverb with the following preposition /baʕi:dan ʕan/ ("far away from") introduces the second opposition, in that they stress the difference between past and present.

On the textual level, as mentioned already, fourteen essays are characterized by repetition and parallelism. The following quotation is an example of lexical repetition. A female student points out how she imagines a "liberated" Palestine would be. Through repetition of the word "Palestine" she expresses her patriotic sentiments very clearly and the emotional effect on the reader is strengthened (Example 11): "Joy spreads in beloved Palestine and the smile returns on the lips of the mothers of Palestine, the elder men of Palestine and the dear children of Palestine" /wataʕumm al-ʔafra:ḥ filasṭi:n al-ḥabi:ba wataʕu:d al-basma ʕala ſifa:h ummaha:t filasṭi:n, ſuju:x filasṭi:n, waʔaṭfa:l filasṭi:n al-ʔaʕizza:ʔ/.

Direct Inclusion of the Reader

The direct inclusion of the reader in seven texts additionally causes the text production of these essays to be involved. Mostly the students address an audience that they imagine. After giving a detailed description of his future dreams, a male student writes (Example 12): "This is everything I dream about, gentlemen!" /ha:ða: kul ma: ʔaḥlum bihi ʔajjuha: as-sa:da/. Only one student addresses the author of this article directly.

b) Situation-dependent versus Situation-independent

All texts tend to be situation-dependent, since all students use verbs, personal suffixes, and personal pronouns in the first person singular or plural to refer to their role in the context of the situation. Some students refer to the role of the addressee in this context by including him.

Reference to the Situation

The majority of the essays contain references to the local or the temporal situation outside the text. It is striking that twelve students refer to the political and the economic situation in the Palestinian areas. These references can be understood only if the reader is able to infer the local and temporal circumstances the writer is referring to. In Example 9 the student refers to the city of Jerusalem and writes, "I imagine Jerusalem resistant, cleansed of the dirt of the usurpers." It is not explicitly stated who the "usurpers" are who make the city dirty. Only with regard to knowledge of the Israeli–Palestinian conflict can one infer what the reader wants to say: that Jerusalem is usurped by the Israelis and that the Palestinians are entitled to get the city back.

c) Abstract versus Non-abstract

Ten texts contain elements of abstract text production, whereas the other ten essays lack abstract elements.

The Agent as a Non-animate Referent

The essays with an abstract component often contain several statements in which the agent is a non-animate referent. In the following example a male student puts forward two different functions of work in the life of a man (Example 13): "Clarification of the meaning of 'reducing responsibility.' It has many meanings. It may mean the work with a high income that provides for the family's keep" /tawdʒiːħan limaʕna taxfiːf al-masʔuːliːja falahu maʕaːnin ʕidda, faqad taʕni: al-ʕamal ðaːt ad-daxl al-ʕaːli: wa-llaði: yuwaffir an-nafaqaːt li-l-ʕaːʔila/.

Passive and Impersonal Statements

In texts with abstract elements, impersonal statements can often be found. In some essays passive constructions also appear. The following quotation contains two sentences. The first is a passive construction that is used to introduce the following sagacious statement as a quotation. In the introductory sentence, the dropping of the agent leads to an emphasis of the verb. The sagacious statement itself consists of an impersonal conditional clause (Example 14): "And as it was said: 'The life of a human being has no value if his existence does not have a meaning'"

/wa kamma: qi:la: la: qi:mata liħaja:t ʔinsa:n ʔin lam jakun liwuʒu:dihi maʕna/.

Results of the Analysis of Twenty German Texts

Field: Textual Means

Advance Organizers

Eight students used advance organizers to structure their texts. One student, for example, subdivided his essay into two parts. The first part is titled "Concerning the profession" (Beruflich), the second is headlined "Concerning the family" (Familiär).

Another student started out each paragraph with a general statement about the topic. These were followed by detailed information about the topic. This structure is demonstrated by the following quotation (Example 1): "In addition much time will be spent in the next years for the fire department, because I signed up for at least eight years. That means that in addition to school, nearly one year's basic training will presumably be coming my way from the fall, which also has to be studied for. Then add to this approximately 130 services a year still. I already dread the subway suicides" (Viel Zeit wird in den nächsten Jahren außerdem für die Feuer draufgehen, da ich mich für mindestens acht Jahre verpflichtet habe. D. h. neben der Schule wird voraussichtlich ab Herbst auch noch eine knapp einjährige Grundausbildung auf mich zukommen, für die auch noch gelernt werden muß. Dazu kommen dann noch ca. 130 Einsätze pro Jahr. Mir graut es jetzt schon vor den U-Bahn-Selbstmördern).

Tenor: Syntactic Means

I-Orientation

On the syntactic level of Tenor, the analysis has shown that all but two essays are written in a personal manner. The next quotation from a female student's text demonstrates a high degree of I-reference. In the center of this passage are the individual objectives of the student (Example 2): "A housewife I will probably never be. I do not want to have children and therefore can work more and thereby have better chances for advancement. Meanwhile I will get along with any job. As soon as I earn my first money I will save something every month. When enough has been gathered together, I will buy myself a car. The driver's license I have already" (Hausfrau werde ich wohl nie werden. Ich möchte keine Kinder haben und kann deshalb mehr arbeiten und habe dadurch bessere Aufstiegschancen. Zwischendurch schlage ich mich mit irgendwelchen Jobs durch. Sobald ich mein erstes Geld verdiene, werde ich jeden Monat etwas sparen. Wenn sich genug angesammelt hat, werde ich mir ein Auto kaufen, den Führerschein habe ich ja schon).

Explicit Argumentation

On the syntactic level of Tenor the analysis brought to light that eight students explicitly justified some of their statements. For example, one student substantiates why he took computer science as a subject in school: "At the same time it is important to be able to deal with the computer, because without the computer almost nothing can be done today and later on all the less. This is why I have chosen computer science for the next school year." (Wichtig ist dabei, mit dem Computer umgehen zu können, denn ohne Computer läuft heute kaum etwas und später erst recht nicht. Darum habe ich für das nächste Schuljahr auch Informatik gewählt).

A female student gives reasons why she is considering studying either architecture or a language: "I could imagine, because of the practical training in an architect's bureau that I have done, to study architecture, because I was pleased with the varied work (drawing, organizing, supervision of construction) very much. As a second consideration the study of a language (Spanish, Russian, English) could come into consideration, because I enjoy languages very much. Moreover, in my later job I want to work in a foreign country . . . ." (Ich könnte mir vorstellen, aufgrund meines absolvierten Praktikums bei einem Architekturbüro, Architektur zu studieren, da mir die abwechslungsreiche Arbeit (zeichnen, organisieren, Bauüberwachung) sehr gut gefallen hat. Als zweiten Vorschlag könnte noch ein Sprachstudium (Spanisch, Russisch, Englisch) in Frage kommen, da mir Sprachen sehr viel Spaß machen. Außerdem möchte ich in meinem späteren Beruf auch im Ausland arbeiten . . . .).

Because of the many causal conjunctions this passage is explicitly argumentative. The argumentation is doubly reinforced by the adverb "very much." The last utterance can be seen as the student's implicit justification for the probable study of a language. By use of the conjunctional adverb "moreover" (außerdem) it becomes clear that the student gives another reason (in addition to the fact that she enjoys languages) for choosing to study a language.

Mode

a) Involved versus Non-involved

In Mode all essays are involved. In the first place, this is due to the use of modals and cognitive and cognitive-affective verbs as well as idiomatic expressions in the first person singular in the present tense in seventeen texts. In eighteen texts the use of many intensifying linguistic devices on the lexical level contributes to an involved text production and to the colloquial character of these writings. Frequently used intensifying linguistic devices are superlatives, adverbs, emphatics, and amplifiers. Moreover, fourteen texts bear words that signal vagueness and uncertainty, like hedges, particles, and indefinite pronouns which contribute to the colloquial character of these essays.

Ellipses
On the syntactic level, nine essays contain ellipses which cause an utterance to be short and imprecise. A female student writes (Example 3): "If I achieve this final examination [the German Abitur] I would like for one year to do something which is not so demanding. What I do not know at all, yet." (Falls ich diesen Abschluß schaffe, möchte ich ein Jahr lang irgend etwas machen, wo man nicht so sehr gefordert wird. Was in etwa, weiß ich noch nicht). The complete final sentence could be: "What I want to do I do not know at all, yet." In this example a verb group is slipped. Only after consideration of the first sentence can the reader infer what the writer wants to say. The reader is forced to fill in the information gap, i.e., to transfer the verb group of the first sentence to the second one.

b) Situation-dependent versus Situation-independent
All of the texts tend to be situation-dependent. By using first personal pronouns in the singular the students refer to their roles in the context of the situation.

Reference to External Physical and Temporal Situations
Many students refer to the local and/or temporal situation outside of the text. One male student writes (Example 4): "The present situation of the labor market does not offer a large choice and one can be happy if one gets a place for vocational training at all." (Die heutige Arbeitsmarkt erlaubt keine große Auswahl und man kann glücklich sein, wenn man überhaupt einen Ausbildungsplatz bekommt). The nominal group "the present situation of the labor market" is a locative and a temporal reference. But the student does not explicitly state what the local and temporal references he is commenting on are. In the text there is no indication that the student refers to the situation of the labor market in Germany in the year 1999.

c) Abstract versus Non-abstract
Fourteen texts are non-abstract. Only six essays contain elements of an abstract text production and, therefore, can be described as partly abstract. The writings with an abstract component feature passive constructions and/or impersonal pronouns (man ["one"] and es ["it"]).

Similarities and Differences between Arabic and German Texts
The similarities and differences between the Arabic and the German texts may be summarized as follows:

Field: Textual Means
Arabic texts
- The Arabic texts often feature repetition and parallelism. Thereby these texts are more cohesive.
- Some of the Arabic texts contain sagacious utterances which are of a universal character.
German texts
- Some of the German texts are clearly structured. This is achieved by the use of advance organizers.

Tenor: Syntactic Means
Arabic texts
- Often the Arabic texts are characterized by a collective, a personal, and an impersonal style of writing.
German texts
- The German texts are characterized by a personal style of writing because the use of the first person singular is predominant.
- In some German texts certain statements, decisions, or considerations are explicitly backed up by reasons that a student gives. These texts are partly argumentative.

Mode
a) Involved versus Non-involved
Arabic texts
- In the Arabic texts the following elements lead to an involved text production:
  —personal style of writing
  —lexical, syntactic, and textual means for emphasis
  —direct inclusion of the reader
German texts
- In the German texts the following elements cause the text production to be involved:
  —personal style of writing
  —colloquialism (ellipses, use of idiomatic expressions, emphatics, amplifiers, hedges, particles)

b) Situation-dependent versus Situation-independent
Arabic texts
- Due to the following factors the Arabic texts are situation-dependent:
  —use of the first person singular and plural
  —direct inclusion of the reader
  —reference to external physical and temporal situations

German texts
- Due to the following features the German texts are situation-dependent:
  —use of the first person singular
  —reference to external physical and temporal situations

c) Abstract versus Non-abstract
Arabic texts
- Half of the texts contain abstract passages. This is due to the following linguistic means:
  —impersonal utterances
  —passive constructions
  —statements in which the agent is a non-animate referent
German texts
- The German texts are mainly non-abstract. Only rarely are impersonal pronouns (es, man) or passive constructions used.

Final Remarks

This study has confirmed my hypothesis that German essays have a stronger tendency toward I-orientation than Arabic essays. This does not mean that Arabic-speaking students prefer an impersonal manner of writing throughout. Rather, it can often be observed that students switch between a personal (I-orientated), a collective (we-orientated) and an impersonal (neither I- nor we-orientated) style of writing. This result is remarkable since all the students were explicitly asked in the task to comment personally upon how they imagine their future to be.

With regard to the Arabic corpus, the writing of the students of the private school contained more I-references than the writings of the students attending a state school for girls. It is hypothesized that the texts of the state school for girls are less personal because they were written for the director of that school. Because the social role relationship between addresser and addressee in this case is largely asymmetrical, these students did not write their essays "from their hearts." Instead, they may have felt the need to compose essays that met the expectations of their director. With this explanation, it is presupposed that essays with many I-references would be contrary to the director's expectations.

Furthermore, this study confirmed the hypothesis that Arabic-speaking students more often address the reader or other participants of the discourse directly in their writings. Another interesting result is that in the Arabic texts there is also a tendency toward an indirect inclusion of discourse participants: the reader is sometimes included by the use of the first person pronoun or by a question.

Moreover, the hypothesis was confirmed that the Arabic-speaking students, in contrast to the German students, make use of parallel constructions. Also, in the Arabic students' writings, repetition is more often found than in the German texts under study. But parallelism and repetition does not occur in all of the Arabic writings. In six Arabic essays, these linguistic means could not be found. It could be observed that all of the students of the state school made use of parallelism and repetition whereas only nine of the fifteen students of the private school employed these linguistic means. This again could be explained by the different context of the situation which may have caused the female state students to include these linguistic "tools" to meet the expectations of the director. This would mean that parallel structures and repetition are looked upon positively by the director.

Finally, it was confirmed that the Arabic-speaking students in contrast to the German students use sagacious statements. Sagacious utterances can be subdivided into three categories—proverbs, parables, and universal statements formulated by the students themselves. Only the proverbs and parables that are marked as quotations are to be seen as indications of a reference to tradition. Individual universal statements often occur at the beginning of an essay and are superordinated to the rest of the text.

With regard to Mode, this study shows that the Arabic as well as the German texts have a tendency toward the spoken mode. In the Arabic texts this is indicated in the first place by lexical, syntactic, and textual means for emphasis and the inclusion of the addressee. In the German texts a personal manner of writing and many different features of colloquialism cause the texts to be somewhat oral. In contrast with the German texts, one half of the Arabic texts contain characteristics of an abstract text production. According to Biber (1988), this tendency is to be seen as an indication of the written mode.[7] Following Biber (1988) in this respect, the Arabic essays have a stronger tendency toward the written mode than the German essays.

Notes

1. For the definition of the register categories see House 1997, p.108 and Halliday/ Martin 1993:32 ff.)
2. For the analysis of this excerpt according to Field see House 1997:147 ff.
3. House (1997) analyzes the English original of this excerpt to compare it with its German translation in terms of the categories of register (Field, Tenor, Mode).

4. For the analysis of this excerpt in terms of Tenor see House 1997, p.148 ff.
5. For the analysis of the excerpt in terms of Mode see House 1997, p.150.
6. However, it has to be taken into consideration that five Palestinian girls did not have as much freedom as the other Palestinian and German students to write a text according to their personal conception since they wrote their essays for the director of the school .
7. According to Sa'addedin (1989:49) abstract generalizations are a characteristic of the *spoken* mode if they are not supported by concrete examples.

References

Biber, D. 1988. *Variation in Speech and Writing.* Cambridge: Cambridge University Press.

Eßer, R. 1996. "Etwas ist mir geheim geblieben am deutschen Referat." *Kulturelle Geprägtheit wissenschaftlicher Textproduktion und ihre Konsequenzen für den universitären Unterricht von Deutsch als Fremdsprache.* Hamburg: Universitat Hamburg.

Goldhagen, D. J. 1996. *Hitler's Willing Executioners. Ordinary Germans and the Holocaust.* New York: Vintage Books.

Halliday, M.A.K. and Hasan, R. 1976. *Cohesion in English.* London, New York: Longman.

Halliday, M.A.K. and Martin, J. R. (1993). *Writing Science: Literary and Discursive Power.* London, Washington D.C.: Falmer.

House, J. 1977. *A Model for Translation Quality Assessment.* Tübingen: Narr.

House, J. 1997. *Translation Quality Assessment. A Model Revisited.* Tübingen: Narr.

Sa'adeddin, M. A. 1989. "Text Development and Arabic-English Negative Interference." *Applied Linguistics* 10, 1 (March 1989), 36–51.

Rhetoric in English Narratives of Native Speakers and Second-language Learners

Miranda Y. P. Lee

Narratives have been analyzed in many different languages, and claims have been made that this particular genre is universal. Certainly the storytelling tradition is strong in most cultures. However, a brief survey of relevant research (Berman 1999; Indrasuta 1988; Matsuyama 1983; Schaefer 1981) shows that rhetorical features adopted by different language groups in narrative are different.

Among the studies, Matsuyama (1983) claimed that while English stories tend to center on actions, Japanese stories are much more concerned with the development of characters, motives, and the relationships between characters. Schaefer (1981) suggested this may be true of Vietnamese narratives as well. Indrasuta (1988) concluded that Thai and American students perceive the functions of narrative differently. American students aim to capture the reader's interest, while Thai writing serves the function of teaching and evaluating. Berman (1999) showed that Arab and American students constructed their narrative texts differently. The results of these studies support the hypothesis that first language (L1) plays a significant role, both linguistically and culturally, in contributing to the differences in rhetoric in writing by different language groups.

Much research on contrastive rhetoric has been done on second-language (L2) English narrative writing by Asian-language speakers but not much has been focused on native speakers of Chinese. The present study therefore compares rhetorical features of narratives written by English and Chinese speakers in order to investigate the influence of L1 in narrative writing.[1] Certain pedagogic implications for L2 writing are drawn as well. More specific objectives of this research are to examine the differences in cohesive devices adopted by native speakers of English (NS) and Hong Kong students (HKS) in their English texts, and to compare informative and evaluative elements given in English narratives of NS and HKS, so as to consider the interpretive responsibility of their texts.

Method

Materials

Narrative was elicited because it allows the researcher to control for content and to see how subjects express the same thing in different ways. It also allows reliable comparison across texts produced by different subjects (Berman 1999). Skills in narrative writing have also been regarded as the basic skills that both L1 and L2 speakers first acquire. This research thus focuses on narrative writing in English and Chinese.

A series of eight pictures, arranged in order of events that make up a story, was used in this paper. The story is about some children playing in a park, as outlined in Table 1.

Table 1. Breakdown of 'Park Story'
1. Two boys and two girls are playing in the park. The boys are chasing one another and the girls are looking at the flowers.
2. A naughty boy suddenly rides across the flowerbed on his bicycle. The two girls are scared.
3. The children look at the mark showing the path of the bicycle.
4. The naughty boy is ripping the flowers out of the ground.
5. He then climbs a tree. The other children are angry with him.
6. He starts swinging on a small branch of the tree.
7. The branch snaps and he falls on the ground with his head hurt.
8. The other children are angry and push him out of the park.

Subjects

Two main groups of subjects were chosen for this study. The first group consisted of forty Hong Kong tertiary-level students (HKS) who are L2 learners of English, and have been exposed to English for fourteen years. They are second-year undergraduate students studying humanities and engineering at the Hong Kong Polytechnic University. The second group encompassed forty native speakers of English (NS) from England, Canada, and the United States. The two subject groups had age (ranging from 20 to 21.5 years) and educational background in common.

Subjects were asked to write down the story according to the picture series. They were given instructions in the language in which they were required to construct the text. The instructions were as follows: "Here is a series of pictures which make up a story. Write a story to a child aged ten, who is a native speaker." HKS were asked to write in both English and Chinese with a three-month interval in order to avoid the possibility of translation, while NS wrote in English. Thus, three sets of data were collected. The Chinese texts serve as a reference for examining the linguistic influence of L1, while the English texts written by NS are regarded as a baseline rather than a model for comparison.

Analytical Approaches

The study adopted two approaches, namely linguistic and discourse analysis. The analysis of cohesion (Halliday and Hasan, 1976), which reveals the semantic and syntactic relationship within a text, was used for the linguistic analysis. Differences in writing by HKS from NS of the target language might be expected because of the linguistic influence of L1 on L2.

Another approach is discourse analysis. A narrative text can consist of at least five constituents in its pattern of organization: orientation, initiating event, complicating event, highpoint, and coda. As first proposed by Labov (1972) and extended by Berman (1997), within these constituents three categories of narrative content can be found, namely, narrative clauses, evaluative elements, and informative elements (Table 2). The analysis is intended to illustrate that the differences in discourse between HKS and NS are mainly due to the cultural influence of L1.

Table 2. Narrative structure and categories

Constituents of Narrative Structure	Categories of Narrative Content
Orientation	Information (+ Evaluation)
Initiating Event	Narrative Clause/s
Complicating action	Narrative Clause/s (+ Eval/Info)
Highpoint	Narrative Clause/s (+Eval/Info)
Coda	Evaluation (+Info)

Findings and Analysis

Text Length

The average text length of HKS English texts is 287 words while that of NS is 451. In addition to text length, a number of T-units[2] and T-unit lengths were used for measurement. The average number of T-units in HKS English texts is less than that of NS texts, and HKS T-unit length is shorter (Table 3). In order to facilitate reliable comparison and to obtain accurate analysis, the data in the sections on conjunctive cohesion and narrative structure will be normalized by comparing with the total number of T-units in each group.

Table 3. Breakdown of 'Park Story' texts by language and length

	Hong Kong students (HKS)		Native English speakers (NS)
Language	Chinese	English	English
Number of words			
Mean	494.3	286.6	450.9
Standard deviation	112.6	68.1	110.7
Number of T-units			
Mean	46.6	34.5	47
Standard deviation	12.5	8.9	13.3
T-unit length			
Mean	10.8	8.6	9.8
Standard deviation	1.3	1.8	1.3

Cohesion

Cohesion is one of the rhetorical devices that binds a text together and signals relations between sentences and parts of texts. Cohesive devices are adopted to tie pieces of text together in specific ways. They can be categorized into reference, ellipsis, substitution, conjunctive cohesion, and lexical cohesion. In this study, I will focus on comparison of the first four categories between NS and HKS texts.

Reference

Two types of relationship are recognized: cataphoric relations look forward for their interpretation, and anaphoric relations look backward. From the data, we find significant differences in use of pronouns and demonstratives between NS and HKS.

a. Pronoun

Both cataphoric and anaphoric relations were examined in this study. No example with cataphoric pronouns was found in the HKS texts, but a certain number were found in NS texts (Table 4), as illustrated in example (1):

(1)   "Once *he* had finish destroying every flower, *Nick* then said 'I don't like any of you.'"

The lack of cataphoric pronouns used by HKS can be explained by the linguistic influence of their L1, as Chinese pronouns are mainly anaphoric. One of the remarkable differences found in the data is the frequency of pronoun usage. The result shows that the number of pronouns in NS texts is twice of that in HKS texts. This may be attributed to the influence of the Chinese linguistic system. Chinese prefers simplicity, and pronouns are not recommended when meaning can be easily interpreted from the context.

b. Demonstrative

In a result similar to that obtained for pronouns, the number of demonstratives found in HKS texts is half that in NS texts (Table 4).

Table 4. Average number of tokens (against average number of words) of referential items

Reference		NS	HKS	Ratio (NS:HKS)
Pronoun	anaphoric	36.25	20.8	6.35:3.65
	cataphoric	15	0	—
Demonstrative		0.01	0.003	7.3:2.3

(2) "John and his classmates only shouted at *that* naughty boy and never care the painful felling of *that* naughty boy."

The data illustrate that HKS applied fewer referential devices, such as pronouns and demonstratives, for cohesion. To counter the lack of cataphoric pronoun use by HKS, L2 teachers are recommended to introduce the usage of cataphoric reference and encourage students to use it as an alternative to anaphoric demonstratives, in order to widen their variety of sentence structure. L2 teachers may show that there are two ways in using pronouns—cataphoric and anaphoric—and give students pairs of examples for illustration, as in (3a) and (3b):

(3a) "After *he* finished his homework, Jack watched television."
(3b) "After Jack finished his homework, *he* watched television."

Students will then learn that sentences can be constructed in both ways.

In addition, L2 teachers are recommended to be aware of the significant difference in frequency of referential devices and to show L2 students the cases in which these devices are necessary.

Ellipsis

Ellipsis is regarded as one of the most difficult rhetorical devices in application for L2 learners. Not surprisingly, no record of ellipsis was found from HKS texts while a few were found from NS (Table 5). An example with verbal ellipsis from an NS text is shown below:

(4) "'I'm going to get you,' shouted Jamie laughing. 'No you *won't,*' laughed Jo as he ran across the park."

Table 5. Number of texts with ellipsis and substitution

Ellipsis	NS	HKS
Verbal	1	0
Clausal	3	0
Substitution		
Nominal	23	21
Verbal	2	0
Clausal	0	0

Ellipsis was found only in dialogues from the samples. Dialogues make the narrative texts look more vivid, and are more common in NS than in HKS texts. In fact, ellipsis is common in Chinese dialogues but Chinese seldom use dialogues in narratives. Therefore, no ellipsis was recorded in HKS texts.

Substitution

Substitution can be made for nominals, verb groups, and clauses. Example (5) is a nominal substitution from an HKS and (6) is a verb group substitution from an NS:

(5) "Four children were very angry about *that* and wanted to fight him."

(6) "'I hate Alex,' shout Mandy. 'We all *do,*' growled Jeff."

Both HKS and NS texts have a similar frequency of nominal substitution, but HKS have no record of verb group substitution (Table 5). L2 teachers can introduce to advanced L2 learners the fact that use of verb group substitution is common, especially in informal or oral English, as in example (6).

Ellipsis and substitution, which are typically found in dialogues, are underused by HKS. The inadequate awareness of the presence of these features in dialogues in narrative writing might be one of the reasons contributing to this result. Therefore, more attention should be paid to the use of ellipsis and substitution for L2 writing.

Conjunctive Cohesion
The study focuses on additive, causal, adversative, non-contrast and expansion conjunctions, and temporal connectors, and differences in their use were examined.

a. Coordination
1. Additive Conjunction

A remarkable difference was found in the usage of coordination between HKS and NS English texts. HKS used about 70 percent more additive conjunctions than NS (Table 6). NS showed coordination without frequently using overt connectors, while HKS tended to use the connector "and" for coordination.

Table 6. Average number of conjunctions (against average number of T-units) of coordination and subordination

Conjunction	NS	HKS	Ratio (NS:HKS)
Additive	0.071	0.124	3.6:6.4
Causal	0.007	0.011	3.9:6.1
Adversative	0.003	0.011	2.0:8.0
Non-contrast and expansion	0	0.003	—
Temporal	0.009	0.008	5.3:4.7

b. Subordination
In general, HKS used more connectors in subordination.

1. Causal and Adversative Conjunctions
HKS observed strict cause-effect order by applying overt connectors. The number of causal conjunctions used by HKS is 60 percent more than that of NS. In addition, the frequency of adversative conjunctions used by HKS in their English texts is four times of that of NS.

2. Non-contrast and Expansion Conjunctions
Aligned with the results obtained from causal and adversative conjunctions, HKS used more non-contrast and expansion connectors, such as "moreover" and "for example." Fifteen percent of HKS used non-contrast and expansion conjunctions, as in examples (7) and (8), but no record of these was found in NS texts.

(7) "*Moreover*, all of us have to take others and others' properties into consideration all the time."

(8) *"For example,* while other children are playing around the park, Joe likes riding his bicycle, persuits them and will pretent to crash them."

Non-contrast and expansion conjunctions are typical in academic or expository discourse but not in narrative discourse. However, the finding that some HKS used these types of conjunctions in narratives reflects the fact that HKS are not aware of the different usage of conjunctions in different discourses. It is recommended at this stage that L2 teachers show students that the usage of certain types of conjunctions is generally confined to a particular discourse. For instance, non-contrast and expansion conjunctions are more widely used in academic and expository writing than in narrative writing. Advanced L2 learners should note this difference in order to improve their written rhetoric.

3. Temporal Conjunctions

While HKS used more conjunctions in general, the temporal conjunction is the only type of conjunction that NS used more than HKS. This may be explained by the awareness of the importance of temporal sequencing in narratives by both NS and HKS.

The above data on conjunctive use indicate that HKS tend to use more overt connectors for causal, adversative, non-contrast and expansion coordination, and subordination. On the other hand, NS expressed this conjunctive cohesion in various ways. In addition to using connectors, NS used action verbs and relative clauses in the sentential and discourse levels, as in example (9):

(9) "He had ridden his bicycle straight through the beautiful 'purple jeepers' flower, leaving poor Katy brushed out of the way."

Narrative Structure

Since both groups of subjects were adults of similar age and level of education, I assumed that they would not reveal any difference in their ability to construct narrative texts. It turned out to be the case that texts written by both groups show a comparable command of 'action structure' with a setting, reference to an enabling situation, a complicating event, a high point, and a coda.

HKS produced well-constructed narrative texts with overt temporal sequencing, a high point, and a coda. On the other hand, NS combined this level of narrative structure with informative details and evaluative comments. Significant differences were found in the content and location of informative and evaluative elements. NS incorporated additional information and a moral that summarizes or evaluates the story's relevance not only in their coda but also within other constituents of the text, while HKS were more confined to the information given from the picture series.

Informative Elements

Informative elements are the basic component found in orientation. Orientation includes the time of the story, its spatial setting, and character identification. Both HKS and NS groups provided the above information but the samples show that HKS gave more specific information on time orientation while NS gave more specific information on character identification.

a. Time Setting

From the data, no specific time was found in NS texts, while 30 percent of HKS offered a specific time orientation in their texts. For example:

(10) *"Last Sunday, May and Susan went to the park."*

b. Character Identification

One of the marked differences between the two groups relates to a particular narrative convention, i.e., the introduction of and reference to the characters (Table 7).

Table 7. Number of nexts with character identification

Character identification	NS	HKS
Referring with names	36	26
Relationships among characters	35	26

HKS texts are less specific in referring to the characters and in addressing the relationships among them. When referring to the characters, only 65 percent of HKS used English names, while 90 percent of NS texts used them. NS preference for naming the children may reflect a cultural difference in narrative conventions, particularly in what is customary in storytelling to children. Many HKS used non-specific phrases, like 'some children,' to refer to the characters instead of giving names for them individually.

HKS lower specificity in writing may be attributed to the influence of their L1, since both their English and Chinese texts recorded fewer cases of referring to characters with names. The different degree of specificity between HKS and NS is therefore worth highlighting in L2 teaching.

Another informative element of character identification is relationships among characters. HKS texts are shown to be less specific. Eighty-eight percent of NS and 65 percent of HKS addressed the relationships among characters, exemplified in (11) and (12) respectively (Table 7):

(11) "*The Appleton family* decided to have a picnic in Stanley Park. Not wanting to go alone, they invited *their neighbours, the Waltons,* to join them.

(12) Jenny dated *her best friend, Windy,* to a garden near her home to play and appreciate flowers."

The less specific approach adopted by HKS might be due to the influence of Chinese convention, as it is always the responsibility of the reader to interpret the text, rather than of the writer to give all the information.

c. Background Information

Good storytellers may give additional information about the actors and their motives, and about other activities that may be going on in parallel with the story. Only 68 percent of HKS gave background information in their English or Chinese texts while 78 percent of NS did so. Example (13) illustrates this:

(13) "Not far away and not long ago there lived a man called *Mr. Green.* Mr Green was a gardener and he worked at a nearby park called Pleasant View Park. The park was very beautiful because Mr Green enjoyed his job and worked very hard. He let all the local children play in the park. They were happy to be there and Mr Green was happy to see them happy. The only rule was the children weren't allowed to damage the plants and flowers."

In this example, a new character—Mr. Green, the gardener— was added in the text. Most of the NS texts offered background information on the park or on reasons for the children to be in the park. In contrast, similar detailed examples are not found in HKS texts. The richest background information in their texts is shown in example (14):

(14) "Yesterday was the day of science study trip of Ben's primary school. The location of the trip was the Flower Garden which is a very famous garden in Canada."

This is not only the case for HKS English texts but also for their Chinese texts. Background information found in Chinese texts is restricted to a limited number of phrases only. This may reflect the convention that Chinese avoid giving uncertain information. Therefore, not much additional information was given.

Evaluative Elements

Evaluative elements were found in different parts of the texts. One of the remarkable differences is that 8 percent of HKS used evaluative elements in the orientation, but no NS used them. Example (15) is from an HKS:

(15) "This story tell us that if a person has done a bad thing, he will be subject to a bad result at the end."

The result might be attributed to the influence of Chinese storytelling convention that narratives serve the purpose of teaching their reader. This convention is common in many Asian language speakers, like the Thai, who consider that writing serves the function of teaching and evaluating (Indrasuta 1988).

Evaluative elements were occasionally found in other constituents of NS narrative texts. Forty-five percent of NS texts have the evaluative elements, like teaching, in the body of their texts, as in example (16):

(16) "*You shouldn't have climbed that tree!* I told you it was dangerous. There are sometimes reasons for rules!" said one of the boys.

However, this kind of teaching element is relatively less common in the body of HKS texts.

Codas may also contain a moral that summarizes or evaluates the story's relevance. Although the number of texts with a moral in the coda is similar in all three sets of data, the content of the moral shows significant differences.

In most NS narratives, interpretive remarks are attributed to the narrator as a principal, who is either addressing himself at the time, or quoting himself as addressing other characters. However, most HKS added other characters who were often senior to the children, such as, in this case, a mother, to provide evaluation devices. We may compare examples (17) and (18) from NS and HKS respectively:

(17) "Therefore, as Tommy The Terror learned the hard way, 'treat your friends the way you want to be treated.'"

(18) "*My mother comforted me* and said 'Boy, your starting point is good, but you really use the wrong method.' She continued, 'You should ask them to play with you if you want to join them, instead try to do something that will damage the garden.'"

This result may reflect the convention that Chinese narrative serves the purpose of teaching and the person who gives the lesson is always senior.

Pedagogic Implications

NS texts are not considered as a model but rather as a reference for comparison in this study. The data obtained from NS and HKS helps us understand the differences in rhetoric adopted by native speakers and L2 learners. The differences in the areas of cohesion and narrative structure in NS and HKS English texts raise awareness of contrastive rhetoric as regards L2 teachers. This study succeeds in showing the areas in rhetoric that L2 teachers might focus on during L2 teaching.

Regarding cohesion, differences in the use of referential items between NS and HKS was noted. HKS lack of cataphoric pronoun use may be attributed to the fact that Chinese pronouns are mainly anaphoric. Therefore, different types of pronouns, cataphoric and anaphoric, may be introduced to L2 learners in order to enhance the variety of sentence structures in their L2 writing. In addition, influenced by the less frequent use of pronouns and demonstratives in Chinese, HKS underused these referential items. L2 teachers need to be more concerned about this case, and to provide their students with illustrative examples when necessary.

Second, HKS use of ellipsis and substitution is relatively low. The findings reveal that L1 linguistic influence does not play much role with regard to this aspect. The result may best be explained by the fact that L2 teachers seldom introduce the usage of these cohesive devices in dialogues or oral English, and L2 learners are not aware of the use of dialogues in written narratives. Therefore, the usage of ellipsis and substitution needs to receive more concern from L2 teachers and learners.

Third, HKS tend to use overt connecting devices, while NS use various devices, such as action verbs and relative clauses, to show cohesion. L2 teachers may show students the alternatives to using connectors—action verbs and relative clauses—which can help express the conjunctive relations.

In respect of narrative structure, although both HKS and NS produced texts with major constituents of narrative structure, remarkable differences were found among the narrative content elements, especially the informative and evaluative elements. The content and location of these elements are different for the different subject groups. NS focus on both the actions of the characters and their relationships, while HKS focus more on time setting and overt conjunctive cohesion. Distribution of background information and evaluative commentary in different narrative constituents characterizes most NS texts in our sample. However, evaluative elements of HKS texts are mainly found in the coda constituent only.

In addition, NS texts are more specific in giving information, like referring to characters by name. In order to improve L2 writing, L2 learners should be aware of the different interpretive responsibility of Chinese and English texts. Writers in English play a more significant role in writing. A more specific approach is necessary in English, not only for narrative but also for other genres such as argumentative and academic writing.

Conclusion and Further Research

The examination of the different use of cohesive devices and of the different content and location of elements between NS and HKS texts helps us to draw considerable pedagogic implications for L2 teachers. It also raises awareness of the significance of contrastive rhetoric in L2 writing for L2 learners, especially advanced ones. The findings support the conclusion that both the linguistic and cultural influences of L1 play an important role in L2 writing. The different use of cohesive devices is mainly attributed to the linguistic influence of L1, whereas the different content and location of elements in narrative structure may be due to the cultural influence of L1 (Chinese). In fact, the influence of L1 on L2 covers both linguistic and discourse levels, from cohesive devices to narrative structure.

Further contrastive rhetoric research on the influences of L2 on L1 writing would help in better understanding L2 writing. In addition, the results obtained from this study could be compared with those from other oriental languages in order to gain more insights into the role that oriental languages play in L2 English writing.

Notes

1. This research was funded by the Departmental General Research Fund, Department of Chinese and Bilingual Studies, The Hong Kong Polytechnic University.
2. T-unit refers to an independent clause with all its dependent clauses; the average T-unit length is often used as a measure of syntactic complexity.

References

Berman, R.A. 1997. "Narrative Theory and Narrative Development: The Labovian Impact." *Journal of Narrative and Life History* 7 (1–4), 235–244.

———. 1999. "Bilingual Proficiency/Proficient Bilingualism: Insights from Narrative Texts," in G. Extra and L. Verhoeven (eds.), *Bilingualism and Migration*. Berlin: Walter de Gruyter.

Biber, D., Conrad, S., and Reppen, R. 1998. *Corpus Linguistics: Investigating Language Structure and Use*. Cambridge: Cambridge University Press.

Connor, U. 1996. *Contrastive Rhetoric: Cross-linguistic Aspects of Second Language Writing*. Cambridge: Cambridge University Press.

———. 1997. "Contrastive Rhetoric: Implications for Teachers of Writing in Multicultural Classrooms," in C. Severino, J. C. Guerra, and J. E. Butler (eds.), *Writing in Multicultural Settings*. New York: Modern Language Association.

Connor, U. and Johns, A. M. (eds.). 1990. *Coherence in Writing: Research and Pedagogical Perspectives.* Alexandria, Virginia: Teachers of English to Speakers of Other Languages.

Extra, G. and Verhoeven, L. (eds.). 1999. *Bilingualism and Migration.* Berlin: Walter de Gruyter.

Halliday, M.A.K. and Hasan, R. 1976. *Cohesion in English.* London: Longman.

Hatch, E. 1992. *Discourse and Language Education.* Cambridge: Cambridge University Press.

Hudelson, S. (ed.). 1981. *Learning to Read in Different Languages.* Washington, D.C.: Center for Applied Linguistics.

Indrasuta, C. 1988. "Narrative Styles in the Writing of Thai and American Students," in C. Purves (ed.), *Writing across Languages and Cultures: Issues in Contrastive Rhetoric.* Newbury Park: Sage Publications.

Labov, W. 1972. "The Transformation of Experience in Narrative Syntax." *Language in the Inner City.* Philadelphia: University of Pennsylvania Press.

Martin, J. E. 1992. *Towards a Theory of Text for Contrastive Rhetoric.* New York: Peter Lang.

Matsuyama, U. K. 1983. "Can Story Grammar Speak Japanese?" *The Reading Teacher* 36, 666–669.

Purves, C. (ed.). 1988. *Writing across Languages and Cultures: Issues in Contrastive Rhetoric.* Newbury Park: Sage Publications.

Schaefer, J. 1981. "Coupling as Text-building, Myth Evoking Strategy in Vietnamese Implications of Second Language Reading," in S. Hudelson (ed.), *Learning to Read in Different Languages.* Washington, D.C.: Center for Applied linguistics.

Severino, C., Guerra, J. C. and Butler, J. E. (eds.). 1997. *Writing in Multicultural Settings.* New York: Modern Language Association.

The Qur'anic Definite Article in Translation
The Case of Citing Animals

Mohamed Farghal
Izzedin al-Zou'bi

The definite article in both English and Arabic is primarily employed to define, determine, individualize, familiarize, etc. Shared knowledge, part–whole relationship, and previous mention constitute the main contexts which discoursally call for the utilization of the definite article in both languages. Being one of the most frequent elements in language, the definite article, as Hewson (1972:131) argues, "affects a tremendous range of discourse." It also, due do its pervasive presence in language, correlates with general competence in other language skills. In this regard, Oller and Redding (1971:93) hold the view that "the learning of article usage goes hand-in-hand with the development of overall proficiency." This being the case, articles in general and the definite article in particular are expected to pose serious problems in foreign language learning. For example, al-Johani (1983:1), while making specific reference to English, states that, "The articles in English have always been a source of difficulty, especially for the foreign learner of the language."

Translation activity, it may be argued, is an advanced application of foreign language learning, where an adequate degree of bilingual and bicultural competence is presupposed. This transnational competence functions as the touchstone in transferring meaning as encapsulated in textual material between any two languages (Catford 1964; Nida 1965). The replacement of textual material in the Source Language (SL) with textual material in the Target Language (TL) involves decision-making at the levels of phonology, morphology, syntax, semantics, pragmatics, and discourse in its entirety. It should be noted that these levels are interrelated and that there is no one-to-one correspondence between languages.

As a consequence, languages may utilize different resources in realizing meaning. For instance, what is achieved morphologically in one language, e.g., negotiable in English, is realized lexically in another language, viz. /qɑːbil li-t-tafaːwud/ ("may be negotiated") in Arabic or, vice versa, what is achieved morphologically in Arabic, e.g., /waladajn/, is realized lexically in English, viz. two boys.

Being a discourse-oriented grammatical marker, the definite article constitutes a problematic area in translation between Arabic and English. While both languages may employ the definite article referentially as well as generically in descriptions whose head is a singular common noun, only Arabic may utilize the definite article both referentially and generically in descriptions whose head is a plural common noun. That is, English, while exclusively employing the definite article referentially in descriptions whose head is a plural common noun, has recourse to the zero article for realizing the generic use in such cases. By way of illustration, consider the following examples:

1. a) /ʔal-ʔasad-u ħajawaːn-un muftaris-un/
   DEF-lion-NOM animal-NOM ferocious-NOM
   "The lion is a ferocious animal."

   b) /ʔal-ʔusuːdu ħajawaːnaːt-un muftarisat-un/
   DEF -lion(pl)-NOM animal(pl)-NOM ferocious(pl)-NOM
   "'Lions are ferocious animals."

2. a) The lion is a ferocious animal.
   b) Lions are ferocious animals.
   c) *The lions are ferocious animals.

The Arabic sentences in (1a and 1b) exhibit the generic use, and so do the English sentences in (2a and 2b). By contrast, the English sentence in (1c) cannot be interpreted as referring to the entire class of lions, hence its ill-formedness insofar as the generic use is concerned. Further, English may utilize the indefinite article for realizing the generic use while Arabic may not, as can be illustrated below (for more details, see Farghal and Shunnaq 1999:49–52):

3. a) A lion is a ferocious animal.
   b) */ʔasad-un ħajawaːn-un muftaris-un/
   lion-NOM animal-NOM ferocious-NOM
   "A lion is a ferocious animal."

The asymmetries between Arabic and English in the use of articles constitute grammatical voids (for more on this, see Farghal and Shunnaq 1998). In particular, the non-correspondence between the generic use involving the definite article plus a plural common noun in Arabic, and the non-generic use featuring the definite article plus a plural common noun in English, is expected to pose serious problems in translation, even to the most professional translators, with Qur'anic translation being no exception. In the case of Qur'anic translation, this mishap may be due to the fact that translators may lack native intuitions about article usage, whether this be in Arabic when the translator is not a native Arabic speaker or in English when he is not a native English speaker, or in both when he is not a native speaker of either language. Consequently, and in the heat of paying optimal attention to form, translators sometimes fall victim to transferring the article when no such correspondence exists. Thus, as Neubert and Shreve (1992:113) argue, "Grammar does more than serve as a structural vehicle for associating words in sentences. Grammatical structures can also serve semantic functions by indicating important relations." With this in mind, one-to-one formal correspondence should be replaced with one-to-many formal correspondence whereby, according to Ivir (1981:55), "a given formal element of the source language, used in different texts produced in different communicative situations, will have several target language formal elements which will correspond to it in translated texts."

The Data

The present study examines the definite article in Qur'anic translation with reference to the citation of animal names in the Holy Qur'an. For this purpose, a select sample of translations of Qur'anic verses involving animal names will be used. The examples will be drawn from three translations by Mohammad Taqiydin al-Hilali and Mohammad Muhsin Khan (1993), Sheikh Izziddin al-Hayek (1996), and Abdullah Yousuf Ali (1964), with an eye to critically evaluating them in terms of definiteness.

To get started, let us consider the Qur'anic verse in (4) along with its translations in (5) below:

4. /qɑ:lu: ʔudʕu lana rabbaka yubajjinu lana ma: hija ʔinna ʔal-baqara taʃa:baha ʕalajna wa ʔinna ʔin ʃa:ʔa ʔallahu lamuhtadu:n/ (al-Baqara 70)

5. a) "They said, 'Call upon your Lord for us to make plain to us what it is. Verily to us *all cows* are alike, And surely, if Allah wills, we will be guided.'" (al-Hilali and Khan).

5. b) "They said: 'Call upon your Lord to tell us what sort of cow she should be; because *all the cows* look alike to us. We hope to be guided if Allah wills.'" (al-Hayek).

Looking at the two translations, it can be readily seen that the generic animal citation in the Qur'anic verse is correctly rendered by al-Hilali and Khan but erroneously by al-Hayek. The Qur'anic verse makes reference to all members of the class (i.e., cows in general), and so does al-Hilali and Khan's translation. However, al-Hayek's translation incorrectly refers to a specific group of cows by employing the English definite article before a plural common noun, a use which is categorically referential in English. This non-correspondence between the definite article when modifying a plural common noun in the two languages seems to account for most of the problems in translating Qur'anic definiteness into English. In other words, in cases like these, syntactic definiteness does not coincide with semantic definiteness in Arabic, whereas it does in comparable cases in English. Below is another illustrative example exhibiting the same kind of problem:

6. /fa?arsalna ʕalajhim ?aṭ-ṭu:fa:na wal-ʒara:da wa-l-qummala wa-ḍ-ḍafa:diʕa wa-d-dama ?aja:tin mufaṣṣala:tin fastakbaru: wa ka:nu: qawman muʒrimi:n/ (al-A'raf 133)

7. a) "So We sent on them: the flood, *the locusts, the lice, the frogs*, and the blood (as a succession of manifest signs), yet they remained arrogant, and they were of those people who were Mujrimun (criminals, polytheists, sinners, etc.)." (al-Hilali and Khan)

    b) "So We sent down on them the flood, *the locusts, the vermins, the frogs* and the blood; these were clear miracles, but they were arrogant and guilty people." (al-Hayek)

    c) "So We sent (plagues) on them: wholesome Death, *Locusts, Lice, Frogs*, and Blood: Signs openly self-explained: but they were steeped in arrogance, a people given to sin." (Ali)

Among the translations in (7), only Ali's translation in (7c) renders the generic animal names in the Qur'anic verse correctly by employing the zero article in English. Both al-Hilali and Khan's and al-Hayek's renditions relay the syntactically but not semantically definite Arabic nouns as both syntactically and semantically definite in English, thus confusing syntactic with semantic definiteness.

In some cases, a pseudo-correspondence may occur between the generic use of the Arabic definite article when it is followed by a singular common noun and the referential use of the English definite article when a singular common noun comes after it. This pseudo-correspondence results from the fact that the generic scope of the definite article modifying a singular noun in Arabic is much wider than that of its English counterpart. By way of illustration, consider the examples in (8) and (9) below:

8. a) /?aḍ-ḍabʕ hajawa:n-un bari:-un/

    b) /?akalahu ?aḍ-ḍabʕu/

9. a) The hyena is a wild animal.

    b) The hyena ate him.

While (8a) and (9a) are equally interpreted generically because they make general statements about the entire class of hyenas, (8b), unlike (9b), has the potentiality of being interpreted generically, in which case it functionally corresponds to 'A hyena ate him,' rather than (9b). It should be noted that the English sentence, 'A hyena ate him' may be interpreted both referentially and generically, given the appropriate context just like the Arabic sentence in (8b).

This area of pseudo-correspondence has apparently caused serious problems to some translators of the Holy Qur'an. The example in (10) along with its translations in (11) is only illustrative:

10. /qa:lu: ja: ʔaba:na ʔinna ðahabna nastabiqu wa tarakna ju:sufa ʕinda mata:ʕina faʔakalahu ʔað-ðiʔbu wama: ʔanta bimuʔminin lana walaw kunna ṣa:diqi:n/ (Yusuf 17)

11.a) "They said: 'O our father! We went racing with one another, and left Joseph by our belongings and *a wolf* devoured him, but you will never believe us even when we speak the truth.'"

b) "They said: 'O our father! We went racing with one another, and we left Yusuf by our things, so *the wolf* ate him. But you will not believe us even though we are telling the truth.'" (al-Hayek)

c) "They said: 'O our father: We went racing with one another, and left Joseph with our things; and *the wolf* devoured him .... But thou wilt never believe us even though we tell the truth.'" (Ali)

As can be noted, al-Hayek and Ali in (11b) and (11c) respectively render the generic animal citation, i.e., /ʔað-ðiʔbu/ by a referential citation, i.e., *the wolf*. By doing so, they communicate the message that Joseph was eaten by one particular wolf, but, actually, the intended meaning of the Qur'anic verse is that Joseph was eaten by one particular species, i.e., wolves, rather than one specific member of the species. The intended meaning is correctly captured by al-Hilali and Khan in (11a), whose rendition of the Qur'anic animal citation can be interpreted generically in this context, that is, it refers to any wolf as representative of the members of the entire class.

Finally, let us cite a situation where the English definite article modifying a singular noun may be correctly employed as an alternative to the generic zero article when relaying a generic Qur'anic citation, as can be illustrated in (12) and (13) below:

12. /waʕala allaði:na ha:du: ħarramna kull ði: ẓufurin wa-mina-l-baqar wa-l-ɣanam ħarramna ʕalajhim ʃuħu:mahuma ʔilla maħamalat ẓuhu:ruhuma ʔaw al-ħawa:ja ʔaw maxtalaṭa biʕ ẓm ðalika ʒazajna:hum bibaɣjihim wa ʔinna laṣa:diqu:n/ (al-An'am 146)

13.a) "To those who are Jews We forbade every animal with claws And of the oxen and the *sheep* We forbade unto them the fat thereof, save what is upon the backs or the entrails, or what is mixed up with the bone, this in recompense for their willful disobedience, and what we say is quite truthful." (al-Hayek)

13.b) "For those who followed the Jewish Law, We forbade every (animal) with undivided hoof, and We forbade them that fat of *the ox* and *the sheep*, except what adheres to their backs or their entrails, or is mixed up with a bone: this is recompense for their willful disobedience: for We are true (in our ordinances)." (Ali)

While Ali succeeds in rendering the generic Qur'anic animal citation by generic English expressions, viz. *the ox* and *the sheep*, al-Hayek, as is often the case in Qur'anic translation, mistakenly employs the definite article instead of the zero article in modifying generic plural nouns in English. This being the case, the animal citation in the context at hand involves one-to-two correspondence between Arabic and English, that is, the generic Arabic animal names /ʔal-baqar/ and /ʔal-ɣanam/ may instantiate two functional equivalents in English, viz. *oxen* and *sheep*, and *the ox* and *the sheep*, respectively.

Conclusion

This paper has examined the citation of animal names as a paradigm example of reference in Qur'anic discourse and translation, with an eye to checking the translator's awareness of the syntactic versus semantic definiteness or the generic versus referential use of the Arabic definite article and its functional counterparts in some English translations of the Holy Qur'an. It becomes clear that these translators have no consistent understanding and/or policy in dealing with the Arabic definite article in translation. In fact, we find the same translator(s) capturing the generic use in one Qur'anic context but missing it in another comparable context. For example, al-Hilali and Khan succeed in relaying the generic function in (2a) but they fail to do this in (4a) above.

The etiology of the translator's confusion has been shown to be twofold. Most importantly, there is the non-correspondence between the frequent employment of the Arabic definite article generically in modifying plural common nouns and the categorical employment of the English definite article referentially in comparable cases. In this regard, functional correspondence exists between the Arabic definite article and the English zero article. This basic mismatch accounts for the bulk of mishaps in the translation of Qur'anic definiteness. Secondly, and also importantly, there is the pseudo-correspondence in some cases between the use of the Arabic definite article modifying a singular common noun generically, and the employment of its English counterpart referentially;

in such cases, English would use the indefinite rather than the definite article generically (see the examples in (11) above).

Finally, the feature of definiteness in language must be viewed as a discourse-oriented feature whose true value is to be sought in the context of situation rather than in decontextualized formal correspondents. With this in mind, one-to-many, many-to-one, many-to-many correspondence between languages becomes the rule, while one-to-one correspondence is relegated to the exception. Only then will translation function as an act of communication.

References

Ali, A.Y. 1964. *The Holy Qur'an: Text Translation and Commentary.* New York: Tahrike Tarsile Qur'an Inc.

Catford, J.C. 1965. *A Linguistics Theory of Translation: an Essay in Applied Linguistics.* Oxford: Oxford University Press.

Farghal, M., & Shunnaq, A. 1998. "Grammatical Voids: A Translational Perspective," in *Perspectives: Studies in Translatology* 6 (1), 79–89.

——. 1999. *Translation with Reference to English and Arabic.* Irbid: Dar al-Hilal for Translation.

Al-Hayek, S. I. 1996. *The Honorable Qur'an in the English Language: An Approximate, Plain and Straightforward Translation.* Beirut : Dar al-Fikr.

Hewson, J. 1972. *Article and Noun in English.* The Hague: Mouton.

Al-Hilali, M. T., & Khan, M. M. 1993. *The Noble Qur'an in the English Language: A Summarized Version of al-Tabari, al-Qurtubi, and Ibn Kathir.* Riyadh: Maktabat Dar al-Salam.

Ivir, V. 1981. "Formal Correspondence vs. Translation Equivalence Revisited," in *Poetics Today* 2, 51–59.

al-Johani, M. H. 1983. "English and Arabic Articles: A Contrastive Analysis in Definiteness and Indefiniteness." Unpublished Ph.D. Dissertation, Indiana University, Bloomington.

Neubert, A., & Shreve, G. M. 1992. *Translation as Text.* Kent (Ohio): Kent State University Press.

Nida, Eugene A. 1964. *Toward a Science of Translating.* Leiden: E. J. Brill, Netherlands.

Oller, J. W., & Redding, E. Z. 1971. "Article Usage and Other Language Skills," in *Language Learning* 21, 85–95.

Verbal Fluency in Bidialectal Settings

The Case of the Greek Cypriot Dialect

Andreas Papapavlou

It has been reported in Cypriot magazines that the majority of Greek Cypriots do not have a complete mastery of spoken Standard Modern Greek (SMG), that their vocabulary is limited, that they feel uncomfortable using SMG, and that their fluency of expression is imperfect and inadequate. That is, when using SMG, especially in formal settings, Cypriots' speech is slow and full of hesitations; they are unable to utter a complete clause without interjecting Cypriot terms.

No empirical evidence has been presented for this claim; however, educators, linguists, and psychologists on the island agree that such a problem does exist (to some degree), but are unable to reach a consensus as to the probable causes of this phenomenon. Some are ready to attribute the problem to the poor teaching of the Greek language in state schools and to the insufficient exposure to and use of SMG, while others seem to relate the problem to Cypriots' ethnic ambivalence and preference for the use of English instead of Greek. Others, however, believe that the problem is psychological and not linguistic. Lastly, there are those who contend that the problem is directly related to the "imposition" of another code or "idioma" on the native language of Greek Cypriots, the Cypriot dialect. As a result of this educational "intervention," Cypriots become bidialectal, able to express themselves in two "codes" or "idiomas," albeit with some difficulties in the formal (official) one.

The aim of the present paper is to examine a) how Cypriot university students view and define the Cypriot dialect and the circumstances under which they find it necessary to vary this code, b) whether the daily usage of this code, along with SMG, affects their oral and written expressive skills (as compared to those of mainland Greeks who normally use one standard code), and c) to identify those factors that are believed to be affecting the oral fluency of Cypriots.

Background

In the first six years of their lives, Greek Cypriot children are mainly exposed to and use the Cypriot dialect in their daily interactions with parents, friends, and neighbors. It may be true that children hear SMG on the radio or on television, but it is not until they begin formal schooling that these children are systematically exposed to SMG. The common practice in schools is for teachers to use exclusively SMG in the classroom and to demand that their pupils use this code throughout the lessons. Teachers consider it their duty to correct pupils when they use certain Cypriot lexical items in place of "proper" Greek terms (such as [tsa'era] instead of [ka'rekla] "chair," [kʰe'lle] instead of [ke'fali] "head"), when they pronounce Greek words with Cypriot phonology ['mitʰi] instead of ['miti] "nose," [mpou'kʰali] instead of [mpou'kali] "bottle," or when substituting Greek phonetic units with Cypriot ones through the application of phonological rules permissible only in the dialect (such as ['ʃeri] instead of ['xeri] "hand," [dʒe'ros] instead of [ke'ros] "weather" (for more details on Cypriot phonology see Newton, 1972a, 1972b). Ordinarily, teachers correct pupils either by repeating the "proper" form of the word or by "ridiculing" them for the way they speak. Often, children are made to feel, perhaps unintentionally, that their own natural way of speaking is wrong, inferior, or impolite. As a result, they appear uneasy when using their native code and gradually come to believe that such a code should only be used by elderly Cypriots living in rural areas (the so-called [xor'kades] "peasants"). Meanwhile, in the school setting, teachers revert to the dialect when interacting with each other during breaks, and children use the dialect among themselves outside the classroom and, of course, at home after school. This rather artificial phenomenon continues throughout the child's formal primary and secondary education and, as a result, the linguistic situation in Cyprus has acquired the following characteristics: a) knowledge of SMG remains academic and superficial for most Cypriots, who frequently feel pretentious and phony when using it; b) those who have to use SMG on formal occasions appear uneasy and uncomfortable with this code; to overcome their uneasiness, Cypriots resort to avoidance strategies and circumlocutions by using longer phrases in place of terms they are not familiar with; c) the majority of Cypriots feel out of place and "inferior" when using SMG in the presence of mainland Greeks; and (d) the language of the heart, for most adult Greek Cypriots, remains always the dialect (Papapavlou 1989, 1998; Papapavlou and Pavlou 1998).

Given the present bidialectal situation in Cyprus, the following questions need to be addressed: a) Should the use of dialects be forbidden in formal education or encouraged? b) Should standard languages be forced on users of non-standard languages and dialects? c) Is the bidialectal situation in Cyprus any different from that in other countries? And d) How does this situation affect the users of the dialect and what problems does it create?

Review of the Literature

Bidialectalism and diglossia are related phenomena and have been studied by several researchers. Diglossia, according to Ferguson (1959), exists in countries whose members use one dialect or code for *formal* purposes and for public events and another dialect in *informal*, everyday situations. In other countries the distinction is between a *high* (H) and a *low* (L) dialect and in some other places the distinction is between the *classical* (literary standard) and the *colloquial* (or local vernacular) form of the language. Richards *et al.* (1985) define a bidialectal person as someone who "knows and can use two different dialects. The two dialects are often a *prestige* dialect, which may be used at school or at work and is often the standard variety, and a *non-prestige* dialect, which may be used only at home or with friends" (237).

Standard or prestigious dialects may have different social functions. In most instances, standard dialects bind people together and are perceived to be highly sophisticated. On the other hand, non-standard languages or dialects are popularly believed "although without any foundation, to be inferior forms, degenerate offshoots from the accepted standard." "Nevertheless," Cripper and Widdowson (1978) continue, "they express a way of life and a sense of cultural identity just as much as do more prestigious language types" (177). Also, according to Fromkin and Rodman (1993), a standard or prestigious dialect "is neither more expressive, more logical, more complex, nor more regular than any other dialect or language" (285). Thus, it may be argued that judgments about the superiority or inferiority of dialects or languages are purely *social* and do not have any *linguistic* basis (Papapavlou 1998, 2001).

The Use of Standard Languages as Mediums of Instruction

Issues related to language policy and planning are very complex and several factors (national, social, political) come into play when choosing a language that is deemed to be "appropriate" and "proper" for schooling purposes. One of the arguments frequently presented by those who advocate the use of standard languages in schools is "to strengthen national unity" among the speakers in a given country. In the case of Cyprus, two more reasons are offered for the use of SMG: a) to deter the possibility of being cut off from the "motherland" (i.e., Greece), and b) to maintain a national identity that is not much different from that of mainland Greece, since the two places share a common history, customs, culture and religion. After Cyprus's independence in 1960, the educational authorities of Cyprus adopted the use of SMG in schools mainly for the reasons stated above. Although the use of SMG in schools was not directly imposed on Cyprus by Greece, it is worth pointing out the following: in 1963 a three-member Educational Commission was sent by the Greek government to Cyprus in order to review the educational system of the island and submit their recommendations. The Commission, along with other recommendations, proposed to the then educational authorities that "they should try to avoid, within the schools term favoring the formation of a *Cypriot national conscience*. To this effect the use of the Cypriot dialect should be avoided in the classrooms" (Persianis 1981:78).

The Use of Dialects as Mediums of Instruction
The use of minority languages as mediums of instruction in schools has received considerable attention recently. For example, Kaplan (1992), in discussing issues of language policy and planning in various countries, makes references to the situation in France. According to Kaplan, speakers of Provençal and Langue d'oc "are unhappy about the imposition of the northern metropolitan (standard) French in their southern regions. Also, the Alsatian people are equally unhappy about the domination of their French/German dialect by French" (146). Furthermore, Kaplan argues that "the policy of the [French] government has consistently been to develop the standard and metropolitan variety of French at the expense of all other languages and French dialects . . . . The language policy of the French government was one of brutal suppression of minority languages and dialects" (146). As a result of this long period, French people from the provinces who had the desire to succeed in French society had to make the effort of learning "good" Parisian French. More recently, several movements have taken place for the use of dialects or local languages in schools, as opposed to "standard" languages. After much effort the French government in 1982 decreed that, in addition to the national language, the languages and cultures of Brittany and other areas would be promoted through schooling, festivals, and exhibitions (Grillo 1989; Press 1994; Temple 1994).

As one might expect, when the child's mother tongue is a non-standard variety and the child is forced to receive education in another form, various educational problems arise. Examples of these situations are found when African American Vernacular English or "Ebonics" (earlier known as Black English) is used in US schools and when English-based creoles of the West Indies are used in UK state schools. In the past, some researchers actually believed in the existence of an intellectual deficit on the grounds that the speakers in such communities are linguistically deficient (Bereiter and Englemann 1966). Other researchers, however, like Labov (1972), who studied Ebonics, refuted the linguistic deficiency theory. Ebonics, many experts would argue, has its own rules and black children do not speak "improper English"; they simply speak another language (Wolfram, 1991; Wolfram and Christian 1989). In the case of Afro-Caribbean (West Indian) children in Great Britain, Edwards (1978a, 1978b) demonstrated that linguistic factors (differences between Creole and standard) and non-linguistic factors (attitudes of peers, teachers, and community members) affect the Afro-Caribbean child's comprehension of Standard British English as well as the child's motivation to learn it. The low academic achievement of these children was first attributed to temporary problems of adjustment, then to negative self-conception, and, of course, to racist teaching. Thus, as noted by Cripper and Widdowson (1978), "by conducting education in the standard version of the language one might change the values of the learners which bind them to their background and thereby cut them off from their cultural heritage" (177). Such situations create numerous problems for the learning attainment and academic success of these children and, therefore, attention should be given to searching for appropriate types of bidialectal education.

Bidialectal Education

Bidialectal education faces extremely complex problems, some of which are socioeconomic, sociocultural, pedagogical, and linguistic in nature. The communities that use the non-standard variety are generally socio-economically and culturally deprived and, in most cases, they are minority groups. In addition, bidialectal education has to fight against attitudes and prejudices developed in the dominant group. Also, the members of these minority groups may need help in order to expel any feelings of inferiority that they may have about themselves and dismiss the notion that their dialect is a stigma, something they should get rid of (Hamers and Blanc 1989). Three types of solutions have been proposed for bidialectal situations: a) the creation of *compensatory programs*, which accept the notion of linguistic deficiency and their aim is to change the linguistic habits of the children and re-educate them into speaking the "proper" language; b) the creation of *bidialectal programs*, which teach the children to use the standard variety at school but these children are also encouraged by the school to use their dialect in their own environment (Fasold and Shuy 1970; Chesire 1987); c) the *eradication of prejudices programs*, which attempt to reduce the attitudes and prejudices of standard speakers of the dominant group, rather than modify the children's behavior (Hamers and Blanc 1989).

Since not all bidialectal settings are identical, it is important to present the major differences between the bidialectal setting in Cyprus and that in other places. First, Greek Cypriots are not a minority on the island and, therefore, they are not in any way socio-economically and culturally deprived (in comparison to other groups living on the island or even in comparison to mainland Greeks). The island is quite wealthy and it has its own long history and rich cultural background. Second, the issue of linguistic deficiency does not seem to apply in this case because when Cypriots are expressing themselves exclusively in the dialect, they appear to be quite fluent, very expressive, and imaginative. Furthermore, a great number of Cypriots hold university degrees and many speak several foreign languages. Also, a substantially rich Cypriot literature and folklore flourished in the past and this literature is mainly written in the dialect (each author writes differently in the dialect since the dialect has never been standardized).

Aims of the Present Study

Some studies cited above suggest that users of dialects may be linguistically deficient, a notion that has not gone unchallenged, and other studies offer various solutions regarding the use of dialects and non-standard codes as mediums of instruction in schools. As far as can be ascertained, there are no studies examining the effects of bidialectalism on fluency of expression when the speakers use the standard form. Thus, this study undertakes such an investigation, to which we now turn.

Method

Subjects

The subjects of the study were 177 Greek Cypriot students, 20 male and 157 female, between the ages of 18 and 20, attending the University of Cyprus (a few mainland Greek students were excluded from the study). These students were randomly selected from six different general required university courses from the humanities, had a similar prior education, and came for the most part from middle-class families.

Instrument

For the purposes of this study a questionnaire was developed in Greek that consisted of three sections with eight Likert-scale questions. In the first section (which contained five questions), participants were given definitions describing six varieties (registers) of the dialect and were instructed to select the definition (variety) that, in their opinion, best describes the dialect (the descriptions of the Cypriot dialect are shown in Table 1). Also, participants were asked to indicate which variety they *use* in their daily interactions and whether they modify this code according to the person they speak to, the topic of their conversation, and the impression (image) they would like to create of themselves. In the second section (which contained two questions), participants were asked to evaluate their own *oral* and *written* skills by comparing themselves to mainland Greeks. Finally, in the third section, participants were asked, in the case that they had indicated that they believed that Cypriots lack oral fluency, to indicate the degree (very much, much, little, very little, nothing) to which each of twelve factors affects this condition (these linguistic or psychosocial variables were selected as factors likely to have an effect on verbal fluency).

Table 1. Varieties of the Cypriot dialect as presented in the questionnaire

Varieties	Descriptions of the Cypriot dialect
1	Like the code used in the radio program known to all as the Cypriot Sketch.
2	Like the Cypriot Sketch, but this code is enriched with vocabulary from Standard Greek and without the conscious avoidance of Cypriot sounds like [tʃ], [dʒ], [ʃ], [ʒ]
3	Like the Cypriot Sketch, but with the conscious avoidance of Cypriot sounds.
4	Like Standard Greek, with the presence of Cypriot terms (loanwords) and with the use of Cypriot sounds.
5	Like Standard Greek, with the presence of Cypriot terms but with the conscious avoidance of Cypriot sounds.
6	Like Standard Greek, without the presence of Cypriot terms and with the conscious avoidance of Cypriot sounds.

Procedures

Students were informed by their instructors that they were randomly selected to take part in a study that examines the linguistic behavior of Cypriots and were asked to complete, in class, an anonymous questionnaire. Students were assured that their answers would remain confidential and be used only for the purposes of the study.

Results and Discussion

The answers to the questionnaires were tabulated and analyzed statistically. The results for each section of the study are presented in various tables.

Definitions of the Cypriot Dialect and Preferred Levels of Daily Usage

The definitions that were selected by participants as being the best descriptions of the Cypriot dialect are presented in Table 2.

Table 2. Definitions (varieties) that best describe the Cypriot dialect

Description (varieties) of the dialect	Number of participants who prefer the description of this variety	Percentage of participants who prefer the description of this variety
1	7	3.9
2	82	46.3
3	0	0.0
4	83	46.9
5	4	2.3
6	1	0.6

The participants' preferences for the frequent *usage* of the dialect are presented in Table 3.

Table 3. Definitions (varieties) of the Cypriot dialect that are used daily

Description (varieties) of the dialect*	Number of participants who prefer the use of this variety	Percentage of participants who prefer the use of this variety
1	2	1.3
2	55	33.9
3	0	0.0
4	81	50.0
5	18	11.1
6	6	3.7

*Of the 177 participants, 162 answered this question

A close examination of the results shown in Tables 2 and 3 reveals that participants differentiate what the dialect is (i.e., the definition that best describes the dialect) from what they actually *use* in their daily lives. Thus, whereas 93% of the participants agree that the definitions that best describe the dialect are 2 and 4 (which, linguistically speaking, are almost identical with each other—see Table 1), only 83% use these two specific levels (2 and 4) and others prefer to use other varieties (including 5 and 6). This result is not surprising, as it reveals that Cypriots, like speakers of other languages, prefer to use varieties of their language or dialect which they consider more "appropriate" or more "sophisticated."

Table 4 presents the changes or variations that participants make in the code according to a) the person they speak to, b) the subject of their conversation, and c) the impression they would like to create of themselves.

Table 4. Variations in the code according to addressee, topic, and the impression participants want to create

Degree to which this code is varied	According to addressee		According to topic		To create a better impression	
	# of participants	% of participants	# of participants	% of participants	# of participants	% of participants
Very much so	84	47.8	47	26.2	46	26.2
A few times	75	42.6	78	44.3	78	44.3
Not consciously	12	6.8	44	25.0	39	21.2
Never	5	2.8	8	4.5	14	7.9

A close examination of Table 4 reveals that participants vary their speech *very much* according to the *person* they speak to rather than according to the topic of their conversation or the impressions they would like to create of themselves. Also, it is worth noting that an equal number of participants code-switch a *few times* in all three conditions (42.6%, 44.3%, 44.3% respectively)

Evaluation of the Oral and Written Skills of the Participants

Participants' evaluations of their oral and written skills in comparison to those of mainland Greeks are presented in Table 5.

Table 5. Participants' evaluations of their oral and written
skills in comparison to those of mainland Greeks (MGs)

Evaluation of skills as com- pared to MGs	Oral skills		Written skills	
	# of participants	% of participants	# of participants	% of participants
Much higher (than those of MGs)	0	0	3	1.7
Higher	2	1.2	9	5.1
Equal	25	14.2	111	63.0
Lower	99	56.2	42	24.9
Much lower	50	28.4	11	6.3

Table 5 shows that 84.6% of the participants consider their own oral skills as being *lower* or *much lower* than those of mainland Greeks. However, they do not feel the same about their own written capabilities. In fact, 63% of the participants (about two-thirds) believe that their written skills are about *equal* to those of mainland Greeks and another 7% as being *higher* or *much higher* than those of mainland Greeks. As can be clearly seen, participants are aware that their skills in oral fluency are limited but do not accept the same for their writing skills.

Factors Affecting Oral Fluency of Expression

Participants were asked if they believed that Cypriots lack oral fluency and to indicate the degree to which each of twelve factors affects this phenomenon. Their responses are presented in Table 6.

Table 6 shows that participants believe that *none* of the twelve factors affects *much* or *very much* Cypriots' oral fluency. Ten factors were evaluated as affecting oral fluency either as very little (7 factors) or nothing (3 factors). Only two factors (out of 12) are declared to possibly affect, to a small degree ('little'), oral fluency and these are a) lack of enriched vocabulary, and b) the presence and use of two codes by the same speaker (i.e., bidialectalism).

Table 6. Evaluation of twelve factors that possibly affect the oral fluency of Greek Cypriots

#	Factors affecting the oral fluency of Cypriots	Very much 5	Much 4	Little 3	Very little 2	Nothing 1
		Average evaluation of all participants for each factor				
1	Incomplete mastery of the Greek language				X	
2	Lack of enriched vocabulary			X		
3	Lack of respect for the Greek language				X	
4	Introversion and shyness				X	
5	Lack of imagination					X
6	Parents' low educational back-ground				X	
7	The presence of a second code (the dialect)			X		
8	The influence of learning for-eign languages				X	
9	Lack of freedom of speech				X	
10	Parents' authoritative behavior					X
11	Feelings of inferiority and mediocrity				X	
12	Ambivalence in ethnic identity					X

Concluding Remarks

In this study an effort was made to examine empirically a) how Cypriots view and define the Cypriot dialect and the circumstances under which they vary this code, b) whether the daily usage of this code, along with SMG, affects their oral and written expressive skills, and c) what factors they believe affect their oral fluency.

Notwithstanding certain limitations (using university students only as participants; participants report on what they think rather than on what they actually do), the results reveal the following important findings: the majority of participants (over 93%) agree with the definitions that best describe the Cypriot dialect (2 and 4), which linguistically are almost identical, and while the majority of participants report that they *use* 2 or 4 more often, others prefer to use levels 5 and 6. This finding is not surprising since speakers of other languages also perceive different levels or registers of their language to be more "eloquent" or "sophisticated."

Cypriots, like other bidialectal speakers, frequently switch from one code to the other. What is important in the present findings is the conditions under which this code varies. It appears that participants vary their code much more depending on *who* their interlocutor is than the topic of their conversation or the impression they would like to create of themselves. This finding is indeed interesting as it shows that, in friendly and intimate circles, participants do not vary their code as much because of the topic of discussion (i.e., from simple chatting and gossiping, to football, to politics) or for the sake of impressing each other. Code-switching in intimate situations (around family members or around familiar people or friends) is perceived by most Cypriots as being either phony or pretentious. On the other hand, the person they speak to appears to be an important factor for code-switching, especially when such a person is perceived to be more educated (and by extension probably more sophisticated), or a person in authority (at the place of work), or a mainland Greek. Under these circumstances, Cypriots find themselves using a level that is probably "higher" than what they are comfortable or feel at ease with. Switching to a higher code may also explain the reported "disturbances" in oral fluency.

The present findings also show that while participants consider their own oral skills as lagging behind those of mainland Greeks, they do not accept the same for their written skills. In fact, a great majority of participants believe that their written skills are at least equal to those of mainland Greeks or, for some, even higher. Furthermore, while participants may admit that their oral fluency may lag behind, they do not accept that their mastery of SMG is in any way imperfect or incomplete and the cause of the problem. Rather, they appear to believe that their oral skills are probably related, to some degree to the lack of enriched vocabulary and to the use of two codes. That is, it may be argued that when speakers have to search from a "pool" of limited vocabulary to satisfy their interactional needs and when these same speakers have to pass the selected lexicon through the "filters" of a) semantic verification, b) phonological correctness, or c) appropriateness of the selected code, certain problems arise in the fluency of these speakers: their speech appears to be slow, full of hesitations, and with many pauses.

It may be concluded that oral fluency may be related to the various choices that a bidialectal person is called upon to make at any given moment. Thus, it appears that more empirical research is needed for the identification of those variables that cause problems in fluency and for the selection of appropriate bidialectal educational programs that can provide the requisite opportunities for the parallel and equal mastery of both codes.

References

Bereiter, C. and Engelman, S. 1966. *Teaching Disadvantaged Children in the Preschool.* Englewood Cliffs, N.J.: Prentice Hall.

Cheshire, J. 1987. "A Survey of Dialect Grammar in Britain," in M. Blanc and J.F. Hamers (eds.) *Theoretical and Methodological Issues in the Study of Languages/ Dialects in Contact at Macro- and Micro-Logical Levels of Analysis.* Quebec: International Center for Research on Bilingualism, B-160, 50–58.

Cripper, C. and Widdowson, H.G. 1978. "Sociolinguistics and Language Teaching," in J.P.B. Allen and Corder, S.P. (eds.) *Papers in Applied Linguistics.* Oxford: Oxford University Press.

Edwards, V.K. 1978a. "Language Attitudes and Underperformance in West Indian Children." *Educational Review* 30, 51–58.

———. 1978b. "Dialect Interference in West Indian Children." *Language and Speech* 21, 76–86.

Fasold, R. and Shuy, R.W. (eds.) 1970. *Teaching Standard English in the Inner City.* Washington, DC: Center for Applied Linguistics, Urban Language Series.

Ferguson, C.A. 1959. "Diglossia." *Word* 15, 125–140.

Fromkin, V. and Rodman, R. 1993. *An Introduction to Language.* New York: Harcourt Brace Jovanovich College.

Grillo, R.D.C. 1989. *Dominant Languages.* London: Cambridge University Press.

Hamers, J.F. and Blanc, M.H.A. 1989. *Bilinguality and Bilingualism.* New York: Cambridge University Press.

Kaplan, R. 1992. "Applied Linguistics and Language Policy and Planning," in W. Grabe and Kaplan, R. (eds.) *Introduction to Applied Linguistics.* Cambridge: Addison-Wesley Publishing Company.

Labov, W. 1972. *Language in the Inner City: Studies in the Black English Vernacular.* Oxford: Blackwell.

Newton, B. 1972a. *Cypriot Greek: Its Phonology and Inflections.* The Hague: Mouton.

Newton, B. 1972b. *The Generative Interpretation of Dialect: A Study of Modern Greek Phonology.* Cambridge: Cambridge University Press.

Papapavlou, A. 1989. "The Language Problem in Cyprus Today." *The Cyprus Review* 1, 137–142.

———. 1998. "Attitudes toward the Greek Cypriot Dialect: Sociocultural Implications." *International Journal of the Sociology of Language* 134, 15–28.

———. 2001. "Mind Your Speech: Language Attitudes in Cyprus." *Journal of Multilingual and Multicultural Development* 22, 491–501.

Papapavlou, A. and Pavlou, P. 1998. "A Review of the Sociolinguistic Aspects of the Greek Cypriot Dialect." *Journal of Multilingual and Multicultural Development* 19, 212–220.

Persianis, K.P. 1981. *The Political and Economic Factors as the Main Determinants of Educational Policy in Independent Cyprus* (1960–1970). Nicosia: Proodos Press.

Press, I. J. 1994. "Breton Speakers in Brittany, France and Europe: Constraints on the Search of an Identity," in M.M. Parry, W.V. Davies, and R.A.M. Temple (eds.). *The Changing Voices of Europe* (chapter 13). Cardiff: University of Wales Press.

Richards, J., Platt, J. and Weber, H. 1985. *Longman Dictionary of Applied Linguistics.* Suffolk: Longman.

Temple, R.A.M. 1994. "Great Expectations? France's Regional Languages," in M.M. Parry, W.V. Davies, and R.A.M. Temple (eds.). *The Changing Voices of Europe* (chapter 12). Wales: University of Wales Press.

Wolfram, W. 1991. *Dialects and American English.* Englewood Cliffs, NJ: Prentice Hall and Center for Applied Linguistics.

Wolfram, W. and Christian, D. 1989. *Dialects and Education: Issues and Answers.* Englewood Cliffs, NJ: Prentice Hall.

Classical and Colloquial Arabic
Are They Used Appropriately
by Non-native Speakers?

Mona Kamel Hassan

The motivation for this study was the researcher's observation that non-native speakers of Arabic (NNS) consider Arabic to have only two varieties: in the case of Egypt, Egyptian Colloquial Arabic (ECA) and classical, or Modern Standard Arabic (MSA). Furthermore, these speakers assume that in formal situations they should use MSA (or a close approximation of it, which is, in fact, not pure MSA), while in informal situations they should use colloquial (ECA). In other words, they do not recognize that in actual use of the language there is a range of formal or informal registers. These registers were explained by Badawi (1973), who divided Arabic into five levels: 1) Classical Arabic (in the Holy Qur'an and classical texts), 2) Modern Standard Arabic (in the media and modern written texts), 3) Educated Spoken Arabic (in conversations among highly educated people to discuss political, social, cultural, and scientific topics), 4) Semi-Literate Spoken Arabic (in conversations among educated people regarding daily life situations), and 5) Illiterate Spoken Arabic (in conversations among illiterate people in daily life situations). Badawi added that each of these levels has specific functions to perform and that their inappropriate use would be considered odd. The purpose of this study is to investigate the varieties of Arabic used by NNS by comparing them with those used by Egyptian native speakers (NS) in the production of two speech acts, namely apology and gratitude.

Theoretical Background

Ferguson (1991:51, 61), discussing diglossia, has stated that in a given situation, speakers may move from a high variety of a language to a different variety. Such a movement is determined by such factors as "relative social position" and "individual interactional strategies." While conversing with each other, speakers sometimes find it more appropriate to use the L (Low) or H (High) variety in specific situations based on the formality of the context. Meanwhile, in one context, the speaker may find it more appropriate to use the H variety while the hearer may use the L variety to "mark power relationships."

Mitchell (1986), however, divided Arabic into three varieties: 1) Vernacular, which has prestige in both urban and rural regions, 2) Written Standard Arabic, which is also spoken on formal occasions, and 3) Mixed Arabic, which is a mixture of written and vernacular Arabic and which functions in formal and informal situations.

Furthermore, Hymes (cited in Walters 1979) has explained that speakers are not limited to a single variety of a language. This was supported by Gumperz (cited in Walters 1979), who clarified that a person may change from colloquial to a formal variety of a language within a single conversation. The researcher, as a native speaker of both MSA and ECA, supports the above-mentioned researchers. Arabic also has formal and informal varieties, and native speakers determine which situations necessitate the usage of either the formal or the informal variety of Arabic . However, certain situations may necessitate using a mixture of both the formal and the informal varieties based on the interlocutors' social class, educational background, and relationship. Thus, it is concluded that it is important for learners to know native speakers' attitudes toward the different varieties of Arabic in order to use them in appropriate situations.

Searle (cited in Schmidt and Richards 1985) has classified speech acts into 1) Representatives, which tell people how things are, 2) Directives, which ask the hearer to do something addressed to him/her by the speaker, 3) Commissives, which commit the speaker to doing something, 4) Expressives, which express attitudes such as regret, thanks, welcome, and apology, and 5) Declaratives, which use a speech act to do something. This was reinforced by Brown and Levinson (1978), who determined that learners have to learn specific contexts where specific speech acts are appropriate; these contexts differ from one society to another and vary according to the addressee.

Leech (1983:195) explained that the function of apology is to remedy an offense and to maintain what he calls "social harmony." Furthermore, Olshtain and Cohen (1983) explain that apology depends upon certain factors such as social status, familiarity, and the age of both the offended person and the one who has to apologize.

And Leech (1983) has identified thanking as an act that has a social goal, which is to create a friendly and polite atmosphere. Leech added that thanking is expressive because through it the speaker's attitude becomes known to the addressee. This is supported by Eisenstein and Bodman (1986), who note that if expressing gratitude is performed successfully, the language function that is used to express gratitude brings feelings of solidarity and warmth. In contrast, if one fails to express gratitude, this will result in negative social results that sever the relationship between the speaker and the hearer.

Research Questions

This study attempts to investigate the following questions:
1. How do NNS assess the six given situations of the study (Appendix) with regard to the formality and informality of the context?
2. Do NNS use the appropriate variety of Arabic while producing the speech acts of apology and gratitude?
3. Do NNS pay the same attention to grammar, pronunciation, and vocabulary while using different varieties of Arabic?

Subjects

The study was first conducted in 1994 with the participation of two groups of subjects, a control group and an experimental group. The control group consisted of fifteen male and female Egyptian NS, whose ages ranged from 20 to 35. They were learning English as a Foreign Language at the Center for Adult and Continuing Education (CACE) at the American University in Cairo (AUC) at the intermediate level. The experimental group consisted of fifteen male and female NNS of different nationalities, whose ages ranged from 19 to 30. They were learning Arabic as a Foreign Language at the Arabic Language Institute (ALI) at the American University in Cairo (AUC).

The study was re-conducted in 2001 with a different experimental group, which consisted of fifteen subjects with the same background as the subjects of 1994. The subjects of the experimental group had studied MSA for from one semester to five years and ECA for from half a semester to one year. They had studied MSA and ECA in different countries, where they were exposed to various methods of instruction and different educational materials. When asked, the reasons they gave for studying colloquial Arabic were to improve their spoken skill, to be able to speak fluently, to be able to communicate, and for pleasure. Their stated purposes for studying MSA were to be able to read and write, to be able to understand people in Arabic-speaking countries, and because MSA is the Islamic language in Arab countries. They also wanted to learn about the culture and traditions of Arab people. These students reinforced their Arabic skills by reading newspapers, watching television, speaking with people, neighbors, and friends, and dealing with colleagues during work time. The rationale for re-conducting the study was to find out if the same results would be obtained, or, in other words, to find out if NNS were still unaware of the existence of the five levels of Arabic as well as the functions performed by each level in appropriate situations as explained by Badawi (1973).

Instrument

All the subjects of the study, both NS and NNS, were given a questionnaire (Appendix) that included a set of six different situations designed to elicit expressions of either apology or thanks. They were asked to respond to the situations at home at their convenience without consulting anyone about their responses. The situations were obtained by surveying NNS living in Cairo for descriptions of actual incidents they encountered, six of which were chosen. These specific situations were chosen to elicit a range of varieties, from formal to informal. Respondents were to determine the appropriate variety/register to be used in each situation. The situations themselves were written (on pieces of paper) in English, while the subjects were asked to audio-tape their responses in Arabic. Situation 1 took place in a restaurant, where someone bumped into a well dressed lady. Situation 2 dealt with burning the seat in a colleague's car. Situation 3 dealt with breaking a door handle in a taxi. Situation 4 dealt with one person complimenting another for delivering a speech. Situation 5 took place in a bank when one of the clients gave another client his/her turn in a long line. And Situation 6 dealt with a taxi driver helping a customer unload numerous packages.

Each of the six situations was analyzed with regard to appropriate or inappropriate choice of a specific variety of Arabic (MSA or ECA) while attention was also given to grammar, vocabulary, and pronunciation while using either MSA or ECA. The responses of the control and the experimental groups were compared in order to examine similarities and differences as well as the factors that might account for these similarities and differences. This was followed by oral interviews, which the researcher conducted (in English) with the experimental groups on 1) their assessment of the given situations as formal or informal, 2) their preference as to whether more attention should be given to grammar, vocabulary, or pronunciation while moving between the two varieties of Arabic. The collected data were analyzed by noting the frequency with which speakers preferred to select a specific type of Arabic (MSA or ECA) in each of the six situations. The responses of all groups of subjects were transliterated and translated into English. Audio-taping the results was a necessary procedure as it gave evidence of the actual language used by the subjects. Interviewing the experimental groups after the audio-taping was also a necessary procedure as it helped in determining the subjects' assessment of the formality or informality of the situations.

Data Analysis, Results, and Discussion

The data of the study were analyzed according to Badawi's (1973) five levels of Arabic, when subjects made their choices as to the use of formal or informal varieties of Arabic.

Table 1. Assessment of the situations by NS and NNS

Situations	NS		NNS 1994		NNS 2001	
	Formal	*Informal*	*Formal*	*Informal*	*Formal*	*Informal*
1. Restaurant	15	0	15	0	13	2
2. Colleague	0	15	0	15	1	14
3. Taxi	0	15	0	15	0	15
4. Speech	15	0	10	5	8	7
5. Bank	0	15	4	11	2	13
6. Driver	0	15	0	15	1	14

As shown in Table 1, the comparison made between the responses of the NS and the two NNS groups (based on the oral interviews conducted with the experimental groups) revealed that NNS were able to assess the situations as formal/informal, as were the NS of Arabic. Both NS and NNS considered it appropriate to use formal language with the well-dressed lady in the restaurant situation (Situation 1) and with the person who delivered the speech in the speech situation (Situation 4), and to use informal language in the other situations. The kind of situations cannot be detached from the choice of a specific variety of Arabic. In other words, preference for the use of one specific variety of Arabic was determined by the context. One of the factors that determined the choice of a specific variety of Arabic was the relative social status of the interlocutor. Both the NS and the NNS used informal language with a colleague because it is more natural and friendly. Other factors that determined the choice of a specific variety of Arabic were the social class and education of the interlocutor and the relationship with the interlocutors. Consequently, both groups of subjects used a formal variety with a well-dressed lady; however, they used informal language with the taxi driver who presumably represents a lower social class. Subjects felt that it would be more comfortable to use informal language with a taxi driver to be closer to his level. Furthermore, both groups of subjects used formal language in the speech situation (Situation 4) because they were dealing with educated people. This reinforces Ferguson's (1991) and Badawi's (1973) claim that each variety of a language performs a certain function.

Table 2. Variety of Arabic used by NS and NNS

Situation	NS			NNS 1994			NNS 2001		
	fus MSA	*f* Edu	*inf* Semi-lit	*fus* MSA	*f* Edu	*inf* Sem-lit	*fus* MSA	*f* Edu	*inf* Semi-lit
1. Restaurant	0	11	4	6	5	4	0	13	2
2. Colleague	0	14	0	0	13	2	0	1	14
3. Taxi	1	1	13	0	11	4	0	2	13
4. Speech	0	12	3	6	5	4	0	11	4
5. Bank	0	4	11	2	11	2	0	1	14
6. Driver	0	1	14	2	13	0	0	0	15

MSA = Badawi's (1973) Level 2 Modern Standard Arabic
Edu = Badawi's (1973) Level 3 Educated Spoken Arabic (ECA)
Semi-lit = Badawi's (1973) Level 4 Semi-Literate Spoken Arabic
fus = *fusha*, or the formal variety of Arabic
f = formal
inf = informal

With regard to the variety of Arabic actually used by NS and NNS, it was found that although the NNS of 1994 managed to assess the situations as formal/informal like the NS, they may have had the misconception that Arabic is a language that has only two varieties, MSA and ECA, where MSA is the formal language while ECA is the informal one. They may have considered that native speakers use pure MSA in formal situations and pure ECA in informal situations.

The following samples from the 1994 data of NNS illustrate this point:

Situation 1:
/ʔana ʔa:sifa giddan waʔargu ʔan tasmaħi li: ʔan ʔaxuðahu li-t-tanẓi:f/
"I am terribly sorry. If you allow me, I'll take it to the dry cleaner's."

Situation 4:
/ʃukran ja: ʔusta:ð ʔana saʕi:dun giddan ʔannaka ʔaħbabta ʔal-muħa:ḍara/
"Thank you, Sir. I am very happy that you enjoyed the lecture."

Since these two situations are formal, NNS assumed that MSA is the most appropriate variety to be used. In other words, they were unaware of the different levels of ECA (Badawi, 1973). However, Egyptians used the formal level of ECA, which suits the formality of those situations.

Situation 2:
/kunt badaxxan wiʕamalt il-xurm da maʕliʃʃ
"I was smoking and I made this hole (because of the cigarette). Sorry."

Situation 6:
/ʃukran iʃ-ʃanṭa tʔi:la ʔawi il-baʔʃi:ʃ da ʕaʃa:nak ʔallah jixalli:k/
"Thank you. The bag is very heavy. This is your tip. God keep you ."

Although both NNS and NS used the informal variety of Arabic (ECA), NNS did not use the different levels of ECA. NS used the variety that was appropriate to the level of informality of those situations based on Badawi's Levels 4 and 5.

This brings up Ferguson's (1991) explanation that native speakers mix the elements of the formal and informal varieties of a language in one context. Thus, NS may use even a single word from MSA in an informal situation, but this is not done by NNS. On the other hand, the similarity of responses of the NNS of 2001 and those of the NS suggests that learners of Arabic as a foreign language may have become more aware of the appropriateness of the Arabic varieties to the context. The following examples are taken from the responses of NNS of 2001, which agree with NS responses:

> *Situation 1:*
> /ʔaːsif giddan mumkin ʔasaːʕid ħadٚritik wiʔarguːki tiʔbali ʔiʕtizaːri/
> "I am terribly sorry. May I help you? Please accept my apologies."

> *Situation 4:*
> /ʃukran limugamlit ħadٚritik ʔana dajman ʔaʔuːl xuṭab musalijja li-n-naːs/
> "Thanks for your compliment. I always deliver interesting speeches."

> *Situation 5:*
> /ʃukran ʕaʃaːn mistaʕgil laːzim ʔaruːħ makaːn taːni fawran/
> "Thanks, as I am in a hurry. I have an urgent errand."

> *Situation 6:*
> /ʃukran wixud il-baʔʃiːʃ da ʕaʃaːnak ʔinta saʕidtini kwajjis/
> "Thanks. Here is your tip. You helped me well."

This increased awareness might be ascribed to Omaggio's (1986:91) "proficiency-oriented approach" in language teaching methodology, where the language curriculum aims at learning language in context and applying this knowledge to coping with authentic language-use situations. Furthermore, Omaggio (1986) suggests that proficiency is the central issue in language teaching, the question being: "How can we help students learning a second language in a classroom setting become proficient in that language?"

The results also support NNS learners' interest in the speaking skill as the primary goal for language learners whose goal is either to achieve personal satisfaction from being able to speak a second language or to get employment in business or industry, as mentioned by Omaggio (1986). Thus, NNS imitate NS in the usage of the actual varieties that are performed in appropriate contexts.

Table 3. Attention given to pronunciation, vocabulary, and grammar in Egyptian Colloquial Arabic (ECA) by NNS

Skill	NNS 1994 N=15	NNS 2001 N=15	Comments
Vocabulary	10	9	Subjects want to respond in a natural way and not think of forms. They will be understood even with incorrect grammar or pronunciation.
Pronunciation	4	6	Pronunciation should be clear in order to be understood by NS and not to sound like foreigners.
Grammar	1	0	Grammar is only for reading and writing. NS prefer sound pronunciation and vocabulary to accurate grammar.

With regard to the attention paid to grammar, vocabulary, and pronunciation as shown in Table 3, both NNS groups agreed that vocabulary is to be given the greatest attention, followed by pronunciation, with no attention given to grammar while conversing in Arabic, reflecting the attitude that grammar is only for reading and writing.

Following are samples of the errors made in grammar, vocabulary, and pronunciation by NNS:

Grammar:
/ʔana ʕajza tixud il-filu:s/ (instead of /ʕayza:k ta:xud/), using a conjugation that does not exist in Arabic.
"I want you to take this money."
/ħadfaʕ il-ħisa:b ʕasha:n naḍḍafhum/ (instead of /ʔanaḍḍafhum/), where a wrong conjugation is used.
"I'll pay for the cleaning."

Vocabulary:
/ʔana kunt bitdixin/ (instead of /badaxxan/)
"I was smoking."
/ʔinta ʔaħbabt il-muħaḍra/ (instead of /kilmiti/)
"You liked the lecture (speech)."

Pronunciation:
/miʃ ʕarfa ʔana izza:j amalt da/ (instead of /ʕamalt/), having difficulty pronouncing the letter ʕ.
"Sorry I don't know how I did this."

/ʔana ʕajza ʔaːxud bustaːnik lit-tandʒiːf/ (instead of /fustaːnik/),
switching the f sound to a b sound.
"I want to take your dress to the dry cleaner's."

This supports Omaggio's (1986:3) explanation that in the early 1970s there
was a distinction between communicative competence and grammatical
or linguistic competence. In other words, L2 learners were "considered
communicatively competent if they got their meaning across to a listener,
even if their grammatical accuracy was relatively low."

On the other hand, Savignon's (cited in Omaggio 1986) definition of
communicative competence did incorporate linguistic competence as
one of its components. Successful communication would depend largely
on individuals' willingness to take a risk and express themselves in the
foreign language, and on their resourcefulness in using vocabulary and
structure under their control to make themselves understood.

Limitations of the Study and Suggestions for Future Research

Since the study was conducted using a small sample, the results cannot
be generalized. It is suggested that the same study be conducted using a
larger sample to be able to generalize the results. Moreover, the situations
used in the present study were limited to the speech acts of apology and
thanks. It is further suggested that other speech acts be used to find out
if the same results will be obtained. NNS subjects represent a variety of
nationalities, a variable that could not be controlled for, and that might
influence NNS subjects' assessment of the formal versus informal situations. It would be useful to conduct the same study using NNS subjects
who are of the same nationality to see if the same results are obtained
when controlling for such a variable.

Since the situations used in this study were obtained through conducting a survey with NNS living in Egypt, the instrument consisted of situations they were familiar with. It would be interesting to include situations
that are not chosen by the respondents.

Conclusion

To sum up, it is apparent that NNS subjects have become more aware of
the functions performed in each variety of the Arabic language in the
appropriate contexts. It is important to reinforce such an understanding

in the teaching of Arabic as a foreign language through the educational materials used. In other words, it is recommended that learners acquire the different registers of Arabic practically by using a variety of authentic materials that introduce such varieties in either written or spoken texts, with emphasis on the distinction between the two varieties.

Furthermore, it became apparent that NNS preferred to pay attention only to grammar when using MSA, but paid more attention to vocabulary and pronunciation when using ECA, and NNS should be taught that mastering grammar and vocabulary is of equal importance for use of both MSA and ECA.

References

Badawi, M. S. 1973. *Mustawayat al-'arabiya al-mu'asira fi Misr*, 89–213. Cairo: Dar al-Ma'arif.

Brown P. and Levinson, S. 1978. "Universals in Language Usage: Politeness Phenomena," in E.N. Goody (ed.), *Questions and Politeness*. Cambridge: Cambridge University Press.

Eisenstein, M. and Bodman, J. 1986. "I Very Appreciate: Expressions of Gratitude by Native and Non-native Speakers of American English." *Applied Linguistics* 7, 2, 167–185.

Ferguson, C.A. 1996. "Diglossia Revisited," in A. Elgibali (ed.), *Understanding Arabic: Essays in Contemporary Arabic Linguistics in Honor of El-Said Badawi*. Cairo: The American University in Cairo Press.

Leech, G.N. 1983. *Principles of Pragmatics*. London: New Harcourt Brace Jovanovich, Inc., 202–213.

Mitchell, T. 1986. "What is Educated Spoken Arabic?" *International Journal of the Sociology of Language* 61, 7–32.

Olshtain, E. and Cohen. A. 1983. "Apology: A Speech-act Set," in N. Wolfson and E. Judd. (eds.), *Sociolinguistics and Language Acquisition*. Rowley MA: Newbury House, 18–36.

Omaggio, A. C. 1986. *Teaching Language in Context*. Boston, Mass: Heinle and Heinle Publishers Inc.

Schmidt, R.A. and Richards, J.C. 1985. "Speech Acts and Second-language Learning," in Jack C. Richards (ed.), *The Context of Language Teaching*. Cambridge: Cambridge University Press, 100–128.

Walters, J. 1979. "Strategies for Requests in Spanish and English: Structural Similarities and Pragmatic Differences." *Language Learning* 29, (2), 277–293.

Appendix

Please respond orally to the following situations in Arabic.
Record your responses on the cassette tape provided:

Situation 1
In a restaurant, you bumped into a well-dressed lady holding a tray full
of food. The tray spilled all over her and stained her clothes. The lady
shouted at you. Apologize to the lady.

Situation 2
While coming back from a party, a colleague offered to accompany you
with his/her car. You were smoking in the car and the cigarette fell and
burnt his/her seat. Apologize to your colleague.

Situation 3
You were in a taxi and unfortunately you broke the door handle. Apologize
to the taxi driver.

Situation 4
You were giving a speech at a general assembly. After the speech, a person
who was attending and who is unknown to you told you that your speech
was wonderful. Thank him/her.

Situation 5
You went to change money in a bank and found a long queue. You looked
worried and in a hurry, so someone gave you his/her turn. Thank him/
her.

Situation 6
A taxi driver helped you unpack numerous packages up to your apart-
ment. Thank the taxi driver.

Diglossic Switching in the Egyptian Speech Community

Implications for Teaching Spoken Egyptian Arabic

Reem Bassiouney

Egypt is a diglossic community, i.e., a community in which two varieties of language exist: a high variety (H) and a low one (L), each with a different function (Ferguson 1959:2). "H" (Modern Standard Arabic, MSA) is the "highly codified" language used in education, while "L" (Egyptian Colloquial Arabic, ECA) is the one used in everyday situations. The concept of diglossia in relation to Egypt has been examined by quite a number of linguists (cf. Holes 1993, 1995; Mejdell 1996, 1999), who concluded that speakers in Egypt tend to switch between H and L in the same stretch of discourse. An attempt to unify this switching into a single linguistic phenomenon was made by Mitchell (1986), who called this switching between H and L in the Arab world "Educated Spoken Arabic." However, he did not try to explain the pragmatic factors governing the occurrence of this kind of Arabic, nor did he assign to this kind of Arabic any syntactic constraints.

This study proposes that the overlap between H and L must be considered if one wants to teach students of Arabic the real language spoken by educated people. Badawi (1995:38), for example, thinks that "The basic difficulty inhibiting the field of teaching Arabic as a foreign language (TAFL) has been and continues to be the absence of a realistic assessment of the language situations prevalent in Arab societies, especially the socio-linguistic characteristics of Arabic, the degree of interaction between each of its varieties . . . and very importantly the language competence of the educated native speakers."

A sociolinguistic theoretical framework is needed to explain diglossic switching in Egypt, a framework that can act as the basis for formulating a way of teaching "the real language used by Egyptians." There are a number of questions that have to be answered to help define this framework:

1. Why do people in Egypt switch between ECA and MSA? What are the sociolinguistic and pragmatic implications of switching?
2. What are the dynamics of switching between H and L? That is to say, is this switching made at random, or does it have a certain pattern? Is it governed by structural constraints that govern larger phenomena, like the phenomenon of code switching?

This study attempts to provide some answers to the second question by studying three morphosyntactic variables: the negation system in MSA and ECA, the system of deixis in MSA and ECA, and the ECA aspectual marker /b/-. I will study the occurrence of these variables in my data in relation to theories of code switching, specifically the Myers-Scotton theory of a matrix language, and examine the syntactic and morphological possibilities of mixing between MSA and ECA in relation to these variables. Having examined the possibilities of mixing, I will also try to find a larger pattern of distribution of these three variables in discourse that is of a mixed variety, and will then show how these findings can contribute to the field of teaching spoken Arabic as a foreign language.

Nature of the Data

My data consist of approximately 9,050 words of spoken contemporary Egyptian monologues, namely four political speeches (P), four mosque sermons (S), and one university lecture (L). First, I would like to point out that MSA and ECA have many shared lexical, phonological, syntactic, and morphological variables. Therefore, it was difficult at times to make a clear distinction between the two. Clyne (1987:754), when working on Dutch, German, and English, also found it difficult to differentiate between two closely linked languages like Dutch and English. Note the following example given by Clyne:

Meestal hier at the local shop en in Doncaster.
"Mostly here at the local shops and in Doncaster."

The preposition "in" is the same in English, German, and Dutch, and so is the word "here" (hier, here). Thus it is sometimes difficult to differentiate two languages or two varieties used together in the same stretch of discourse. Note also that Parkinson thinks that ECA and MSA are both "parts of a single expressive system" (1996:99). Although one should try as hard as possible to study the structural differences between utterances, one should still consider utterances within a larger framework. Every stretch of discourse is unique in itself as well as being a unified whole.

Categorizing the Data

The data are categorized as follows:

Pure MSA (Modern Standard Arabic)
Pure ECA (Egyptian Colloquial Arabic)
Mixed varieties:
   a.   basically ECA
   b.   basically MSA
   c.   MSA with insertions from ECA
   d.   ECA with insertions from MSA
   e.   A mixture of MSA and ECA[1]

The data are categorized into different levels for a number of reasons: first, these levels enable us to describe more accurately the occurrence of the syntactic variables analyzed later. For example, it is not surprising to find an increase in the use of MSA demonstratives in a monologue in which MSA is the prevalent but not the only variety used. It will be more surprising, however, if, in a monologue in which ECA is the prevalent variety, MSA demonstratives are used more than ECA ones. If this happens, then it is a fact worth some attention. Therefore, there is a need to measure the occurrence of MSA and ECA variables in the monologues and to categorize the monologues accordingly.

It is noteworthy, however, that this division is arbitrary, and, as was said before, the only purpose of this division is to understand the dynamics of how switching between MSA and ECA takes place. I neither claim that the notion of levels occurs in the mind of Egyptians when speaking, nor that these are the levels used by Egyptians when speaking. The only difference between my levels is in the quantity of MSA or ECA variables, whether these variables are phonological, morphosyntactic, or lexical in nature. Table 1 summarizes the categories.

Table 1. Classification of the data

Nature of the monologue	Level used
Political speeches	
Political speech 1	
Part i	Basically ECA
Part ii	Basically MSA
Part iii	Mixture of both
Political speech 2	Mixture
Political speech 3	MSA
Political speech 4	
Part i	MSA
Part ii	ECA
Part iii	MSA
Part iv	ECA
Part v	MSA
Religious sermons	
Sermon 1	Basically ECA
Sermon 2	MSA with insertions from ECA
Sermon 3	Basically ECA
Sermon 4	MSA
University Lectures	
Lecture 1	ECA with insertions from MSA

The Three Variables and the Reasons for Choosing Them

The three variables were chosen specifically because they are realized differently in MSA and ECA. They have not been discussed in detail by Ferguson and his successors (cf. Bassiouney 1998, 2000), and they have not been discussed as a single type of variable in Myers-Scotton's terms of system morphemes. Linguists have tended to study these variables separately (cf. Rammuny (1978) (negation), Al-Hassan (1980) (demonstratives), Mitchell and Al-Hassan (1994) (verbal aspect). These variables will also allow us to question some ideas about syntactic constraints on code switching.

Structural Constraints on Diglossic Switching as Part of Code Switching

With very few exceptions (Eid 1988), no one has tried to examine the syntactic rules that govern switching between ECA and MSA. Moreover, there are even fewer studies that attempt to explain syntactic constraints on diglossic switching as part of code switching. Code switching has been defined by Gumperz as "the juxtaposition within the same speech exchange of the passages of speech belonging to two different grammatical systems or subsystems" (1982:59). Therefore, code switching is not restricted to switching between different languages (Myers-Scotton 1998b:18; Mejdell 1999:226). The need for studies that examine diglossia within the framework of code switching is urgent. Walters (1996:181), for example, recognizes that the mixing between H and L that occurs in Arabic can be studied in relation to Myers-Scotton's theory of "matrix language": "Work that considers the nature of diglossic switching in the light of Myers-Scotton's model of the grammatical structure of code switching would also be welcomed . . . . Arabic will provide a fertile ground for testing and refining her model even as her model provides the most comprehensive framework to date for analysing code switching as a formal problem." (1996:193)

There have been a number of theories that try to impose syntactic constraints on code switching. For example, the two-constraint theory by Sankoff and Poplack (1981), the theory of government and binding by Di Sciullo *et al.* (1986), and the theory of the matrix language by Myers-Scotton (1997). I will concentrate on the ML theory as the most promising. This is because it does not rely on a specific theory of grammar, as does the government and binding theory. This means that the ML hypothesis will not be influenced by whatever theory of grammatical structure is adopted. This, in fact, is an essential point since syntacticians are now modifying the government and binding theory, and are opting for a more lexically based theory.[2] More importantly, Myers-Scotton's theory tries, in an unprecedented manner, to combine a theory that can explain both the discourse functions of code switching and the structural constraints on code switching. Myers-Scotton thinks that by having a matrix language, linguists can start addressing the question more clearly of why people switch between languages.

The Matrix Language Hypothesis

Myers-Scotton (1998b:21) thinks that human beings are equipped with an innate language faculty that enables them to assess linguistic choices. Code switching as defined by Myers-Scotton (1997:45) is a phenomenon that allows morphemes from two or more languages in the same projection of a complementizer, by which Myers-Scotton means a subordinate clause (see also Roberts 1997:34).

According to Myers-Scotton, when two languages or varieties are brought together by a bilingual or monolingual speaker, there is a dominant language at work. Thus, one language should be assigned the status of what she terms a "matrix language" (ML). The ML supplies the grammatical frame of constituents. Myers-Scotton's main hypothesis is that there is always an ML in bilingual (or diglossic) communities and there is always only one ML at a time. Thus, one has first to recognize the ML, then analyze a structure, and maybe later assign discourse functions to it.

An ML is defined by "system morphemes." There are two kinds of morphemes, based on the lexical feature of plus or minus "thematic roles." Content morphemes assign or receive thematic roles, like agent, experiencer, beneficiary, etc. This category includes nouns, descriptive adjectives, and most verb stems. System morphemes, on the other hand, cannot assign or receive thematic roles. This category includes inflections, determiners, possessive adjectives, and intensifier adverbs. Thus, an ML supplies system morphemes, which are syntactically relevant. The embedded language (EL) supplies only content morphemes. Myers-Scotton's main hypothesis is that "languages can sustain structural incursion and remain robust, but the taking in of alien inflections and function words is often a step leading to language attrition and language death" (1998a:289).

Examining Structural Constraints on Diglossic Switching

Application of the ML Hypothesis to the Data
In the data there are examples of mixed forms, consisting of:
1. A negative marker in one variety and a verb in another.
2. A demonstrative marker in one variety and a noun in another.
3. An aspectual marker (the /b-/ prefix) in one variety and a verb in another.

All the mixed forms consist of:
1. ECA negative marker + MSA-like verbs
2. ECA demonstrative marker + MSA-like nouns
3. An ECA aspectual marker (/b-/ prefix) + MSA-like verbs

There are no examples of:
1. MSA negative marker + ECA verbs
2. MSA demonstrative marker + ECA nouns
At first glance, one may claim that if the three markers discussed, which are system morphemes, are realized in ECA, then, according to the matrix language hypothesis, the ML is ECA, and the EL is MSA. The

basis of mixing is an ECA syntactic sub-structure, into which MSA lexical elements are inserted. Examples in my data that suggest that this is the case follow (system morphemes are underlined and clauses are divided by a slash).

Negative particles:
1) /wi liða:lik il-ʔima:n miʃ ka:fi/ (S2)
   "That is why believing by itself is not enough."

System morphemes:
/il-/ definite article ECA or MSA
/miʃ/ negative particle ECA

Content morphemes:
/ʔima:n/ noun ("belief") MSA
/ka:fi/ adjective ("enough") MSA

Morphemes that are difficult to classify:
/liða:lik/ (Thus) MSA
(This morpheme is difficult to classify as an MSA content morpheme since it does not seem to assign thematic roles; besides, I do not think that it can be considered an MSA system morpheme because it is more like a frozen conjunctive).

In this example, the ML is ECA since ECA provides the sub-structure of the sentence, while the speaker fills in the lexical gaps with MSA items. The negative marker, which is considered by Myers-Scotton a system morpheme, is in ECA, while the content morphemes that assign thematic roles, like nouns and adjectives, are in MSA.

Demonstratives:
2) /ʔaj ʔanna il-ʕaql da ma:dda bituntiʒ il-fikr/ (S2)
   "That is to say, this mind is a substance that produces thinking."

System morphemes:
/il-/ definite article ECA/MSA
/da/ demonstrative marker ECA
/bi/ aspectual marker ECA
/il-/ definite article ECA or MSA.

Content morphemes:
/ʕaql/ noun (brain) MSA

/maːdda/ noun (substance) MSA
/tuntiʒ/ verb (produce) MSA [as above]
/fikr/ noun (thinking) MSA and ECA
Again, in this example, the morphemes that do not assign theta (thematic) roles, like the demonstratives and the aspectual markers, are in ECA, while the morphemes that assign theta roles, like nouns and verbs, are in MSA. Therefore, the ML in this example is ECA.

The /b-/ prefix:
   3) /jaʕni kull il-duwal illi bitaqaʕ ʕala ħawḍ il-baħr il-
      mutawassiṭ/ (L1)
      "That is to say, all the countries that lie on the Mediterranean
      Sea."

System morphemes:
   /kul/ specifier ECA or MSA
   /il-/ definite article ECA or MSA
   /illi/ relative marker ECA
   /bi/ aspectual marker ECA
   /ʕala/ preposition ECA and MSA
   /il-/ definite article ECA or MSA
   /il-/ definite article ECA or MSA

Content morphemes:
   /jaʕni/ verb ("to mean") ECA
   /duwal/ noun ("countries") ECA or MSA
   /taqaʕ/ noun ("fall") MSA
   /ħawḍ/ noun ("area") MSA
   /baħr/ noun ("sea") ECA or MSA
   /mutawassiṭ/ adjective ("middle") ECA or MSA
The system morphemes in this example, like the aspectual marker /b-/, occur in ECA rather than MSA, while the content morphemes like nouns, verbs, and adjectives are from both ECA and MSA.

   In the above examples, the system morphemes are realized in ECA, while the content morphemes are realized in MSA. Apparently then one may conclude that the ML in the Egyptian speech community is ECA, and the EL is MSA. However, there are a number of examples in my data that pose problems for the ML hypothesis, and these examples suggest that the situation in the Egyptian community is more complicated than that. Therefore, one may have to abandon the idea of an ML in favor of a more sophisticated framework that can explain more precisely what takes place in the Egyptian community.

Problems with the ML hypothesis

Examples that pose problems for the ML hypothesis:

4) /wi kaːn fiːh ʔittifaːqaːt bitunaffað/ (P1, 2)
   "And agreements were being applied."

System morphemes:
/fiːh/ ("there is/are") ECA verbal existential complement.
/bi/ aspectual marker ECA
/u/ and /a/ in the verb /tunaffað/, denote the MSA passive
form of the verb (discontinuous passive morpheme).

Content morphemes:
/kaːn/ verb ("to be") both MSA and ECA
/ʔittifaːqaːt/ noun ("agreements") MSA
/tunaffað/ verb ("to be applied") MSA

If we accept the ML–EL hypothesis, then, in this example, it is very difficult to decide what the ML is. As the aspectual marker on the verb is in ECA, one might expect the other ML variables to be ECA also, as was the case in the previous examples. In this example, though, one cannot claim that there is only one ML at work. In fact, there are one discontinuous system morpheme taken from MSA and two taken from ECA. The speaker uses the existential /fiːh/, which is ECA, and also uses the /b-/ prefix, which is an ECA feature, but he still uses the discontinuous passive morpheme /u-a/, which is quintessentially MSA. This "internal" form of the passive is not available for him in ECA, in the sense that it cannot be applied to ECA passive verbs, which have the /it-/ prefix. To clarify this point further, I will give the ECA and MSA counterparts of this example:

5) /wi kaːn fiːh ʔittifaʔaːt bititnaffiz/ (ECA)
   "And agreements were being applied."
6) /wa kaːnat hunaːka ʔittifaːqaːt tunaffað/ (MSA)
   "And agreements were being applied."

Existence is expressed in ECA by a morpheme that is etymologically a locative adverb /fiːh/, which has no morphosemantic analogue in MSA. In MSA it is /juːʒad/ (a passive verb) or /hunaːk/ (an adverb). This means that there is no possibility of mixing between the two systems to express existence—the two systems do not overlap at this point of morphosyntactic structure. The ECA form has been selected. Similarly, as far as the verb (being applied) is concerned, the passive form is expressed in MSA by structures that have no morphosemantic analogue in ECA. Here the

MSA form has been selected.[3] If this is the case, one cannot say that, in a sentence like that quoted, the ML is ECA. The speaker obviously knows specific morphosyntactic forms of both ECA and MSA and uses them in this example. The example is particularly interesting because it has intra-word code switching: in the same word we have an aspectual morpheme from ECA, and a passive morpheme from MSA.

Other examples that pose problems for the ML hypothesis are as follows:

7) /ʔana bataṣawwar ha:ða: il-kala:m lajsa ka:fijan/ (P2)
    "I think this is not enough."

System morphemes:
  /ʔana/ 1st person pronoun ECA or MSA.
  /b/ aspectual marker ECA
  /ha:ða:/ demonstrative MSA
  /il-/ indefinite article ECA or MSA
  /lajsa/ negative marker MSA
  /-an/ case marker MSA

Content morphemes:
  /taṣawwar/ verb (to think) MSA
  /kala:m/ noun (talk) ECA or MSA
  /ka:fij/ [/ka:fi:/—see above] adjective ("enough") MSA

In this example, we find system morphemes from both MSA and ECA. The aspectual marker is an ECA system morpheme, while the demonstrative as well as the negative marker are MSA system morphemes. Moreover, there are two system morphemes in this example that are not exclusive to one variety. It is very difficult to decide, in this example, whether the pronoun /ʔana/ or the article /il-/ (both are system morphemes) belong to MSA or ECA. They are, in fact, items shared by both varieties.

8) /jaʕni bijibʔa fi:h hima:ja fi: ha:ðihi il-mana:ṭiq/ (L1)
    "That is to say, there is protection in these regions."

System morphemes:
  /b/ prefix ECA aspectual marker
  /fi:h/ existential adverb ECA
  /fi:/ preposition ECA or MSA
  /ha:ðihi/ demonstrative MSA
  /il/ indefinite article MSA or ECA\

Content morphemes:
/jaʕni/ verb ("to mean") ECA
/jibʔa/ ("to become") ECA
/ħima:ja/ noun ("protection") MSA or ECA
/mɑnɑ:ṭiq/ noun ("regions") MSA
In this example, the content morphemes that occur are from both
varieties. This is predicted by the ML hypothesis. The problem is that the
system morphemes that occur are also from both varieties. The existential adverb, which does not assign theta roles, and is therefore a system
morpheme, is in ECA, but the demonstrative, which is also a system morpheme, is in MSA. There are system morphemes from more than one variety in the same projection of a complementizer. Besides, as with example
7, there are system morphemes that are difficult to classify as MSA or ECA,
like the preposition /fi:/ and the article /il-/.

9) /wa jurfaʕ ʕanhu il-takli:f da ʔiðɑ lam jakun ʕa:qilɑn/ (S2)
"And this responsibility is lifted off his shoulders if he is not
sane."

System morphemes:
/u/ passive morpheme MSA
/ʕan/ preposition (from) MSA
/-hu/ 3rd person pronoun MSA
/il-/ indefinite article MSA or ECA
/da/ demonstrative ECA
/ʔiðɑ/ (if) MSA
/lam/ negative particle MSA
/jakun/ Jussive MSA
/-an/ accusative marker MSA

Content morphemes:
/jurfaʕ/ verb ("raised") MSA
/takli:f/ noun ("responsibility") MSA
/jakun/ verb ("to be") MSA
/ʕa:qilɑn/ adjective ("sane") MSA
In this example, the speaker uses only MSA content morphemes. He
also uses mostly MSA system morphemes. The negative marker is in MSA,
and he uses MSA pronouns and case markers. However, he uses system
morphemes from both varieties. Moreover, as with the previous examples,
there are system morphemes that are difficult to categorize as ECA or
MSA. The article /il-/ is a case in point.

10) /il-mawdˤuːʕ da kaːn ʕuridˤ ʕala il-muʔtamar il-ʔislaːmi/ (P1,2)
"This issue was presented at the Islamic Conference."

System morphemes:
/il-/ indefinite article ECA or MSA
/da/ demonstrative ECA
/u/-/i/ discontinuous passive morpheme MSA
/il-/ indefinite article MSA or ECA
/ʕala/ preposition ("at, on") MSA or ECA
/il-/ indefinite article MSA or ECA

Content morphemes:
/mawdˤuːʕ/ noun ("issue") ECA or MSA
/kaːn/ verb ("to be") ECA or MSA
/ʕuridˤ/ verb ("to be presented") MSA
/muʔtamar/ noun ("conference") ECA or MSA
/ʔislaːmi/ adjective ("Islamic") ECA or MSA

In this last example, the speaker uses an ECA system morpheme, the demonstrative /da/, as well as an MSA system morpheme, the discontinuous passive morpheme /u/-/i/. Again, in this example, it is difficult to categorize the definite article as MSA or ECA. The content morphemes that occur in this example are from both varieties MSA and ECA. But even with content morphemes, one encounters the same problem, namely that many items are shared by both varieties.

These examples resist interpretation within the framework of diglossia and challenge ideas about syntactic constraints on code switching. First, as noted earlier, linguists studying diglossia have not explained cases of mixing of this sort and have tended to study ECA and MSA variables separately. There have been few attempts to study the use of these variables in mixed speech (ECA and MSA). The two constraints theory (Sankoff and Poplack 1980) and the government principle (Di Sciullo *et al.* 1986) fall short of explaining the above examples. For example, both would predict that there is no switch between an aspectual marker like the /b-/ prefix and a verb. More importantly, the ML hypothesis cannot explain the above examples. The ML hypothesis predicts that all the system morphemes will be in the ML, and in these examples we see system morphemes from two different varieties being used together in the same word. There are two MLs at work here:, ECA and MSA.

One might expect, as I did initially, that the basis of mixing in these monologues is an ECA syntactic substructure, into which MSA lexical elements are inserted. But some examples proved to be more problematic. The idea of a basic substructure (an ML) falls short of explaining the last examples for a number of reasons. First, the ML hypothesis is based on the idea that there is always only one ML at a time. That is to say, once there is more than one ML at a time, then this is an indicator of language death. For example, the taking of inflections and function words from a language other than the ML is a step toward language attrition and death. As was shown in the examples above, there sometimes seems to be more than one ML at work. Although the theory of ML is indeed valid in certain cases, it does not seem to give a clear-cut picture of what goes on in this diglossic community.

Another problem with this theory is the fact that in certain examples it is very difficult to decide whether a certain morpheme belongs to ECA or MSA. The MSA definite article /(v)l/, where v stands for vowel, has no fixed vowel quality, since the latter changes according to its position in the sentence, and so it is sometimes difficult to classify the article as MSA or ECA. Moreover, some prepositions (which are system morphemes) are shared by both varieties.

ECA and MSA are different varieties with many shared content and system morphemes, and it is almost impossible sometimes to say whether a certain morpheme belongs to ECA or to MSA. Thus it is not easy to come up with one ML, since it is sometimes difficult to decide which variety is being used in the first place.

The Composite ML Hypothesis

Myers-Scotton has recently, however, proposed another idea to explain some cases of code switching. This is the idea of a composite matrix language (1998a:289). She posits that when there is a change in progress in a bilingual community, the ML is a composite, based on structures from both languages, but moving toward the new ML. Usually the change in progress is completed, and a language shift follows, with the new language playing the role of an ML.

The idea of a composite ML can help us explain what is going on in the Egyptian speech community. The problem with this hypothesis is that one cannot just claim that there is change in progress in Egypt, either in the form of language shift or of language death.[4]

Having established the fact that the Egyptian community has a composite ML, I would like to examine how different system morphemes from both varieties are distributed in the data.

The Pattern of Distribution of the Three Variables

I found that speakers tend to alternate between ECA and MSA demonstratives in the same speech performance, while they find it difficult to use

MSA and ECA negative systems in the same speech performance. This fact will be explained below.

Consider Table 2, in which the frequency of the use of negation and demonstratives in Political speech 2 (which is in a mixed variety, i.e., there is equal frequency of variables from MSA and ECA) is contrasted.

Table 2. The frequency of occurrence of demonstratives and negation in Political speech 2.

Morphosyntactic variables	MSA	ECA
Negation	1	4
Demonstratives	5	5

One can see from Table 2 that MSA demonstratives and ECA demonstratives occur with the same degree of frequency. The same is not true for MSA negation and ECA negation. Here are some examples:

ECA negation

12) /il-riqa:ba ʕala iṣ-ṣa:dira:t ja: sija:dat il-wazi:r ʕamalit ḥa:ʒa ɣari:ba giddan wi ʔiʒra:ʔ ʔana mi∫ fahmu/ (P2)[5]
"The export inspectors, Mr. Minister, did something very strange. They followed a procedure I do not understand."

MSA negation

13) /ha:ða: il-kala:m lajsa ka:fijan/ (P2)
"This statement is not enough."

MSA demonstratives

14) /it-taḥði:r is-sa:biq ʔa:l ʔinn ha:ðihi il-shirka tuwarrid silaʕ fasda/ (P2)
"The last notification says that this company imports spoiled products."

ECA demonstratives

15) /wi ja: laha min ka:riθa wi kaʔinn da il-ʕuqu:ba di na:s bitaqtul ʔaṭfalna/ (P2)
"And what a catastrophe! It is as if this is the punishment! These are people that are killing our children."

In the first pair of examples, the whole sentence (phonologically, morphologically, syntactically) is either in MSA or in ECA. There is no switching within a sentence. In the second set of examples, the speaker switches, sometimes beginning his switching from ECA to MSA and sometimes vice-versa. In example 17, /ʔɑːl ʔinn/ is an ECA sentence (phonologically, morphologically, and lexically). This sentence is then followed by the MSA demonstrative /haːðaː/ and the rest of the sentence following it is in MSA. Thus the MSA demonstrative initiates a switch from ECA to MSA. The opposite is true for example 18, where the MSA noun /ʕuquːba/ is followed by an ECA demonstrative /di/, and the rest of the sentence following is in ECA.

The demonstratives here are used to initiate a switch. This is not true in the case of negation, which is not used to initiate a switch. Apparently, this speaker finds it easy and convenient to use MSA and ECA demonstrative systems with the same frequency in the same speech performance. Egyptians alternate between the MSA and the ECA demonstrative systems in the same speech performance. This is not true in the case of negation.

Now consider the following figures taken from Sermon 2, and the contrast between the distribution of demonstratives and negation in Table 3.

Table 3. The frequency of occurrence of demonstratives
and negation in Sermon 2

Morphosyntactic variables	MSA	ECA
Negation	26	1
Demonstratives	10	7

In Sermon 2, the speaker is speaking mainly in MSA, with occasional insertions from ECA. As one can see from Table 3, the speaker uses ECA negation only once, in contrast to twenty-six uses of MSA negation. This is expected, since, as was said before, the speaker tries to stick to MSA throughout his speech. However, when it comes to demonstratives, MSA and ECA demonstratives occur with almost the same degree of frequency. This is an interesting finding, especially since this extract is geared toward MSA.

Note that Political speech 2 is in a mixed variety. It seems strange that MSA negation does not occur to any great degree, compared to ECA negation. However, the case is different with demonstratives: MSA demonstratives and ECA demonstratives seem to occur with approximately the same frequency. This equal usage of both systems in Political speech 2, as noted above, suggests that this speaker finds it easier to alternate between MSA and ECA demonstratives in the same speech performance. However, the situation in Sermon 2 is even more interesting. This sermon is not in a mixed variety; the speaker basically speaks MSA. Nevertheless, he uses MSA demonstratives ten times, and ECA demonstratives seven times; i.e., he uses both systems with almost the same degree of frequency. This is interesting in its own right. One could argue that the reason for this is that the speaker finds it simpler to use vernacular morphosyntactic variables. However, negation is also a morphosyntactic variable and the speaker clearly has no problem with the MSA negation system, given his heavy use of it. Thus it is unlikely that the reason for his mixed use of the MSA/ECA demonstrative systems is anything to do (for this speaker at least) with ease or difficulty of usage of MSA/ECA morphosyntactic variables *per se*. The argument that speakers use ECA demonstratives more because ECA demonstratives are a deeply embedded mother tongue morphosyntactic feature, like negation, and that they seem to prefer to realize morphosyntactic variables in their mother tongue, explains nothing in this case.

In the case of Sermon 2, we should not expect to find ECA demonstratives, since the whole sermon is basically MSA. Yet again, we find almost equal use of MSA and ECA demonstratives. Lecture 1 provides an instructive parallel, since, unlike Sermon 2, it is basically ECA with insertions from MSA. In this speech, we should not expect to find MSA demonstratives, or if they do occur we would expect them to occur very rarely. This, however, is not the case, as Table 4 illustrates.

Table 4. Distribution of demonstratives and negation in Lecture 1

Morphosyntactic variables	MSA	ECA
Negation	0	10
Demonstratives	5	8

MSA and ECA demonstratives occur in Lecture 1 with roughly the same degree of frequency. This is not the case for negation, as no single MSA negative variable occurs. Again, it seems that the negation system differs in its use from the demonstrative system (MSA and ECA).

16) /maʕnaːha: ʔinnuh wazzaʕ il-firaʔ wil-saraːja ħasab il-manaːṭiʔ illi miħtaːga ħimaːjit ig-gunuːd jaʕni bijibʔa fiːh ħimaːja fi haːðihi il-manaːṭiq, ħimaːja ʕaskarijja ʔaw gunuːd ħaːriṣiːn [ħaːriṣiːn? ħaːriṣiːn?] ʕala il-manaːṭiʔ di maːjihṣalʃ fiːha: θawra/ (L 1)

"This means that he distributed the groups according to the places that need the protection of the soldiers. That is to say, <u>these places</u> are protected. They are protected by armed forces, or by soldiers who make sure there are no riots in <u>these places</u>."

In this example from Lecture 1, the speaker alternates between the MSA and the ECA demonstrative systems, using both in the same example. Note also that although the prevalent variety is ECA, the speaker still makes use of MSA demonstratives.

The /b-/ prefix on the other hand is the most dominant variable of all, occurring with both ECA-like and MSA-like verb forms (see examples). Table 5 illustrates the use of the /b-/ prefix with MSA verbs in all the data. The table counts p-stems, where "p" stands for "prefix," denoting the imperfect tense in MSA verbs (cf. Holes 1995), in which it is possible for the /b-/ prefix to occur, and states the number of times it actually occurs with MSA p-stem verbs and the number of times it could have occurred but did not do so.

Table 5. The use of the /b-/ prefix with MSA verbs in the data

Nature of the monologue	MSA p-stem verb + /b-/ prefix	MSA p-stem verb without the /b-/ prefix	Total
Political speech 1			
Part i (basically ECA)	3	1	4
Part ii (basically MSA)	2	3	5
Part iii (mixture)	2	1	3
Total			12
Political speech 2 (mixture)	3	2	5
Political speech 3 (MSA)	0	0	0
Political speech 4			
Part i (MSA)	0	0	0
Part ii (ECA)	1	0	1
Part iii (MSA)	0	0	0
Part iv (ECA)	0	0	0
Part v (MSA)	0	0	0
Total			1
Sermon 1 (basically ECA)	3	3	6
Sermon 2 (MSA with insertions from ECA)	3	16	19
Sermon 3	0	0	0
Sermon 4	0	0	0
Lecture 1 (ECA with insertions from MSA)	11	6	16

One can see from Table 5 that the /b-/ prefix can occur in both monologues that are geared toward MSA and those that are geared toward

ECA. Therefore, one may conclude that a pattern of distribution of these variables within a monologue can be predicted. For example, in a monologue in which the speaker uses a mixed variety (ECA and MSA with equal frequency), one can predict that while the speaker may use MSA as well as ECA demonstratives, he will tend to use ECA rather than MSA negative particles. One can also predict that the ECA /b-/ prefix can and will be used with MSA-like verb forms.

In a monologue in which MSA is the dominant variety, one can predict that the speaker will tend to use MSA negative particles rather than ECA ones, but he may still use ECA demonstratives with the same frequency as MSA ones. Again, in this type of monologue the /b-/ prefix can occur with MSA-like verb forms.

In a monologue in which ECA is the dominant variety, one can predict that the speaker will tend to use ECA negative particles rather than MSA ones, but he may still use MSA demonstratives with the same frequency as ECA ones, and again the /b-/ prefix could occur with MSA-like verb forms. Therefore, while with negation, there seems to be a consistent use of one negation system at a time, the same is not true for demonstratives or the /b-/ prefix.

Conclusions

This study has attempted to examine switching between ECA and MSA in relation to three morphosyntactic variables by applying the ML and the composite ML theories of code switching to the data. It has also tried to examine the pattern of distribution of the variables analyzed, and we have found that:

1. The composite ML hypothesis can explain the situation in the Egyptian speech community. Students must be aware that they can use system morphemes from both varieties, ECA and MSA, in the same stretch of discourse.

2. There is a specific pattern of distribution of all the system morphemes studied. Students can use the /b-/ prefix with MSA-like verbs as well as with ECA verbs, since this system morpheme is very flexible. Students can also use MSA and ECA demonstratives in the same stretch of discourse, but they should stick to one negation system or another, depending on the dominant variety used.

3. A negation marker in ECA with a verb in MSA is a possible combination, while a negation marker in MSA with a verb in ECA does not occur in these data. The same is true with demonstratives:

a demonstrative in ECA with a noun in MSA is possible, but the reverse does not occur in these data.

Foreign students of spoken Arabic, especially advanced ones, must understand the dynamics of switching by knowing, for example, what system morphemes can occur in MSA or ECA and the significance of this occurrence. Students of spoken Arabic can benefit from studies that explain structural constraints and try to place them within a larger framework. Studies that do so with more system morphemes are needed, as well as studies that explain why people switch in the first place.

Notes

1. The terms "mixture of both varieties" and a "mixed variety" are used to refer to inter-sentential code switching (switching within a sentence), while later on I will use the verb "to mix" to discuss switching within a word.
2. See also Chomsky (1993), "A Minimalist Program for Linguistic Theory," in Hale and Keyser (eds.), 1–52.
3. Just as there is no hybrid possible between /fi:h/ and /juːʒad/ or /hunaːk/, so there is none possible between /tunaffað/ and /titnaffiz/.
4. I do not think there is language death in Egypt, since the diglossic situation in this community is definitely an old one, but this needs another study which is more diachronic in nature.
5. The "g" is mostly used in both MSA and ECA, but sometimes speakers use "ʒ" when speaking MSA.

References

Badawi, A. 1995. "The Use of Arabic in Egyptian T.V. Commercials: A Language Simulator for the Training of Teachers of Arabic as a Foreign Language." *Georgetown University Round Table on Language and Linguistics*, 33–39.

Bassiouney, R. 1998. *Functions of Diglossic Switching in the Egyptian Community*. Unpublished M.Phil. thesis, University of Oxford.

———. 2000. "Diglossic Switching and the Phenomenon of 'Blending': Evidence from Egypt." *Proceedings of the Thirteenth International Symposium on Theoretical and Applied Linguistics*. Thessaloniki (1999), 243–254.

Chomsky, N. 1993. "A Minimalist Program for Linguistic Theory," in *The View from Building 20*, by K. Hale and S.J. Keyser (eds.) 1–52. Cambridge, Mass.: Massachusetts Institute of Technology Press.

Clyne, M. 1987. "Constraints on Code-Switching: How Universal Are They?" *Linguistics* 25, 739–64.

Di Scuillo, A.M., Muysken, P. and Singh, R. 1986. "Government and Code-mixing." *Journal of Linguistics* 22, 1–24.

Eid, D. M. 1988. "Principles of Code Switching between Standard and Egyptian Arabic." *Al-Arabiyyah* 21, 51–79.

Ferguson, C. 1959. "Diglossia," in Hymes, D. (ed.) 1964. *Language in Culture and Society.* New York: Harper and Row.

Gumperz, J.J. 1982. *Discourse Strategies.* Cambridge: Cambridge University Press.

Hale, K. and Keyser, S.J. (eds.) 1993. *The View from Building 20.* Cambridge, Mass.: Massachusetts Institute of Technology Press.

Al-Hassan, S. 1980. "Variation in the Demonstrative System in Educated Spoken Arabic." *Archivum Linguisticum* 8, No 3, 32–57.

Holes, C.D. 1993. "The Uses of Variation: A Study of the Political Speeches of Gamal Abdul-Nasir." *Perspectives on Arabic Linguistics* 5, 13–45.

——. 1995. *Modern Standard Arabic: Structure, Functions and Varieties.* London: Longman.

Mejdell, G. 1996. "Some Sociolinguistic Concepts of Style and Stylistic Variation in Spoken Arabic (with Reference to Naguib Mahfouz Talking about His Life)."*Tradition and Modernity in Arabic Language and Literature* by J.R. Smart (ed.). London: Curzon Press.

——. 1999. "Switching, Mixing-code Interaction in Spoken Arabic," in B. Brendmoen, E. Lanza and E. Ryen (eds.) *Language Encounters across Time and Space.* Oslo: Novus Press.

Mitchell, G. 1986. "What is Educated Spoken Arabic?" International Journal of the Sociology of Language 61, 7–32.

Mitchell, G. and Al-Hassan, S. 1994. *Modality, Mood and Aspect in Spoken Arabic.* London: Kegan Paul International.

Myers-Scotton, C. 1997. *Duelling Languages.* Oxford: Clarendon Press.

——. 1998 (a). "A Way to Dusty Death: The Matrix Language Turnover Hypothesis." *Endangered Languages: Language Loss and Community Response,* L. Gernoble and L.Whaley (eds.). Cambridge: Cambridge University Press.

——. (ed.) 1998 (b). *Codes and Consequences: Choosing Linguistic Varieties.* Oxford: Oxford University Press.

Parkinson, D. 1996. "Variety in Standard Arabic Grammar Skills," in *Understanding Arabic,* A. Elgibali (ed.). Cairo: The American University in Cairo Press.

Rammuny, R. 1978. "Functional and Semantic Developments in Negation as used in Modern Literary Arabic Prose after World War Two." *Journal of Near East Studies* 37/3, 245–264.

Sankoff, D. and Poplack, S. 1981. "A Formal Grammar for Code-switching." *Papers in Linguistics* 14, 3–56.

Walters, K. 1996. "Diglossia, Linguistic Variation, and Language Change in Arabic." *Perspectives on Arabic Linguistics* 8, 157–193.

The Debate over Grammar Instruction

Accommodating Both Positions

Georgette Ioup

The value of form-focused instruction in second language acquisition has been the subject of intense discussion. The issues center on whether the formal aspects of the classroom, namely rule isolation and error feedback, can aid the development of a learner's linguistic system in the new language. These issues are of concern in the teaching of both writing and oral communication. The initial arguments against a major role for form-focused instruction were put forth by Krashen in several publications (see esp. 1980, 1985). Krashen argued that the role of the classroom is primarily to provide comprehensible input and is useful only at the beginning stages of L2 acquisition, where students find the input generated outside the classroom too difficult to comprehend. According to Krashen, explicit knowledge of the language gotten through conscious enhancement of the input can only become part of a metalinguistic or *learned* system and will not influence the shape of the subconscious linguistic system responsible for producing natural speech. Only primary linguistic data—the type of input that drives child first-language acquisition—is available to build the underlying or *acquired* grammar. This reasoning is behind the acquisition/learning distinction central to Krashen's theory.

The counter position is articulated in studies that endeavor to establish the positive effects of a focus on form (Day and Shapson 1991; Carrroll and Swain 1993; Doughty 1991; Doughty and Varela 1998; Eckman, Bell, and Nelson 1988; Gass 1982; Harley 1989; Lightbown and Spada 1990; Pica 1983; Pienemann 1984; Schachter, Rounds, Wright, Smith, and Magoto 1995; Weslander and Stephany 1983; White 1991; White, Spada, Lightbown, and Ranta 1991; for excellent reviews, see Long 1988 and Long and Robinson 1998.) These studies demonstrate that form-focused instruction facilitates short-term gains on particular constructions but leave open the question of whether it influences ultimate attainment.

Few studies have examined ultimate attainment. Pavesi (1986) compared learners with many years of ESL experience and found that instructed learners outperformed naturalistic learners on selected grammatical measures. Since her two groups were not matched with respect to socioeconomic background and level of education, the findings may not be entirely the result of differences in formal training. Ioup (1995), however, did control for socioeconomic and education factors and found that the near-native ultimate attainment levels of her two subjects, one instructed and one naturalistic, were almost indistinguishable.

Those who see a benefit from form-focused instruction attribute it to several factors. Some argue that adult learners need to have their attention drawn to forms in the L2 that have little communicative value and, therefore, tend to be ignored, such as the -s on the 3rd person singular present tense verb in English. Ellis (1990) stated that, for the adult learner, "conscious awareness of forms that contribute little to communicative effectiveness may be necessary to ensure that they are eventually acquired" (169). He further observed that instructed forms may not appear immediately in spontaneous speech; however, when learners reach the point in development where they are ready to acquire these features of the language, they will perceive them more easily in the input if they have conscious awareness of their existence.

Others note that adults, unlike children, do not continuously restructure L2 rules until they become native-like. Schmidt and Frota (1986) argued that unless an adult consciously notices a discrepancy between the form of a structure in the input and the non-target version of it produced by his or her rule system, the non-native construction will resist restructuring and may eventually become a fossilized form. Some support for their position comes from data on Schmidt's own adult language learning experience. He spent several months learning Brazilian Portuguese in both a formal and an informal context, all the while keeping an observational diary of his language-learning experience. The authors found that during this brief period of language learning, only those constructions in the input that had been consciously noted in Schmidt's diary were subsequently incorporated into his grammar.

White (1990) argued that certain aspects of the L2 necessitate attention to their formal properties. She explained that two types of input are available to the learner, but only one of these is associated with conscious awareness. The first is input giving information that something is possible in the target language. This is referred to as positive evidence and is the information that can be inferred from natural speech. The other is input giving information that something is not possible. Referred to as negative evidence, this input must be explicit in nature, either as a formal rule or as corrective feedback—the two essential components of formal instruction. She explains why.

Often an L1 rule is more general than its counterpart in the L2, but since the rules are partially similar, the learner assumes that there is a complete overlap. The aspects of the L1 rule that do not appear in the L2 input are perceived to be accidental gaps. For example, assume an L1 French speaker is learning L2 English. Adverb placement is relatively free in both English and French, but there are some restrictions that occur only in English. In English the adverb may never separate the verb and its direct object, while in French it can. The French rule, therefore, is more general in this respect. The examples in (1) illustrate the contrast.

1) a. Jean lit des romans souvent.
   b. Jean lit souvent des romans.
   c. John reads novels frequently.
   d. *John reads frequently novels.

According to White, without explicit negative evidence that forms like (1d) are impossible, French-speaking learners of English will assume these structures are as grammatically correct in English as they are in French.

Two Types of Form-Focused Instruction

Researchers now distinguish between two approaches to a formal presentation of grammatical information. The two constructs were first defined in Long (1991). Traditional grammar presents rules one paradigm at a time, divorced from meaningful context. The syllabus is determined by factors other than the immediate needs of each learner. More importantly, the timing of the presentation is not triggered by perceived problems arising from a communicative event. When an isolated grammar lesson is the objective, the instruction is referred to as *Focus on FormS*. On the other hand, if meaningful communication is taking place and within this context students exhibit faulty rule acquisition, the instruction that ensues in response to this need is referred to as *Focus-on-Form* instruction. The crucial defining feature of Focus-on-Form instruction is the connection that is drawn between the form discussed and the meaning expressed in the context under consideration. Many researchers maintain that Focus on Form is the only valid approach to formal rule presentation (Doughty and Williams 1998; see especially the article by Long and Robinson).

Form-Focused Instruction and L2 Writing

The debate on the validity of Focus on Form is carried into L2 writing instruction with discussion of whether there is any benefit to be gained from overt correction of written grammatical errors. The research investigating this issue has produced conflicting results (Cardelle and Corno 1998; Doughty and Varela 1998; Fathman and Whalley 1990; Kepner 1991; Lalande 1982; Semke 1984; Sheppard 1992). Most recently the debate has been articulated in a series of articles and replies by Ferris (1999) and Truscott (1996, 1999). The issue is whether grammar correction in any form can impact grammatical accuracy in subsequent writing.

Truscott (1996) argued that grammatical correction is useless from both a theoretical and a practical perspective. On the theoretical side, he cited research describing how metalinguistic knowledge imparted by formal instruction is not the type of input that can be utilized by the internal linguistic system. This system can respond only to implicit knowledge gained through language use, not to explicit knowledge provided by grammatical correction (Ellis 1993; Schwartz 1986, 1993). From a practical perspective, Truscott maintained that there was no experimental evidence to support grammatical correction in L2 writing. Instead, the empirical research either favored the no-correction alternative or was neutral . He noted that grammatical correction is normally treated as a simple transfer of information from teacher to student, which cannot be effective because "the acquisition of grammar is a gradual process, not a sudden discovery" (342).

In defense of grammatical correction, Ferris (1999) cited studies that demonstrated benefit from it. She concluded that in light of the inconclusive nature of the empirical research and students' demonstrated preference for error correction (Leki 1991; Ferris 1995), one should hesitate before abandoning correction altogether.

An Exploratory Study

Most of the research investigating the value of grammar feedback covers periods of short duration. The time periods for the studies range in length from one week (Carroll and Swain 1993) to one year (DeKeyser 1993), with an average of six to ten weeks. Perhaps the mixed results are due to the variation in length of the studies. It may also be the case that some learners respond to feedback quickly and others require repeated feedback over a longer duration. If a learner has reached a highly stabilized plateau in language development, as is true of many of the learners in language classes, then even grammar feedback over the course of one year may not be sufficient to allow grammatical forms to restructure—if such feedback is found to be capable of having an impact on the internalized form of a rule.

I would like to report the results of an exploratory study on one subject that covered a period of seven consecutive semesters. This learner, whom I will refer to as "Jenny," had entered a university ESL program with an L2 English grammar that was rigidly stabilized, following a long period of informal acquisition. Although she was fluent, her grammatical control was far from native-like. In an attempt to determine whether formal learning after years of informal acquisition can be effective, this study examines the impact of formal ESL instruction on her written productions. The question addressed is whether form-focused instruction can improve her written grammatical control.

The Subject

Jenny is a native speaker of Mandarin Chinese who enrolled in the English as a Second Language (ESL) program of an urban university. When she was ten years old, her family emigrated from Taiwan to the United States, where she was enrolled in a public elementary school at the fifth grade. Since at that time there was no ESL instruction available in her school system, she was immediately mainstreamed into the regular classroom. In the absence of a Chinese-speaking community in her new environment, Jenny quickly became dependent on English as the medium of communication outside her immediate family. At the time of the study, she used Chinese only with her parents; communication with her siblings (two younger sisters and a younger brother) was entirely in English.

After graduating from a parochial high school at age nineteen with a good academic record, Jenny enrolled in the university. At the time of her enrollment her grammatical development in English had become rigidly stabilized, containing many partially or incorrectly specified rules. She spoke fluently and with ease, but non-natively.[1] Because of her scores on a placement exam administered by the university, Jenny was required to enroll in ESL. She was placed into the third and last level of the university's intensive ESL program.[2]

An Overview of Jenny's ESL Experience

The ESL program at Jenny's university consisted of two divisions, one intensive and one non-intensive. The emphasis of the instruction in the program was the development of an effective expository writing style. The writing instruction at all levels was reading-based and emphasized a process approach requiring several drafts, with extensive peer review, editing, and revision. This was combined with individualized instructor conferencing to discuss writing and grammatical problems specific to the student. Throughout the program, grammar was taught both from a grammar text and contextually with focus directed toward the individual problems that arose. The actual structures that were taught varied from semester to semester depending on the text in use, which the instructor selected. Grammatical awareness was also self-directed, as students edited and reworked their own written prose. Typically, when teachers addressed errors in writing, these errors were pointed out but left for the student to correct. Though the content and style of the classes varied with the instructor, the two essential components of form-focused instruction—rule explanation and error feedback—were always present.

Jenny's courses made extensive use of both approaches to form-focused instruction discussed earlier. Lessons from the grammar text were most certainly Focus on FormS. However, a large part of the grammatical input was contextually centered, addressing only the structural errors that were problematic for the learner in her writing and always in relation to the meaningful context. This input included peer reviews, editing work, revisions, and individual student/teacher conferencing. These aspects of her grammatical instruction exemplify Focus on Form. Both types of form-focused instruction attempted to raise awareness of grammatical structure, the former in the abstract, and the latter in relation to meaning as the need arose.

After one semester in the intensive program, Jenny tested into the lower level of the non-intensive program. However, because of the stabilized nature of the non-native forms in her writing, six additional semesters of enrollment (three at each level) were required before she was finally able to exit the program.[3] It was clear that Jenny was not the type of student who could monitor structural correctness in her written productions.

Analysis of Jenny's Development
To determine whether Jenny had restructured her most problematic grammatical forms, her written productions at the entry, midway, and exit levels were compared. Samples of 200 words were randomly selected from four different essays at each level. Five grammar points were examined to determine if there was a change in error control over time: preposition choice, tense selection, article usage, verb form, and use of the plural -s morpheme. These five were selected for two reasons. First, they were among the structures that received extensive Focus-on-FormS instruction during Jenny's entry-level intensive ESL class. The instruction included both rule explanation and form-focused practice. Additional

class work supplemented the textbook units on the formation and use of
the English tenses, regular and irregular plural noun formation, normal
use of the definite and indefinite article, and the semantics of the common English prepositions.

The second reason these structures were selected was that they were
among the ones that produced errors in Jenny's written compositions.
Since the ESL classes are, to some extent, individualized through teacher/
student conferencing and awareness of self-generated written errors,
these forms would have received Focus-on-Form instruction throughout
her seven semesters. It is also the case that these structures occur with
enough frequency in her writing to make comparison across levels meaningful.

Any preposition, article, plural, verb formation, or tense usage within
the selected passages that deviated from native usage was tabulated as an
error. Verb form errors (as opposed to tense errors) consisted of verbs that
were structurally ill-formed. Because the compositions providing the data
consisted of original writing, the errors in each category covered a wide
range of semantic functions. The results are presented in Table 1.

Table 1. Comparison of selected errors by level

	Preposition	Tense	Article	Verb form	Plural -s
Entry	4	18	19	15	9
Midway	1	4	6	4	6
Exit	4	2	1	6	4

The results indicate that the grammatical feedback had a beneficial effect
on Jenny's grammar. Four of the five grammar structures show improvement. Tense and article errors were dramatically reduced. At the entry
level her writing samples contained eighteen tense and nineteen article
errors; these fell to two and one, respectively, at the exit level. Both categories require semantic knowledge, evidence that Jenny was getting a better grasp on the form–meaning relationship in English. The reduction in
verb form and plural -s errors is not as dramatic, although each declined
by more than half. Preposition choice also requires a form–meaning correspondence. Although the data show no improvement in this category,
there were relatively few errors to begin with.

Pica (1983) observed that while more advanced proficiency may not
be reflected in the total number of morphological errors produced by

the learner, the type of error tends to change as the learner progresses. At the beginning stages the tendency is to overgeneralize morphological suffixes, often resulting in double morphological markings (e.g., *childrens* as the plural of *child*). At the more proficient levels, the morphological error is more often one of underspecification, where the learner omits the morphological marking altogether (e.g., *has eat* as a perfect tense verb). Jenny's writing exhibited just such a change in error type as she progressed. Her entry-level writing included verb form sequences like *would talks, should built, to built, does stayed, don't wanted, is torned, lefted,* and *cutted.* At the exit level, when she produced verb-form errors, they were likely to be underspecified: *is always worry, keeps me inform, was base on, I finally finish, everyone shout and clapped hands, should of go, glasses that shaped like cat eyes.*

After leaving the ESL program Jenny completed two semesters of freshman English and two sophomore level literature courses. Her literature teacher indicated that her writing was fine and that she did well in both courses. It appears, then, that her stabilized errors were overcome.[4]

In this study the subject received both Focus-on-FormS and Focus-on-Form instruction, which included extensive grammar correction of written productions. It is impossible from this limited research to claim with absolute certainty that one of these alone, or some combination, was responsible for her progress, for one could argue that she would have improved just as much with no form-focused instruction. However, since she had ample exposure to academic discourse before she entered ESL and had written all through her secondary school without eradicating her persistent basic errors, one can theorize that the "extra" factor her ESL classes provided was the form-focusing instruction. I will argue below that it was indeed her classroom grammar focus that allowed her internal grammar to restructure, but I will do so in a way that is consistent with the position of Krashen, Truscott, and other researchers who argue that formally presented grammar cannot penetrate a language system.

Discussion

Now let us turn to an exploration of how attention to grammar is able to effect a change in a learner's internal system. Jenny had extensive exposure to academic English while her grammatical structures were in a frozen state. Not only did she have teachers who lectured to her in the educated standard throughout her high school and early college years, but she was an avid reader of novels and weekly news magazines in English. If questioned on the content of what she read, Jenny showed full comprehension. Even so, the input she received through her reading and lectures was not able by itself to affect a change in her stabilized grammatical state. What the ESL classes provided that her other academic work did not was the ability to place selective attention on features of the input that needed restructuring in her own internal grammar.

Sharwood Smith (1986) noted that language learners process input in two different ways: they may use the information contained in the message to construct the meaning of the whole, or they may process the structure of the input to help in the development of their grammars. L1 children process for meaning without conscious attention to structural properties. Nevertheless, they are able to incorporate the structural information contained in the message into their evolving grammars. L2 adults, like children, have difficulty consciously processing for meaning and structure simultaneously. However, unlike children, they are not assured of acquiring structural properties that they have not noticed. Skehan (1996) observed that for the L2 learner, "processing language to extract meaning does not guarantee automatic sensitivity to form" (41).

Just as there are two modes for processing input, dual processing modes are available in L2 production (Skehan 1996). Normally, when time pressures are great or communicative needs are paramount, learners will be preoccupied with the content of their productions rather than the form. On the other hand, whenever exactness is a priority, concern for the form of the message will take precedence. Learners who have become accustomed to focusing on content rather than form are not able to adapt easily to a form-focusing mode of production. Their inability derives from the processes that give rise to fluency: rule-generated sequences that are used frequently come to be stored as whole lexical units (Skehan 1996). During communicative interactions these lexicalized exemplars are retrieved to produce rapid, fluent L2 output. In a developing L2 grammar, non-native sequences that have been stored as exemplars are replaced by more native-like ones as the system evolves. Fossilization results when ill-formed exemplars cease to restructure.

When the grammar contains rigidly stabilized structures, attention to form becomes crucial. A learner has limited attentional resources and therefore must be selective in what to attend to (VanPatten 1990). If the learner is under pressure to communicate successfully, attention must focus on the elements of the message that are the major contributors to meaning. It is only when there is attention to spare that the formal properties that are not crucial to meaning can be attended to. As the learner becomes more fluent, attentional resources are freed up. But if grammatical structures are stabilized, the learner will no longer utilize these resources to notice form. At this point the formal classroom can play a key role. Schmidt (1990) observed that when attention is directed properly, features of the input become available for intake, in the sense that previously unnoticed elements are made accessible to the internalized grammar. Structuring the learning experience allows learners to notice generalizations that might have been overlooked.

This course of learning describes Jenny's experience. It appears that her stabilized forms had become well-entrenched. Thus the instruction she experienced had to serve two purposes: 1) it had to make her aware of the differences between the standard English system and the forms she was producing, and 2) it had to assist her in replacing her ill-formed exemplars with more native-like ones. Both tasks were accomplished through the repeated attention-focusing practice she experienced. Because her forms were so entrenched, she required much more practice to modify them than learners with rule systems that have not stabilized. The results lend support to Schmidt and Frota's (1986) conclusion that an ill-formed L2 rule cannot be altered without conscious awareness of the discrepancy between the input form and the form produced by the L2 system.

Observe that in this account both noticing and practice are required. This appears to contradict the arguments by Krashen (1982, 1985), Truscott (1996), and Schwartz (1986, 1993) that formal grammar is not the sort of input that can be utilized by the internal language module. Formal knowledge is *explicit* knowledge about the language—metalinguistic information. The learning that takes place using the innate language module requires *implicit* knowledge—knowledge of the rules that is unconsciously acquired from natural speech. As Winter and Reber (1994) explain, "implicit learning refers, in the most basic sense, to the human ability to derive information about the world in an unconscious, non-reflective way ... without awareness of the learning process" (117). Certainly, knowledge imparted through formal rules cannot function as implicit learning.

When implicit knowledge is used efficiently and automatically, it is referred to as *procedural* memory and contrasts with *declarative* memory— that which can be accessed consciously. Procedural memory consists of processes and skills; declarative memory consists of facts and concepts. Paradis (1994) detailed the neurological correlates of the two memory systems, outlining how declarative memory, which subserves formal language learning, is functionally distinct from procedural memory, which subserves naturally acquired language. Clinical evidence indicates that discrete patterns of cerebral lesions are associated with the impairment of each memory system, leaving the other intact. Paradis is clear that one type of memory cannot translate into the other since each is associated with a separate neurofunctional system. This would support Krashen's position that learning cannot become acquisition. Learned grammar is a type of declarative knowledge, while acquired grammar is procedural knowledge. How can I claim, then, that it was the formal training that Jenny received that helped her internal language system improve?

Though declarative memory cannot transform itself into procedural memory, there is a way in which formal training can build the natural language system. Paradis (2000) explains that each time one uses metalinguistic knowledge to construct a declarative routine, one simultaneously produces a procedure of the same type. In this way explicit knowledge is used to construct output that in turn functions as implicit input (see Ellis 1993, 1994). Consider the analogy of learning to operate a standard transmission vehicle. At first the learner must think through every movement of the hands and feet to shift the gears. In time the process becomes automatic—proceduralized. The automatic control comes about not because a conscious routine converts to an automatic one, but because simultaneously, implicit procedures are unconsciously being established each time the shift routine is consciously executed. The same process occurs in learning new grammar rules. Each time a structure is articulated using a formal rule, implicit knowledge of the structure is independently acquired.

McLaughlin (1990) described the way in which knowledge shifts from controlled to automatic. In cognitive theories of learning, complex skills are initially learned as controlled processes that require attention and time. Through practice they become routinized, freeing up the controlled processes to tackle new difficult learning.[5] In this theory, practice has a central role. "From a practical standpoint, the necessary component is overlearning. A skill must be practiced *again and again and again*, until no attention is required for its performance" (115, emphasis added). This is how error correction functioned for Jenny. The same errors occurred over and over in her work. Each time she corrected them she unconsciously established procedural memory of the correct forms.

Conclusion

These cognitive theories, then, provide a basis for my claim that the formal training that Jenny received helped her internal language system improve. Jenny's long period of stabilization meant that she had well-established rules specifying ungrammatical constructs. One or two semesters were not enough to bring about a change. Many hours of formal classroom work were needed for her to develop alternative rules for her frozen structures, and then to use them to restructure her internal grammatical system. It was this practice that allowed her to rely on the restructured rules for automatic, correct retrieval by providing abundant output, which, in turn, served as the implicit input that effected change in the internal grammatical system. Thus, grammatical instruction serves to build a language system without undermining the theoretical dimensions of language acquisition.

Notes

1. It is interesting to note that her phonological accent was native-like.
2. While at the university Jenny continued to live at home and commute, all the while working part-time at the family restaurant. Thus, in many ways the university can be seen as an extension of her high school experience.
3. During her seven semesters Jenny never experienced the same teacher twice. As a result, she was exposed to a number of different teaching styles, although all teachers in the program shared the same basic teaching philosophy.
4. To see the actual improvement in her writing, refer to the sample entry and exit essays provided in the Appendix.
5. McLaughlin does not specify the cognitive mechanisms that allow the change from controlled to automatic processes. However, they must certainly function along the lines described in the preceding paragraphs.

References

Cardelle, M. and Corno, L. 1981. "Effects on Second Language Learning Of Variation in Written Feedback on Homework Assignments." *TESOL Quarterly* 15, 251–261.

Carroll, S. and Swain, M. 1993. "Explicit and Implicit Negative Feedback: An Empirical Study of the Learning of Linguistic Generalizations." *Studies in Second Language Acquisition* 15, 357–386.

Day, E. and Shapson, S. 1991. "Integrating Formal and Functional Approaches to Language Teaching in French Immersion: An Experimental Approach." *Language Learning* 41, 25–58.

DeKeyser, R. 1993. "The Effect of Error Correction on L2 Grammar Knowledge and Oral Proficiency." *The Modern Language Journal* 77, 501–514.

Doughty, C. 1991. "Second Language Instruction Does Make a Difference: Evidence from an Empirical Study of Second Language Relativization." *Studies in Second Language Acquisition* 13, 431–469.

Doughty, C and Varela, E. 1998. "Communicative Focus On Form," in C. Doughty and J. Williams (eds.) *Focus on Form in Classroom Second Language Acquisition* (114–138). Cambridge: Cambridge University Press.

Doughty, C. and Williams J. 1998. *Focus on Form in Classroom Second Language Acquisition.* Cambridge: Cambridge University Press.

Eckman, F., Bell, L., and Nelson, D. 1988. "On the Generalization of Relative Clause Instruction in the Acquisition of English as a Second Language." *Applied Linguistics* 9, 1–20.

Ellis, R. 1990. *Instructed Second Language Acquisition.* Oxford: Blackwell.

———. 1993. "The Structural Syllabus and Second Language Acquisition." *TESOL Quarterly* 27, 91–114.

———. 1994. "Implicit/Explicit Knowledge and Language Pedagogy." *TESOL Quarterly* 28, 166–172.

Fathman, A. and Whalley, E. 1990. "Teacher Response to Student Writing: Focus on Form versus Content," in B. Kroll (ed.), *Second Language Writing: Research Insights for the Classroom.* Cambridge: Cambridge University Press.

Ferris, D. 1995. "Student Reactions to Teacher Response in Multi-draft Composition Classrooms." *TESOL Quarterly* 29, 33–53.

———. 1999. "The Case for Grammar Correction in L2 Writing Classes: A Response to Truscott (1996)." *Journal of Second Language Writing* 8, 1–11.

Gass, S. 1982. "From Theory to Practice," in W. Rutherford and M. Hines (eds.), *On TESOL '81* (129–139). Washington, DC: TESOL.

Harley, B. 1989. "Functional Grammar in French Immersion: A Classroom Experiment." *Applied Linguistics* 10, 331–359.

Ioup, G. 1995. "Evaluating the Need for Input Enhancement in Post-critical Period Language Acquisition," in D. Singleton and Z. Lengyel (eds.), *The Age Factor in Second Language Acquisition* (95–123). Clevedon: Multilingual Matters.

Kepner, C. 1991. "An Experiment in the Relationship of Types of Written Feedback to the Development of Second-Language Writing Skills." *The Modern Language Journal* 75, 303–313.

Krashen, S. 1980. "Theoretical and Practical Relevance of Simple Codes in Second Language Acquisition," in R. Scarcella and S. Krashen (eds.), *Research in Second Language Acquisition* (7–18). Rowley, MA: Newbury House.

———. 1982. *Principles and Practice in Second Language Acquisition.* New York: Pergamon.

———. 1985. *The Input Hypothesis: Issues and Implications.* London: Longman.

Lalande, J. 1982. "Reducing Composition Errors: An Experiment." *Modern Language Journal* 66, 140–149.

Leki, I. 1991. "The Preferences of ESL Students for Error Correction in College-level Writing Classes." *Foreign Language Annals* 24, 203–218.

Lightbown, P. and Spada, N. 1990. "Focus-on-form and Corrective Feedback in Communicative Language Teaching: Effects on Second Language Learning." *Studies in Second Language Acquisition* 12, 429–448.

Long, M. 1988. "Instructed Interlanguage Development," in L. Beebe (ed.), *Issues in Second Language Acquisition: Multiple Perspectives* (115–141). Rowley, MA: Newbury House.

———. 1991. "Focus on Form: A Design Feature in Language Teaching Methodology," in K. de Bot, R. Ginsberg, and C. Kramsch (eds.), *Foreign Language Research in Cross-cultural Perspective* (39–52). Amsterdam: John Benjamins.

Long, M. and Robinson, P. 1998. "Beyond Focus on Form: Cognitive Perspectives on Learning and Practicing Second Language Grammar," in C. Doughty and J. Williams (eds.), *Focus on Form in Classroom Second Language Acquisition* (15–41). Cambridge: Cambridge University Press.

McLaughlin, B. 1990. "Restructuring." *Applied Linguistics* 11, 113–128.

Paradis, M. 1994. "Neurolinguistic Aspects of Implicit and Explicit Memory: Implications for Bilingualism and SLA," in N. Ellis (ed.), *Implicit and Explicit Learning of Languages* (393–420). London: Academic Press.

———. 2000. "Cortical and Subcortical Contributions to L2 Acquisition and Learning." Paper presented at the meeting of the American Association of Applied Linguistics, Vancouver.

Pavesi, M. 1986. "Markedness, Discourse Modes, and Relative Clause Formation in a Formal and an Informal Context." *Studies in Second Language Acquisition* 8, 138–155.

Pica, T. 1983. "Adult Acquisition of English as a Second Language under Different Conditions of Exposure." *Language Learning* 33, 465–497.

Pienemann, M. 1984. "Psychological Constraints on the Teachability of Languages." *Studies in Second Language Acquisition* 6, 186–214.

Schachter, J., Rounds, P., Wright, S., Smith, T., and Magoto, J. 1995. "A Dual Mechanism Model for Adult Syntax Learning." Paper presented at the Second Language Research Forum, Ithaca, NY.

Schmidt, R. 1990. "The Role of Consciousness in Second Language Learning." *Applied Linguistics* 11, 17–46.

Schmidt, R. and Frota, S. 1986. "Developing Basic Conversational Ability in a Second Language: a Case Study of an Adult Learner of Portuguese," in R. Day (ed.) *"Talking to Learn": Conversation in Second Language Acquisition* (237–326). Rowley, MA: Newbury House.

Schwartz, B. 1986. "The Epistemological Status of Second Language Acquisition." *Second Language Research* 2, 120–159.

———. 1993. "On Explicit and Negative Data Effecting and Affecting Competence and Linguistic Behavior." *Studies in Second Language Acquisition* 15, 147–163.

Semke, H. 1984. "Effects of the Red Pen." *Foreign Language Annals* 17, 195–202.

Sharwood Smith, M. 1986. "Comprehension versus Acquisition: Two Ways of Processing Linguistic Input." *Applied Linguistics* 7, 239–256.

Sheppard, K. 1992. "Two Feedback Types: Do They Make a Difference?" *RELC [Regional Language Center] Journal* 23, 103–110.

Skehan, P. 1996. "A Framework for the Implementation of Task-based Instruction." *Applied Linguistics* 17, 38–62.

Truscott, J. 1996. "The Case against Grammar Correction in L2 Writing Classes." *Language Learning* 46, 327–369.

———. 1999. "The Case for 'the Case for Grammar Correction in L2 Writing Classes': A Response to Ferris." *Journal of Second Language Writing* 8, 111–122.

VanPatten, B. 1990. "Attending to Content and Form in the Input: An Experiment in Consciousness." *Studies in Second Language Acquisition* 12, 287–301.

Weslander, D. and Stephany, G. 1983. "Evaluation of an English as a Second Language Program for Southeast Asian Students." *TESOL Quarterly* 17: 473–480.

White, L. 1990. "Implications of Learnability Theories for Second Language Learning and Teaching," in M. Halliday, J. Gibbons, and H. Nicholas (eds.), *Learning, Keeping and Using Language* (271–286). Amsterdam: John Benjamins.

———. 1991. "Adverb Placement in Second Language Acquisition: Some Effects of Positive and Negative Evidence in the Classroom." *Second Language Research* 7, 133–161.

White, L., Spada, N., Lightbown, P., and Ranta, L. 1991. "Input Enhancement and L2 Question Formation." *Applied Linguistics* 12, 416–432.

Winter, B. and Reber, A. 1994. "Implicit Learning and the Acquisition of Natural Languages," in N. Ellis (ed.), *Implicit and Explicit Learning of Languages* (115–146). London: Academic Press.

Appendix

Writing Samples from Entry and Exit Classes

Entry Class

During Han Dynasty there was a man named Pan Ch'ao, known for his exploits in the Western Region, was a man with couriage and ambition. Very often, he got alot of merits done. At the end, he became a writer in his 70's. During Han Dynasty #16, Pan was sent to the western region in Chinese Turkestan. When he and his 36 soldiers arrived, the king treated with politeness and courtesy. However, after a period of time the king has begun to neglect them. Pan asked his soldiers if they also felt the same. He went on saying that this is because of the barbarian had sent a representative here which has made the king neglected them. Only the smart people could predict something before any matter happens, not to mention that the matter is very clear! Pan wanted to prove his theory, then take an effective action. So he called in one of the servant and asked him where does barbarian's representative stay now. When the servant heard that, was shocked, thought that Pan knew everything. So the servant told Pan everything. Pan has proven his theory is true, then he locked up the servant, just in case he let out of the information. At the same time, he gathered up his 36 soldiers to have a drink. When they became half drunk, Pan used words to get them angry. He said that they came to this far away place to seek riches and fame. Now that the barbarian's representative is here just for a few days, and the king started to neglect them. If the King's soldiers captured Pan with the others and gave them to the barbarians. They will feed their corps to the wolves. So they wonder what should they do. Everyone agreed that they are in such dangerous situation, either life or death, they will listen to Pan.

Exit Class

In the article "An 'Official Language' for California?," Geoffrey Nunberg expresses negatively on the issue concerning English being the official language of the United States. I feel that English is already the official language of the U.S.; why should anyone make it a law? In the article, the author states two states already voted "yes" to that issue, but before I decide on the issue, I like to look at it more carefully. Should English be the official Language of the United States?

Since the 17th century, people have been immigrating from other countries to the United States. The Dutch people settled in the Missouri area; the Spanish in Florida, Texas, and California; and the French in the Louisiana territory. These European people originally spoke their own languages. Generations after generations, people lost their languages. The only thing they might know is where their ancestors came from. To complete the transition, schools teach in English, but not in other languages. As I can see, English is already rooted in the United States. True, there will be other language speakers; however, in today's society, people feel good about learning another language. They feel great when they can understand what other people are saying in another language. Yet, there are also some raticles feel differently about having different language in the US.

My brother is another good example of this topic. He is the first generation in my family who was born in the United States. He can not speak Chinese or say any simple sentence. Everything is just English. Even though English was the only language he speaks and writes, he is having a problem with it at school. My family speaks to him in English and barely one or two words in Chinese. He still doing bad in English. Making English as an official language is the United States doesn't solve any of the grammatical problems the children have.

A Constructivist View of Learning Strategies

Zuhal Okan

In line with the recent movement within educational theory and practice toward a learner-centered view of pedagogy, studies on learner strategies have highlighted the importance of accommodating different beliefs and attitudes that students bring into the classroom (see, for example, Wenden and Rubin 1987; O'Malley and Chamot 1990; Oxford 1990). In particular, there is a growing interest in defining how learners approach the language-learning task and in clarifying how teachers can help students identify strategies that work best for them.

Defining "Learning Strategies"

There is little consensus in the literature concerning the definition of language learning strategies. Oxford (1990) defines learning strategies as "specific actions taken by the learner to make learning easier, faster, more enjoyable, more self-directed, and more transferable to new situations." Williams and Burden (1997) make a distinction between a skill and a strategy. They explain that "learning strategies are conceived of as operating at a level above skills; they can be seen as the executive processes which manage and coordinate the skills" (145). They further state that a learning strategy "is a series of skills used with a particular learning purpose in mind. Thus, learning strategies involve an ability to monitor the learning situation and respond accordingly. This means being able to assess the situation, to plan, to select appropriate skills, to sequence them, to co-ordinate them, to monitor or assess their effectiveness and to revise the plan when necessary" (145).

Research on Classifying Learning Strategies

Most of the early studies on learning strategies emerged from a concern for identifying the characteristics of "good language learners" (Rubin

1975; Stern 1975). The principal aim was to demonstrate that effective students apply learning strategies while learning a second language, and that once identified, such strategies could be made available to less successful learners (Naiman *et al.* 1978; Chamot *et al.* 1988). Reiss (1985), however, argues that an active learner is not necessarily engaged in language production. Many successful classroom learners have been observed as "silent speakers"; in other words, they rehearse and practice silently while listening to others. Recent research also suggests that effective language learners, instead of using a single strategy pattern "use an array of strategies, matching those strategies to their own learning style and personality and to the demands of the task." In other words, they "find ways to tailor their strategy use to their individual needs and requirements; they develop combinations of strategies that work for them" (Oxford and Ehrman 1995:362).

I also feel that labeling students as good and poor language learners according to the strategies they use is a rather simple approach to a very complex issue and raises several questions: is it possible to differentiate between good and poor learners on the basis of strategy use only? What if the reason for unsuccessful learners not employing the same strategies as those used by successful learners has to do with more complex issues such as cultural background or the proficiency level of the learners? When a particular strategy works with an individual, does it mean it will work for another as well?

Instruction in Learning Strategies

In recent years the notion of learner training, i.e., the explicit teaching of strategies, has received a considerable amount of attention in English Language Teaching (ELT). Procedures for strategy training have been suggested by a number of researchers (Hosenfeld *et al.* 1981; O'Malley and Chamot 1990). What is common in all of these is the role the teacher assumes: identifying the strategies students are already using, presenting new strategies used by successful students, modeling them, and providing opportunities to practice.

Apparently, one should be aware of a number of issues before implementing strategy training. O'Malley and Chamot (1990), for example, draw attention to the question of whether learners should be made conscious of the strategies they are taught, or whether it is sufficient to provide students with practice opportunities. Wenden (1987), on the other hand, points out that learners' own preferred learning strategies should be taken into account before any instruction is provided.

In fact, how we cater for individual differences in strategy training, i.e., different characteristics such as age, gender, personality, motivation, self-concept, life experience, and cultural background that learners bring to the task of learning, has been one of the major concerns in our experience. And these issues link our discussion to constructivist perspectives on learning.

Personal Construct Psychology

We first need to clarify the concept of construct and constructivism as a general approach to learning. Personal Construct Psychology was developed by George A. Kelly (1955). Kelly uses the term "construct" to refer to bipolar concepts we use to construe the world— that is, to interpret our reality and to predict future events. He suggests that people use their construct systems "to observe, classify, explain, predict and control the events they are interested in" (Sendan 1995:24).

As for the major tenets of constructivism, first we need to mention that the constructivist perspective recognizes the personal dimension of learning. It helps us understand personal change since it explains why "each individual constructs his or her own reality and, therefore, learns different things in very different ways even when provided with what seem to be very similar learning experiences" (Williams and Burden 1997:2).

To Roberts (1998:23), a constructivist approach suggests the following learning cycle:

- The person filters new information according to his or her expectations and existing knowledge of the world;
- S/he constructs the meaning of the input;
- This meaning is matched with her prior internal representations relevant to the input;
- Matching confirms or disconfirms existing representations;
- If there is a match, then s/he maintains the meaning as presently constructed (assimilation);
- If there is a mismatch, s/he revises her representation of the world to incorporate the new information (accommodation).

This principle of constructivism has a direct bearing on strategy training concerning the teachers' role, in particular. It implies that teachers, before embarking on teaching new strategies, should be aware of the fact that students, when they step into the classroom, bring with them a variety of strategies. What is to be done, therefore, is to let the students look at themselves from the outside, see what they already have at their disposal, reflect on how they learn, and see how the others learn.

The second principle that the constructivist view upholds is that reflection on experience is central to learning: "Learners can reconstruct their knowledge through reflection. Meta-cognition is an important part of learning and can involve reflection on the degree of understanding or the nature of thoughts" (Bell and Gilbert 1996:58). This principle is highly compatible with reflective thought, which has influenced thinking in education in recent years. Sendan (1995) discussing Schön's (1983, 1987) theoretical construction of reflective practice, finds the latter to be consistent with Kelly's Personal Construct Theory in that while Schön views professional learning as "engaging in reflective conversation with one's own practice through which practitioners test out, reframe and reconstruct their implicit understanding of professional situations," Kelly proposes that "individuals utilize hypotheses to anticipate events, and perpetually revise or reconstruct their construct systems based on validation or invalidation of their anticipations of their experiences" (Sendan 1995:36).

Kaufman and Brooks (1996) accept constructivism as a theory of human development. In the constructivist classroom, the teacher's role is to create dynamic learning environments that promote interplay among students, materials, and ideas. Kaufman and Brooks (1996:234–235) summarize the characteristics of constructivist-based classrooms (based on Grennon Brooks and Brooks [1993]):

- Use raw data and primary sources, along with manipulative, interactive, and physical materials.
- When framing tasks, use cognitive terminology, such as *classify*, *analyze*, *predict*, *create*, and so on.
- Allow student thinking to drive lessons. Shift instructional strategies or alter content based on student responses.
- Inquire about students' understandings of concepts before sharing your own understandings of those concepts.
- Ask open-ended questions of students and encourage students to ask questions of others.
- Seek elaboration of students' initial responses.
- Engage students in experiences that might engender contradictions to students' initial hypotheses and then encourage a discussion.
- Provide time for students to construct relationships and create metaphors.

To Kaufman and Brooks (1996), in the constructivist classrooms, teachers pose problems of emerging relevance for which the teacher and the student jointly search for answers. Secondly, teachers structure lessons in such a way that learning occurs in context. Thirdly, teachers value students' point of view and create opportunities for students to reflect on their assumptions, beliefs, etc. Finally, constructivist teachers find ways of assessing student learning within the context of teaching. When evaluating students' work they avoid using judgmental responses.

With these issues in mind, now let us look at the study itself.

The Study

I would like to say a few words about my general aims for organizing the Language Learning Strategies course. First, I wanted to avoid approaches that talk of "good language learner–bad language learner." I wished to make it clear that all learners are capable of learning a second language as long as appropriate teaching occurs, where the emphasis is on helping learners to develop appropriate cognitive skills and strategies.

Secondly, from my years of teaching experience, I have come to believe that identifying and drawing the attention of the learners to the processes they go through as they do an activity helps the students become better learners in the long run. To me, what is important and remarkable is not the product, i.e., what is done, but the process, i.e., how an individual achieves the result.

For the purpose of this chapter I shall limit my discussion to one language learning task my students and I worked on, which I hope will suffice to illustrate our experience.

The Setting and the Participants

The data I shall draw on come mainly from one particular class that I taught during the fall term of 2000. The participants consisted of thirty-two Turkish freshman students (twenty females and twelve males aged between nineteen and twenty-two) studying at the ELT Department, Faculty of Education, Çukurova University. At the time of the study, the students were all at the upper-intermediate level in proficiency, as defined by both university and department placement procedures.

The program provides initial training in the teaching of English as a Foreign Language to students majoring in primary and secondary education. It comprises both academic courses (courses in subject matter, general culture, and pedagogy) and practice teaching of twelve weeks, which typically consists of a school experience phase in the second term of the fourth year.

The Language Learning Strategies course that we are focusing on lasts for twenty-eight hours spread over fourteen weeks in one semester. The language of the classroom is English. All discussions except for group work, when students tend to speak in Turkish, take place in English.

Assumptions

The study started with the following assumptions:

1. Learners do not generally stop and think about what learning a language, or learning in general, involves. They need help to conceptualize learning as thinking, which will eventually lead them to monitor and evaluate their own performance.

2. What is apparent from a constructivist view of learning is that individual characteristics such as age, gender, motivation and cultural background may play an important role in how the learner perceives the learning process. Therefore, rather than instructing them to use particular strategies, it would be more useful to help individuals to discover and develop what strategies they already have at their disposal.

3. Individuals will choose to use certain strategies if they are genuinely engaged in a learning task, which they find relevant to their needs.

4. Learners need to be provided with opportunities to look back on what they have done and reflect on it.

Procedure

Now let us take each assumption stated above in relation to the work done by the students. In terms of methodology, what I have done was to follow the arrows, as seen below, and clarify each concept with the involvement of the students:

LANGUAGE

↓

LEARNING

↓

STRATEGY

↓

LANGUAGE LEARNING STRATEGIES

Language

The first week of the course was primarily directed toward encouraging learners to understand and develop an awareness of the nature of language, native or foreign , its structure and the possibilities for its use. I considered it important that students should go beyond the classic definition of language: language is a system of communication among people. The students were invited to come up with alternative views of language and they were all noted on the board. Then we had a discussion on how language is central to the processes of teaching and learning. The aim was to help the students see that language is not a simple tool, as they may think, but that it is essential to pay conscious attention to the role it plays in our lives.

Learning

Having explored with the learners the nature of language, the course went on to consider "learning" as a thinking activity. At this stage, for the purpose of clarifying the concept of "learning" itself, students were encouraged to suggest what they understood by the term and how it applied to their day-to-day lives. Together we worked on definitions of learning and talked about the essential components of the learning process in the light of recent research on cognitive psychology. We discussed the following research-based statements about learning (for further information see Jones *et al.* 1987):

1. Learning is goal oriented.
2. Learning is linking new information to prior knowledge.
3. Learning is organizing information.
4. Learning is acquiring a repertoire of cognitive and metacognitive structures.
5. Learning occurs in phases, yet is non-linear.
6. Learning is influenced by development.

Strategy

As a further step in the course, I attempted to encourage students to be conscious of how they go about learning something—that is, what they do when they face a task or a problem and what skills and strategies they make use of. Here, I wanted to establish the meaning of the notion of "strategy" by inviting students' active participation. They came up with interesting descriptions of the ways ("techniques," as they put it) that ease the process of learning.

Identifying the Learners' Strategies

Then came the time to identify the learners' strategies. Holmes and Ramos (1991) have developed a checklist of reading/summarizing/writing strategies on the basis of previous research of a similar nature, from teacher observation of the writing process, and from scrutiny of the finished products. I opted for a more ethno-methodological technique and relied on the learner only in my attempt to take the teacher from the center-stage of the learning process.

Following Holmes and Ramos, I provided students with learning tasks such as preparing a summary, reading and listening for study purposes, test taking, and communication, and I observed them as they worked on their own or in groups. During the task hour I was there to help and to answer their questions. Among the tasks students worked on, I present here the reading task and the checklist, the results of my observations, and the discussions, in which students proposed some modifications.

The text we worked on was entitled "Global Warming," which was followed by simple comprehension questions.

The Checklist

Before reading:

- Planning: at this stage students decided if they wanted to work alone or in groups. They also had a look at the text and the questions that follow and made guesses about the content.
- Collective reading, if they are working in groups
- Reading the title and making inferences about it
- Examining illustrations: the students added this particular strategy to the checklist during our discussion periods. They rightly stated that the text they worked on did not contain any illustrations but if it had, they could have made use of them to anticipate the content along with the title.
- Skimming
- Recognizing the type of the text
- Looking for key words in the questions that indicated what kind of answer to expect. I was surprised to see students make use of this strategy before they even started reading, but in our later discussions they stated that that was the way they had prepared for the university entrance exam. In this way, they said, they could save time and answer more questions.

While reading:

- Underlining the unknown words
- Starting to read at the beginning and reading right through
- Using context
- Taking notes on a separate sheet of paper
- Looking up words in the dictionary
- Looking for key words in the questions that indicated what kind of answer to expect. Some students used this strategy during reading. They later explained that they wanted to know what they would be tested on—despite my numerous attempts to state that the purpose of the task was not to measure in any way their ability to read and that no evaluation on the comprehension questions would take place.

Previous knowledge: students stressed the importance of this strategy in understanding the text, referring to the discussions we had had on the learning process and how essential the linking of new information to prior information is for real learning to take place.

- Continuing, if unsuccessful at decoding a word or a phrase
- Stopping, if unsuccessful at decoding a word or a phrase
- Consulting their grammar book: students added this strategy afterwards and stated that they were very concerned about grammatical accuracy.
- Translating

After reading:
- Returning to the text to look for the correct answer, sometimes rereading the text
- Locating the area in the text that the question referred to and then looking for clues to that answer in that context.
- General knowledge outside the text called up by the reader in order to cope with the written material
- Guessing
- Paraphrasing
- Checking the grammatical accuracy of the answers

Immediately after students finished answering the comprehension questions, they were asked to mark the strategies they had used while their recollections of the task were still fresh. The students were then asked the following questions to initiate the discussion on their learning processes:

What strategies did you use?
Were they successful?
Would you use the same strategies the next time? (Holmes and Ramos
    1991:208)

Throughout the discussions, students not only had an opportunity to recognize the strategies they used but could also hear about the different procedures used by others. In addition, they could evaluate their own learning and see what they already knew, and what they needed to know.

There is no doubt that more items could be included in the checklist and the analysis of a particular text could be taken further. The intention here, however, has been to present an illustrative, rather than exhaustive, set of items in order to see constructive principles at work.

Students' Views on the Course

In line with the constructivist principle that reflection on experience is central to learning, I asked students to evaluate the course at the end of the term. I told them to feel free to write whatever they wanted to. I encouraged them to reflect on the processes used in carrying out the tasks, as well as on their feelings and emotions. A selection of students' comments follows:

"To me this course is essential for language learners. Most of us study through out-of-date methods and techniques. We succeed to some extent but never become aware of what we already have. Now I understand how important strategy is and that it will lead me to success."

"I learned one thing: to become aware of what I know and how I can use them."

"Your teaching strategies are different. You do not like giving any information directly. Instead, you push us to notice what we already know, to be critical. This is nice. And difficult because this is not the way we have trained so far. I am appalled when I first encountered your questions. I wish we could get away from memorization."

"We were told to memorize before. I cannot comment on anything."

"I found it very effective not to follow a specific textbook but do activities all the time. We have participated in the lesson actively."

"What I like most about this course is that it teaches how to become a good learner. We were not given piles of photocopies to memorize. No stress, a very comfortable atmosphere. This is how I like to learn. I remember everything we talked about because I wanted to listen and I enjoyed it."

"When I think about it I see that what we have learned was already known to us. We were using them everyday but unknowingly. Now we can use them in other lessons too."

Not all students expressed positive attitudes, as indicated by the following:

"The only problem I had with this course is that I didn't have any sources to work for the exam. I am not used to this. I have got to have something in my hand."

"Why do we have this course? We already know the techniques we talked about and we use them. So what is the point of making it much harder and complicated?"

Conclusions

It is obvious that learning strategies hold an important place in the teaching/learning process. What is proposed in this study, on the basis of constructivist principles, is a move from an interventionist approach to a descriptive one, since the latter has more to offer to gain insights into the learning process.

We believe that in order to help learners assume greater control over their own learning, it is important to help them to become aware of and identify the strategies that they already use or could potentially use. This study has confirmed Holmes and Ramos' (1991) finding that checklists can be powerful tools to draw students' attention to the learning process and help them to identify the learning strategies they use. They can also act as reference points for the teacher in designing appropriate learning tasks for the students since, in this way, the teacher has first-hand information as to how the students go about a task through their choices of learning strategies.

My students' comments have persuaded me that such a focus on learning processes is well worth the time we spend on it. Students could reflect on their own experience, which is the first step toward turning personal experience into metacognitive awareness.

References

Bell, B., and Gilbert, J. 1996. *Teacher Development: A Model from Science Education.* London: Falmer Press.

Chamot, A., Kupper, L. and Impink-Hernandez, M. 1988. *A Study of Learning Strategies in Foreign Language Instruction: Findings of the Longitudinal Study.* McLean, Va.: Interstate Research Associates.

Grennon Brooks, J. and Brooks, M.G. 1993. *In Search of Understanding: The Case for Constructivist Classrooms.* Alexandria, Va.: Association for Supervision and Curriculum Development.

Holmes, J. and Ramos, R. 1991. "Talking about Learning: Establishing a Framework for Discussing and Changing Learning Processes," in C. James, and P. Garrett (eds). *Language Awareness and the Classroom.* London: Longman.

Hosenfeld, C., Arnold, V., Kirchofer, J., Laciura, L., and Wilson, L. 1981. "Second Language Reading: A Curricular Sequence for Teaching Reading Strategies." *Foreign Language Annals* 14(5), 415–22.

Jones, B.A., Palincsar, A., Ogle, D. & Carr, E. (1987). *Strategic Teaching and Learning: Cognitive Instruction in the Content Area.* Alexandria. Va.: Association of Supervision and Curriculum Development.

Kaufman, D. and Brooks, J. G. 1996. "Interdisciplinary Collaboration in Teacher Education: A Constructivist Approach." *TESOL Quarterly*, 30(2), 231–251.

Kelly, G. A. 1955. *The Psychology of Personal Constructs: A Theory of Personality*, 2 vols. New York: W.W. Norton and Co. Inc.

Naiman, N., Fröhlich, M., Stern, H., and Todesco, A. 1978. *The Good Language Learner. Research in education series, No.7.* Toronto: Ontario Institute for Studies in Education.

O'Malley, J. M. and Chamot, A. U. 1990. *Learning Strategies in Second Language Acquisition.* Cambridge: Cambridge University Press.

Oxford, R. L. 1990. *Language Learning Strategies: What Every Teacher Should Know.* New York: Newbury House/Harper and Row.

Oxford, R. L., and Ehrman, M.E. 1995. "Adults' Language Learning Strategies in a Foreign Language Program in the United States." *System,* 23, 359–86.

Reiss, M. 1985. "The Good Language Learner." *Canadian Modern Language Review* 41, 511–23.

Roberts, J. 1998. *Language Teacher Education.* London: Arnold.

Rubin, J. 1975. "What the 'Good Language Learner' Can Teach Us?" *TESOL Quarterly* 9, 41–51.

Schön, D. A. 1995. *The Reflective Practitioner: How Professionals Think in Action.* Aldershot: Arena.

Schön, D. A. 1987. *Educating the Reflective Practitioner: Towards a New Design for Teaching and Learning in the Professions.* San Francisco: Jossey-Bass.

Sendan, F. C. 1995. *Patterns of Development in EFL Student Teachers' Personal Theories: A Constructivist Approach.* PhD Thesis, University of Reading.

Stern, H. H. 1975. "What Can We Learn from the Good Language Learner?" *Canadian Modern Language Review* 31, 304–18.

Wenden, A. and Rubin, J. (eds.) 1987. *Learner Strategies in Language Learning.* Englewood Cliffs, NJ: Prentice Hall.

Williams, M. and Burden, R.L. 1997. *Psychology for Language Teachers: A Social Constructivist Approach.* Cambridge: Cambridge University Press.

A Learner-Based Approach to Writing Improvement

Using "Repertory Grid Technique" as a Learning Tool

Hülya Yumru
Jülide İnözü

Attempts to improve students' written products often fail, as the starting point for improvement is provided by the teachers themselves or the institutions. That is, the focus has been only on the teachers' transmission of predetermined content with the hope of standardizing writing courses in the institution. However, this approach has not started the process of "perspective transformation," for it is the teachers who provide students with ready-made solutions for the predetermined problems (Swan 1993). As a result, this "solution-centered" approach to learner development activities gave rise only to marginal, short-term results (Eraut 1972). For this reason, we believe that at the beginning of any development program the focus should be on helping learners to uncover their perceived need for improvement, as only in such a condition will development be directly relevant to personal needs. The philosophy of involving the learners in the learning process is highlighted in Kelly's (1955) personal construct theory.

A fundamental postulate of personal construct theory holds that if we want to understand a person (in our case a student), then we have to understand how s/he perceives the world (in our case the features of a good piece of writing), and so how s/he construes personal choices and decisions (in our case his/her perception of strengths and weaknesses regarding writing and the possible action steps to be taken to overcome those perceived weaknesses for improvement). To summarize, Kelly (1955) points out that "if you want to help people to change, you must first understand the construction they are placing on their world, the theories they hold and the questions they are asking" (Burr and Butt 1992:3). In other words, change is believed to take place when individuals explore and understand their personal constructs (Diamond 1991).

In line with the above reasoning, the basic premise of this study is that students are more capable of improving their writing if they are actively involved in identifying, analyzing, and solving the problems hidden in their written products. Thus, this study seeks answers to the following exploratory questions:

1. What are the students' personal constructs regarding the features of a good writer?
2. How do the students perceive themselves as writers?
3. What are the students' perceived needs for improvement in their writing ability?
4. Do changes occur in the students' perceived needs for development if they are actively involved in identifying and analyzing problems in their written products?
5. If there occurs any change in students' perception of "self as a writer" as compared to "ideal self," is this change reflected in their written products?

The Study

The Participants
In this fourteen-week study, we worked with ten randomly selected freshman students of the ELT Department of Çukurova University, Adana, Turkey. However, three of these students dropped out of the study during the term for various reasons.

Data Collection
The data of our study came from two main sources: holistic evaluation of the portfolios kept by the students throughout the semester (see Appendix 1 for the checklist used) and repertory grids (see Appendix 2). The aim of using Kelly's Repertory Grid technique (Pope and Keen 1981) was to involve the students in the identification of:

- their personal constructs regarding the features of a good writer
- their perception of "themselves as writers" (which meant self as a writer at the beginning of the study), and their "ideal selves as writers" (which meant the writers they would like to be in the future)
- their perceived needs for improvement in writing.

Repertory Grid Elicitation Procedures

At the beginning of the study, we held a conference with the students to inform them about the aim and the procedures involved in repertory grid elicitation. We also explained to the students the meanings of the vocabulary used in the grid, such as *element*, and *implicit* and *emergent constructs*. In literature, elements are defined as "an individual's personal observations or experience of the world," which are "used to define the area of the topic" (Repertory Grid 2 Manual 1993:6). Following this definition, we explained to the students that their elements were the writers who were well known to be personally meaningful to them. Constructs are defined as a person's "classification of his personal observations or experience of the world (Repertory Grid 2 Manual 1993:6). Drawing on this definition, we pointed out to the students that constructs refer to the features of a writer who they thought was good at writing. We also explained to them that each construct had two poles, emergent and implicit. As a result, we indicated that the way (considering the feature identified) in which two of the elements were alike constituted the emergent construct, while the other feature which differed from the emergent pole stood for the implicit construct.

Elicitation of Elements

We followed Pope and Keen's (1981) method in the elicitation of elements. That is, we elicited both the elements and the constructs from each of the students. This elicitation procedure was completed in the researchers' office with the students, which took approximately forty minutes. When eliciting elements, we asked the students to think of nine writers, three of whom they believed to be Effective, three Typical (Average), and three Ineffective. As the main concern of the procedure was to elicit the students' views on the features of effectiveness in writing, they were asked not to provide the researchers with the identity of the writers they considered, but rather to use codes for their names. They were then advised to code the Effective writers from the most effective to the least effective, such as E1, E2, and E3. They were asked to apply the same procedure to Typical and Ineffective writers.

Elicitation of Constructs

Using the nine writer codes written on nine cards, the students employed a triadic elicitation technique. In other words, they selected three cards randomly, in order to identify the triads. They then recorded the identified triads (e.g., E1, T2 and I3) on the triad column in their grid forms. Having completed this, the students were asked to articulate which two of the three writers were similar to each other and different from the third regarding the features of a good writer. The similar pairs (e.g., E1 and T2) were then marked on the triad column in the grid form and their construct (e.g., rich vocabulary use) was recorded on the emergent (similarity) pole. Next, the construct (e.g., repetition of the same vocabulary items) that distinguishes the third writer from the two on the same dimension was recorded on the implicit (contrast) pole. The students were allowed to make as many comparisons as possible for the triads randomly selected. The same elicitation procedures were repeated until either the students pointed out that they were not able to propose any other constructs, or when they started repeating the constructs they had already dealt with.

We also used a five-point rating scale for the constructs in the grids. In this scale, "1" represented the closest value to the emergent (similarity) pole, "3" the mid value, and "5" the closest value to the implicit (contrast) pole. Having elicited the students' elements and constructs, the students were asked to rate each of their elements on each construct that they came up with. After the completion of the ratings, the students were asked to rate themselves as "self as a writer" and "ideal self as a writer" on the same constructs.

At the end of the study, the students were given their completed grid forms without the original ratings on them. They were asked to read their original constructs so as to make any necessary additions, deletions, or modifications. As a final step, the students were asked to re-rate the elements on each of the constructs that they had identified.

Holistic Evaluation of Student Portfolios

The second group of data came from the holistic evaluation of students' portfolios, which includes the writing tasks done throughout the term. The checklist (see Appendix 1) used for this purpose was prepared in accordance with the weaknesses identified by the students themselves. The aim of this checklist was to evaluate whether the students had improved their identified weaknesses in practice. ·

Findings of the Study

Analysis of the First Repertory Grid Data

We subjected the students' repertory grids to content analysis to find out the answer to our first research question, which aimed at uncovering the personal constructs held by the students about the features of a good writer. The content analysis of the first repertory grid data produced a total of eight constructs from seven students. At the beginning of the study, the students in our study perceived good writers as those who:

- are good at using grammar
- discover the topic before they begin to write.
- formulate their topic sentence before they go any further
- exclude irrelevant ideas regarding the topic
- use a variety of vocabulary
- support their ideas effectively
- organize their thoughts at the beginning of a writing process
- make use of transitions for a smooth flow of ideas

Another concern of this study was to find out how the students perceived "themselves as writers" at the beginning of the study, as compared to their "ideal self as writers" (i.e., their role models). The analysis of the students' ratings of "themselves as writers" and their "ideal selves as writers" on the constructs that they came up with revealed the students' perceived need for improvement in all of the constructs that are mentioned above. On the whole, the most problematic issues seemed to be the appropriate use of grammar , vocabulary use and knowledge, supporting their ideas, organizing their thoughts, excluding irrelevant ideas regarding the topic, and formulating their topic sentence.

Having analyzed the repertory grid forms, we interviewed the students to confirm whether our view of their needs for writing improvement matched their views. At the end of our interviews with the students, we came up with the following conclusions to be considered when preparing our learner-based writing syllabus:

- Students have problems in deciding the amount of detail that should be included while writing.
- Students have a concern related to the problem of eliminating sentences that are not related to the topic.
- Students experience problems in organizing their thoughts/ideas.
- Students do not know how to begin writing.
- Students have problems in the correct use of grammar.
- Students want to increase their word power.

In the light of the writing course syllabus topics that we negotiated with the students, we designed the tasks that specifically focused on the factors that lead to writing effectively, such as unity, support, coherence, and sentence skills. Moreover, the tasks included practice in pre-writing strategies such as brainstorming, outlining, free-writing, listing, diagramming, and in making a point supporting that point with examples, facts, or statistics and then organizing and connecting the specific evidence. All through these activities, we also focused on writing error-free sentences and vocabulary improvement. That is, we tried to remedy the problems that occurred in individual student papers, such as run-on sentences, fragments, subject–verb agreement, dangling modifiers, and verb consistency, and the mechanics of language use. Regarding vocabulary improvement, we could only deal with developing the habit of selecting words that are appropriate and exact for the context chosen.

Analysis of the Second Repertory Grid Data

At the end of the fourteen-week period, we subjected the second repertory grid forms to content analysis, to explore a) the changes in the content of personal constructs held by the students, and b) the changes in the students' perception of "self" and "ideal self" as a writer. The analysis of the second repertory grid data indicated two types of change:

1. changes in the content of personal constructs
2. changes in the perception of "self as a writer"

To illustrate these two types of changes, we present specific examples from students' repertory grid forms. The first type of change observed was the integration of the new constructs into the whole system of construction regarding the features of a good writer. For example, the second student in our study group added five new constructs into her existing construction system regarding the features of a good writer. These five new constructs were "good command of grammar," "good at expressing the controlling idea in the topic sentence," "good at writing supporting ideas related to the topic sentence," "good at punctuation," "good at using words that are appropriate to the context." Two out these five constructs ("good at punctuation," "good command of grammar") were newly formed ones, which we assume were acquired through personal experience of writing instruction and the writing tasks involved, and the consequent feedback given by either peers or the teacher. The other three constructs ("good at expressing the controlling idea in the topic sentence," "good at writing supporting ideas related to the topic sentence," "good at using words that are appropriate to the context"), on the other hand, took the form of attaching new meanings to the already existing labels. That is, during the writing instruction process, Student 2 seems to have gone through a reflection and restructuring period within which she further clarified the already acquired constructs. For example, at the beginning of the term, this student had only one construct concerning vocabulary use in writing ("good at using a variety of vocabulary"). However, as a result of the new experiences in which she had been involved in the writing course, she elaborated this construct and added a new meaning onto her already existing construct system regarding vocabulary use in writing (i.e., "good at using words that are appropriate to the context").

The analysis of change with regard to the students' perception of "self" and "ideal self" as a writer indicates the changes in the students' perception of the qualities of a good writer, and themselves as writers. Although the seven students' perception of "ideal self as a writer" (i.e., their role models) seems to reflect no change, there seems to be a considerable change in the students' perception of themselves as writers. And this change was realized in two ways: either a) the students perceived themselves closer to their ideals, or b) they thought they were far from possessing the features of their role models. For instance, at the beginning of the study, Student 5 perceived "self as a writer" far from her "ideal self as writer" regarding the effective use of grammar in writing. However, at the end of the study, she perceived "self as a writer" very close to her "ideal self as a writer," in the correct use of grammar (see Appendix 3). Therefore, we assume that she thinks she is going to be an effective writer concerning the use of grammar; however, she does not think she is an ideal one yet. The same student, on the other hand, perceived "self as a writer" as being average in terms of using a variety of vocabulary at the beginning of the term. But at the end of the study, she associated "self as a writer" with a writer far from her "ideal self." In fact, she linked her "self as a writer" to the ineffective writers, regarding vocabulary use. Thus, we can assume that at the end of the course, she became more aware of the features possessed by effective writers and her needs in writing as regards to vocabulary use.

Holistic Evaluation of Students' Portfolios

The last group of data emerged out of the holistic evaluation of students' portfolios, which include the writing tasks done throughout the term. We evaluated the students' portfolios to find out whether or not the changes in the students' perception of "self as a writer" as compared to "ideal self as a writer" were reflected in their written products. That is, we wanted to find out whether the students improved their identified weaknesses in practice. To achieve this aim, the papers of the students were ranked as "poor," "fair," "average," "good," and "excellent," using a holistic evaluation checklist (see Appendix 1) that focused on content, organization, vocabulary, language use, and mechanics of a written piece.

Holistic evaluation of students' papers indicated that the changes in the students' perception of "self as a writer" regarding the correct use of grammar and producing coherent and unified paragraphs were the most common areas of improvement reflected in students' written pieces. For example, at the beginning of the study, Student 3 viewed "self as a writer" as average in terms of using grammar correctly. However, at the end of the study, she identified "self as a writer" as being very close (i.e., good at the use of grammar) to her "ideal self as a writer." The holistic evaluation of this student's collection of written products with a specific focus on language use revealed that she had gone through a process of improvement especially in writing simple but effective constructions.

In another case regarding the issue of producing coherent pieces of writing, Student 6, for example, rated "self as a writer" as average at the beginning of the study. But then her view of "self as a writer" changed and she perceived herself as good in writing coherently. The holistic evaluation of this student's written products in terms of coherence showed that while the previous writings of this student lack organization, i.e., the ideas were confused and disconnected, her later works were well organized and cohesive.

Conclusions

The basic premise of this study was that students are more capable of improving their writing skills if they are actively involved in identifying their own strengths and weaknesses, rather than having their needs articulated for them by the teachers. Following this line of reasoning, we have tried to negotiate the writing course syllabus with the students considering the weaknesses as identified through repertory grid forms.

This study demonstrates that the repertory grid technique may be one of the beneficial tools in the identification of the students' needs by having them articulate their own weaknesses. The information obtained through this technique may be a sound starting point in preparing a learner-based syllabus and, accordingly, the writing tasks to be used to remedy the problems identified. In effect, as the students take part in decision-making (syllabus negotiation), they take on the responsibility for and ownership of change (i.e., writing improvement), rather than developing a resistance to the writing course.

Finally, we suggest that at the outset of any course (e.g., reading, literature, structure, etc.), the focus should be on uncovering students' personal theories (i.e., beliefs) so as to design a variety of activities that build on the students' perceived needs for development.

References

Burr, V., and Butt, T. 1992. *Invitation to Personal Construct Theory*. London: Whurr Publishing Ltd.

Diamond, C.T.P. 1991. *Teacher Education as Transformation*. Milton Keynes: Open University Press.

Eraut, M. 1972. *In-service Education for Innovation* Occasional Paper 4. National Council for Educational Technology.

Kelly, G.A. 1955. *The Psychology of Personal Constructs: A Theory of Personality*,Vol. 1. New York: W.W. Norton and Co. Inc.

Pope, M.L. and Keen, T. 1981. *Personal Construct Psychology and Education.* London: Academic Press.

Repertory Grid 2 Manual. 1993. Canada: Centre for Person-Computer Studies.

Swan, J. 1993. "Metaphor in Action: The Observation Schedule in a Reflective Approach to Teacher Education." *English Language Teaching Journal* l, 47:3, 242–249.

Appendix 1

Composition Profile

Content

Excellent to very good: knowledgeable, substantive, thorough development of thesis, relevant to assigned topic

Good to average: some knowledge of subject, adequate range, limited development of thesis, mostly relevant to topic but lacks detail

Fair to poor: limited knowledge of subject, little substance, inadequate development of topic

Very poor: does not show knowledge of subject, non-substantive, not pertinent, or not enough to evaluate

Organization

Excellent to very good: fluent expression, ideas clearly stated, supported, succinct, well organized, logical sequencing, cohesive

Good to average: somewhat choppy, loosely organized but main ideas stand out, limited support, logical but incomplete sequencing

Fair to poor: non-fluent, ideas confused or disconnected, lacks logical sequencing and development

Very poor: does not communicate, no organization, not enough to evaluate

Vocabulary

Excellent to very good: sophisticated range, effective word choice and usage, word form mastery, appropriate register

Good to average: adequate range, occasional errors of word form, choice, usage but meaning not obscured

Fair to poor: limited range, frequent errors of word form, choice, usage, meaning confused or obscured

Very poor: essentially translation, little knowledge of English vocabulary, idioms, word form, or not enough to evaluate

Language Use

Excellent to very good: effective complex constructions, few errors of agreement, tense, number, word order/function, articles, pronouns, prepositions

Good to average: effective but simple constructions, minor problems in complex constructions, several errors of agreement, tense, number, word order/function, articles, pronouns, prepositions but meaning seldom obscured

Fair to poor: major problems in simple/complex constructions, frequent errors of negation, agreement, tense, number, word order/function, articles, pronouns, prepositions, fragments, run-ons, deletions, meaning confused or obscured

Very poor: virtually no mastery of sentence construction rules, dominated by errors, does not communicate, or not enough to evaluate

Mechanics

Excellent to very good: demonstrates mastery of conventions, few errors of spelling, punctuation, capitalization, paragraphing

Good to average: occasional errors of spelling, punctuation, capitalization, paragraphing but meaning not obscured

Fair to poor: frequent errors of spelling, punctuation, capitalization, paragraphing, poor handwriting, meaning confused or obscured

Very poor: no mastery of conventions, dominated by errors of spelling, punctuation, capitalization, paragraphing, handwriting illegible, or not enough to evaluate

Appendix 2

Repertory Grid

Construct No	Triads	Emergent Constructs (similarities) Elements	Rating Scale 1 2 3 4 5										Implicit Constructs (contrasts) Elements
			E1	E2	E3	T1	T2	T3	I1	I2	I3	Self	Ideal	
1														
2														
3														
4														
5														
6														
7														
8														
9														
10														
11														
12														
13														
14														
15														

Appendix 3

Table 1. The number of constructs and the students' perception of themselves and their ideals as these emerged in the first administration of the repertory grid

Constructs	S1		S2		S3		S4		S5		S6		S7	
	Ideal	*Self*	*Ideal*	*Self*	*Ideal*	*Self*	*Ideal*	*Self*	*Ideal*	*Self*	*Ideal*	*Self*	*Ideal*	*Self*
1	1	2	—	—	1	3	1	2	1	4	1	2	—	—
2	1	2	—	—	—	—	1	3	—	—	—	—	—	—
3	—	—	1	2	—	—	—	—	—	—	—	—	—	—
4	—	—	1	2	—	—	—	—	—	—	—	—	1	2
5	—	—	1	3	—	—	—	—	1	3	—	—	1	3
6	—	—	—	—	—	—	1	3	1	3	—	—	1	2
7	—	—	—	—	—	—	—	—	—	—	1	3	1	3
8	—	—	—	—	—	—	—	—	—	—	1	3	—	—

Table 2. The number of constructs and the students' perception of themselves and their ideals as these emerged in the second administration of the repertory grid

Constructs	S1		S2		S3		S4		S5		S6		S7	
	Ideal	*Self*	*Ideal*	*Self*	*Ideal*	*Self*	*Ideal*	*Self*	*Ideal*	*Self*	*Ideal*	*Self*	*Ideal*	*Self*
1	1	1	1	1	1	2	1	2	1	2	1	2	—	—
2	1	3	—	—	—	—	1	3	—	—	—	—	—	—
3	—	—	1	2	—	—	—	—	—	—	—	—	—	—
4	1	1	1	2	—	—	—	—	—	—	—	—	1	2
5	1	2	1	3	—	—	—	—	1	4	—	—	1	2
6	1	1	1	2	—	—	1	2	1	3	—	—	1	2
7	1	2	—	—	—	—	—	—	—	—	1	2	1	2
8	1	1	—	—	—	—	—	—	—	—	1	2	—	—
9	—	—	1	3	—	—	—	—	—	—	—	—	—	—
10	—	—	1	2	—	—	—	—	—	—	—	—	—	—

Politeness and Pragmatic Failure
Speakers' Intentions and Hearers'
Perceptions in L2 Apologies

Mona M. Osman
Paul B. Stevens

The Problem and Its Setting

The focus of this study is the speech act of apology in English as a second language. Specifically, the problem that we address here is the relationship between 1) the level of L2 English proficiency and 2a) the degree of *directness* and 2b) the degree of *politeness* in the production of the speech act of apology by native Arabic speakers.

The Variables

This study investigates the relationship between one independent variable and two dependent variables. The independent variable is L2 English proficiency. Since the study was conducted in the English Language Institute (ELI) at the American University in Cairo (AUC), L2 proficiency was operationally defined according to the ELI levels. For the purposes of this study, native English speakers are considered the highest level of proficiency.

The two dependent variables are politeness and directness. Since this study is concerned with the misunderstanding or pragmatic failure that occurs between L1 and L2 speakers and because this misunderstanding happens when the intention of the speaker does not match the perception of the hearer, politeness is operationally defined as speakers' own judgments regarding their *intended* degree of politeness and the judgment of the hearers regarding the hearers' *perceptions* of the politeness of the utterances on a Likert scale. This definition of politeness is different from what has been done in most previous research, where the basis for defining politeness derives from looking at the modality markers.

Directness here is operationally defined according to an objective, five-point nominal scale designed by the researchers, who were guided by House and Kasper's (1981) eight-point directness scale for complaints and Haverkate's (1988) three-point directness scale for directives. The scale designed for this study depends upon a) acknowledgment that the offense is bad, b) implicit or explicit acknowledgment of responsibility for the offense, and c) an implicit or explicit expression of apology. The scale is detailed in Appendix 1.

The study involves one moderating variable, namely the *degree* of offense in each situation. This variable is operationally defined according to the ratings of both Americans and Egyptians on a three-point scale (minor offense, average offense, and major offense). As for extraneous variables, the degree of dominance and familiarity of the interlocutors are controlled for in the questionnaire items. Age, the time spent in an English-speaking country, and educational background are controlled for through sampling.

The Research Questions

Because this is an exploratory study, there are no hypotheses, but two research questions are asked:

1. Is there a relationship between the level of L2 English proficiency and the degree of *directness* in the production of the speech act of apology in English by L1 Arabic speakers?

2. Is there a relationship between the level of L2 English proficiency and the degree of *politeness* in the production of the speech act of apology in English by L1 Arabic speakers?

These questions are broken into six sub-questions that are dealt with below.

Significance of the Study

The study is significant, as it is related to two problems in EFL. The first is that of miscommunication between L1 and L2 speakers. The study undertakes a new approach that attempts to find out whether the speaker's *intentions* of politeness meet the hearer's *perceptions* of the politeness of the utterances. If an L2 speaker intends to be impolite to an L1 hearer, or an L1 speaker intends to be impolite to an L2 hearer and the hearer perceives the utterance as impolite, there is no linguistic problem. Linguistic problems arise when the speaker's intentions to be polite are misread by the hearer as impolite, due to some deficiency in the foreign language proficiency.

The second problem is one of curricula, for if there is no positive relationship between L2 proficiency and speech act production, perhaps curriculum developers should rethink the curricula if communication with L1 speakers is one of the goals of the foreign language program.

Rationale for the Problem

Since several studies, such as Stevens (1991), Stevens (1994), and Thomas (1983) have supported the point of view that there is miscommunication or pragmatic failure between L1 and L2 speakers, it is important to look for the reasons for this miscommunication in the speech acts of L2 learners. Several other studies, including Blum-Kulka (1983) have supported the notion that languages differ in assigning illocutionary force to indirect speech acts, which may lead to miscommunication, that there are differences in the degree of directness and politeness across languages, and that fluent L2 speakers can comprehend direct, but not indirect, speech acts. Those results should be checked across various proficiency levels. Blum-Kulka (1987) maintains that directness and politeness are not the same and that for requests the most direct utterances are the least polite, but, at the same time, the most indirect are not necessarily the most polite. Now, since requests are face-threatening acts, whereas apologies are face-supportive, Blum-Kulka's results need to be verified for apologies. Koike (1989) supports the viewpoint that L2 beginners can comprehend and produce speech acts, but, unlike L1 speakers, they tend toward clarity at the expense of politeness. Koike's results need to be investigated at other proficiency levels as well.

Concerning the speech act of apology, it has already been supported that L2 learners are like L1 speakers in the production of the *main* apology strategies, but not their modifications (Trosborg, 1987; and Cohen, Olshtain, and Rosenstein, 1986). In an analysis of modality markers, Trosborg (1987) claims that L2 speakers appear to be less polite than L1 speakers in the production of the speech act of apology. However, generalizability was limited due to the number of subjects. Moreover, modality markers should not be the only measure of politeness, since it is the intention of the speaker and the perception of the hearer that really count where miscommunication is concerned. To the researchers' knowledge, no one has yet investigated the relationship between the level of L2 proficiency and the degree of directness and politeness in the production of the speech act of apology. In addition, previous studies have assumed that the impolite-sounding utterances of L2 learners have been due to some kind of linguistic deficiency, specifically pragmatic failure. This study attempts to measure subjects' pragmatic intentions regarding politeness and compare these to raters' perceptions of the politeness of the learners' pragmatic production. Only where learners mean to be polite but are perceived to be impolite can pragmatic failure be said to have occurred. Hence, this study, through its design, aims at improving on previous designs, and at filling a gap in the literature.

Methodology

Subjects
Subjects are made up of twenty-five subjects from each of four levels: English native speakers (Cairo American College (CAC) high school students), and three proficiency levels of non-native English learners in the ELI at AUC, namely students from English 100, upper-level Intensive English Program (IEP) (English 99), and intermediate-level IEP (English 98). The mean age of American subjects was 16. That of the three non-native levels was eighteen. The mean time spent in an English-speaking country was 10.5 years for the Americans and a few months for the three non-native levels. Most of the non-natives in all three levels rated their use of English with native English speakers as occasional. Regarding the educational background, most of the English 100 and upper-level IEP subjects came from schools where the principal language of instruction was English, whereas most of the intermediate-level IEP subjects came from schools where the main language of instruction was Arabic.

Instruments
The starting point for the questionnaire was one designed by Cohen, Olshtain, and Rosenstein (1986) and is composed of eight apology situations. However, six other speech act situations were included as distracters to avoid response sets. There were some modifications to the original questionnaire to make the situation the subjects were asked to put themselves in more relevant to the here and now, to avoid ambiguity, and to control for the degree of familiarity. The eight apology scenarios in the questionnaire are detailed in Appendix 2. In addition, an attitudinal survey was used to measure the degree of politeness according to the speaker's intentions on a Likert scale of 1 to 5, with 1 meaning very impolite, and 5 very polite. Subjects wrote their responses on machine-scorable answer sheets. Three volunteer raters from each of the four proficiency levels were asked to rate the hundred responses according to their perceptions of *politeness* on a Likert scale of 1 to 5 similar to that of intentions. Then, as far as *directness* is concerned, three volunteer raters from among friends were trained to rate directness according to the directness scale for apologies designed for the study. The overall inter-

rater reliability of the three directness raters as obtained from the pilot study data was 0.941. The responses were mixed up before giving them to the raters, to avoid order effect. The Cronbach Alpha for the attitudinal survey of politeness intentions was 0.89 and that for perceptions was 0.74, which means that the surveys were quite reliable (that is, internally consistent).

Procedures

A thirty-minute meeting with the students was scheduled through the teachers of each level. A thirty-minute meeting was also scheduled with the American CAC students during their free time where they take their breaks at school. During the meeting with each group, the first five minutes were spent explaining the instructions. The subjects were given the questionnaire to complete in fifteen minutes. (The time allowed was intentionally short so as not to give time for thinking or modifying the answers, in an attempt to make the answers more spontaneous). Subjects were then given the Intentions Attitudinal Survey to complete in ten minutes. Before running the experiment, three Egyptian volunteer raters for the Politeness Perceptions Survey were recruited from each level with the help of their teachers. Three American raters (AUC faculty and graduate students) were also recruited for the same purposes. After the experiment was completed, the politeness raters were asked to rate all the responses according to their perceptions on machine-scorable answer sheets. Simultaneously, the three directness raters rated the directness of the responses according to the scale designed for the study.

Data Analysis and Interpretation

Statistical Analysis

All the data were collected on machine-scorable answer sheets. ASCII files were created, and the data were analyzed using SYSTAT.

Sub-question 1):

Are all four proficiency levels of speakers (natives, English 100, upper level IEP, and intermediate level IEP) equal in their politeness intentions?

To answer this sub-question a 4x8 repeated measures ANOVA was used. Results revealed a significant main effect for level only between the native English speakers and the other three levels. This main effect was moderated by the interaction between level and situation. The results indicate that the native English speakers intended to be less polite than all three levels of L2 speakers. This cannot be interpreted as a main effect for proficiency level, but rather as a main effect for language group (L1 versus L2).

Sub-question 2a):

Do the native speakers perceive the degree of politeness of all four levels as equal?

A one-way repeated measures ANOVA was applied to the data. Results revealed a significant main effect for proficiency level. The Americans rated upper-level IEP as most polite, followed by English 100 and intermediate-level IEP and rated the native English speakers as least polite. This indicates that Americans perceive of themselves as less polite than they do L2 Egyptian English speakers. Upper-level IEP were rated as more polite than English 100 (even though English 100 is a higher level of proficiency), and were also rated more polite than intermediate level IEP (which is a lower level of proficiency).

Although we do not offer this as an explanation for what is going on here, it is as if L2 English speakers become more polite as they acquire more language proficiency up to a certain limit and then they fall back into being less polite as they become closer to native language proficiency. There is a certain logic to this, as it may be the case that intermediate-level IEP students do not have the means to express the degree of politeness they wish to convey. As they move into upper-level IEP, they gain the skills that enable them to express this politeness. As they move into English 100, they start to imitate native English speakers in their speech, thus becoming less polite once more. This is in keeping with the politeness intentions of L1 English speakers being less than that of L2 English speakers. However, there may be other factors that better explain this.

Sub-question 2b):

Are the politeness intentions of all four levels the same as native speakers' perceptions?

A series of independent t-tests were applied to the data. There was no significant difference between the intentions and the perceptions. As these results contradict all previous research they contribute to our understanding of the cross-cultural aspect of pragmatics. The findings of this study support the hypothesis that L1 English speakers do not misunderstand L2 English speakers, at least within the context of apologies.

Sub-question 3a):
Do all four levels equally perceive the degree of politeness of the native English speakers?
A one-way ANOVA was employed. The results revealed no significant effect for proficiency level.

Sub-question 3b):
Are the perceptions that the three levels of the non-natives have of the natives' utterances the same as the natives' politeness intentions?
A series of independent t-tests were employed. The results revealed that there is no difference between intentions and perceptions. This indicates that L2 English speakers do not misunderstand L1 English speakers, at least within the context of apologies.

Sub-question 4):
Are the four levels equal in their degree of directness?
A one-way repeated measures ANOVA was administered. The results revealed no significant effect for level. Probably, this is because the speech act of apology as a face-supportive act is inclined to being direct. Most of the subjects, regardless of level, chose to offer an explicit apology (e.g., "I'm sorry"), or at least to offer repair (e.g., "I'll pay for the damages").

Sub-question 5):
Does the degree of offense make any difference as a moderating variable?
A one-way ANOVA was employed to detect any difference in perception between Americans and Egyptians. None was detected, indicating that the degree of offense had no effect on the relationship between politeness intentions and proficiency level.

Sub-question 6):
Is there any relationship between the degree of directness of the utterances and that of politeness?
A Spearman Rank procedure was applied to the data to detect any correlation. The matrix showed that the correlation coefficient for English 100 is the only statistically significant one. Thus, the results revealed that there is a positive correlation between directness and politeness in relation to apologies, at least for English 100. However, one can speculate that the other coefficients might have increased if there had been more than eight situations, or if it had not been necessary to average across the 100 responses. In order to avoid order effect, the researchers mixed up the responses of the 100 subjects and, in order to reorder them, they had

to average across the responses of each level. They also had to average across raters. Thus, the researchers were left with only the eight apology situations to correlate between politeness and directness. The speech act of apology is a face-supportive act to the other, and it is only in face-threatening acts that we need to resort to indirectness. More accurately, though, the speech act of apology is both face-threatening (embarrassing) and face-saving (preventing further complaint) to the self, which explains why some people resort to indirectness if they see it as more face- threatening than face-saving to the self.

Pragmatic Analyses

A few words may be in order regarding the linguistic data themselves, looking at some of the kinds of pragmatic strategies that the subjects were employing. This is meant to be illustrative only, as a thoroughgoing pragmatic analysis of the strategies used by the subjects would go beyond the scope of the study.

It seemed that subjects typically apologized by saying "sorry" and/or by giving an explanation and/or by making some offer of repair. This may have been especially true of the English 100 subjects (the most proficient non-native group).

"Sorry!"

Many subjects used "Sorry!" or "I'm sorry!" as part of their apologizing strategy. However, it is notable that "Sorry!" was used in various ways.

(a) In examples (1) and (2) from the"chairs at swimming pool" scenario, some subjects said "Sorry!" to express regret or apologize for the offense, with an explanation of how the offense happened.
  (1) "Sorry, I did not notice that."
  (2) "Sorry, I didn't recognize this."

(b) In (3) and (4), other subjects expressed regret or apologized for the offense, then offered repair or promise of forbearance. This was the case in the "spilled coffee" scenario:
  (3)"I'm very sorry; let me help you."
as well as in the "meeting at library" scenario:
  (4) "Sorry, I really forgot to come yesterday. I won't forget today."

(c) Others, as in (5), apparently said "Sorry!" to express regret or apologize for their offense, then tried to justify their actions, as in the "wrong bus directions" scenario:
  (5) "I'm very sorry; I only tried to help."

(d) Still others, in (6) and (7), expressed regret or apologized for the offense, but then went on to reprimand their imagined interlocutor, as for example, in the "chairs at swimming pool" scenario:

(6)   "Sorry, I didn't see 'em, but you could've said it in a better way."

This was also true in the "it's a she, not a he" scenario:

(7)   "Sorry, why don't you put to her an earring because babies at this age can't be differentiated."

(e) In (8), it is also possible to say "Sorry!" to express regret or apologize for an offense, while at the same time justifying why the offense happened and even refusing to redress the "wrong" (if indeed from the speaker's viewpoint it is a "wrong"):

(8)   "I'm sorry, when I saw them there were no bags. You have to find others."

It seems that "I'm sorry!" here is not an *apology* for having committed an offense, but rather an expression of *regret* that the interlocutor has taken offense or has a problem, or perhaps a statement of regret that the speaker is *about* to say something which the hearer will not like.

(f) In (9), a similar expression of regret or apology for an offense *which is about to happen* is found in this example of the "chairs at swimming pool" scenario:

(9)   "Sorry, but you have to be polite when talking to me."

Insufficient/Unacceptable Explanations

Part of what can make an apology acceptable or polite is the part of the apology that explains how the offense occurred in the first place and/or tries to compensate for the offense, whether by stating one's regret for what has happened or by promising to do better in the future. However, some subjects chose to be impolite by explicitly or implicitly criticizing the interlocutor. Thus, in the "it's a she, not a he" scenario, the response

(10)   "But she looks like a boy"

is impolite, since it does not apologize at all and, at the same time, gives a justification that the girl's parents presumably would not want to hear. Moreover, in (11), we see that even with "I'm sorry!" the response is impolite, since it tells the parent something he or she would not welcome hearing:

(11)   "I'm sorry; she looks like a boy."

On the other hand, in (12)

(12)   "Sorry, why don't you put to her an earring because babies at this age can't be differentiated"

the presence of "Sorry!" is not enough to make up for the implicit reprimand of the rest of the response, which taken as a whole is impolite.

Acceptable Explanations

However, in (13), (14), and (15), an acceptable explanation and/or a promise to rectify the wrong may be enough to make the apology "polite," even in the following examples (the "meeting at the library" and "forgot the medicine" scenarios) where the respondent is apologizing for having broken a promise:

(13) "I went to the chemist, but I found it closed."

(14) "No, I forgot, but I'm leaving now and I'll get it after a short time."

(15) "I'm sorry, I had other things which filled my mind. Don't worry, I'll pass by and hand it to you."

"I forgot!"

Since the "meeting at the library" and "forgot the medicine" scenarios, involve breaking a promise, it should be difficult to apologize in these situations. Indeed, this is the case in the following examples, where the explanation given is too flimsy an excuse to justify having broken a promise:

(16) "I am sorry, I forgot."

(17) "I'm sorry; I forgot because I was too busy."

On the other hand, examples (18) through (21) show that begging forgiveness, promising repair (i.e., fulfilling the promise), or self-deprecation all are ways for the respondent to redeem his/her reply, making it into a "polite" one:

(18) "I really forgot. Please forgive me."

(19) "Oh my God, I forgot. I can return and buy it now. Please wait for me."

(20) "I'm sorry, I really forgot. Can we meet tomorrow?"

(21) "I'm sorry, it was stupid of me to forget."

Some Impolite Responses

A number of respondents answered impolitely in the "chairs at the swimming pool" scenario. In this scenario, subjects were apparently responding to the prompt when it was phrased in a somewhat aggressive tone:

(22) "Hey! Those are our chairs. Can't you see our clothes on the ground next to them?"

Thus, the impoliteness of the subjects' responses is probably explicable by the aggressive tone of the prompt, and subjects actually seemed to be reprimanding their interlocutor. Responses included:

(23) "Sorry, but you can say it in a nice way."

(24) "Please do not shout; I thought that these chairs belong to nobody."

(25) "Sorry, but you have to be polite when talking to me."
(26) "Sorry, I didn't see 'em, but you could've said it in a better way."
A particularly interesting response was that of one subject who wrote:
(27) "Shut your mouth."
What is interesting here is that this particular subject, in spite of the aggressiveness of this response, is for the most part quite cooperative or polite in the other scenarios. It appears, therefore, that the subject is reacting here to the tone of the complainer and that this aggressive tone overrides the subject's potential obligation to apologize or any obligation to be "polite."

"*It doesn't matter!*"
A couple of respondents answered the "it's a he, not a she" scenario in an impolite fashion. Note that, in both cases, the informant said "It doesn't matter."
(28) "It doesn't matter. She's [a] cutie."
(29) "It doesn't matter, I wanted only to know the age of the baby."
Now, in this case, if an interlocutor is expecting an apology, to say, "It doesn't matter" is impolite. It may be the case, however, that the respondent is attempting to apologize by using the English equivalent of /maʕleːʃ/ which, in some cases is "I'm sorry!" but in others is "It doesn't matter!" In other words, while it *may* be the case that the subject has chosen the wrong formula here, resulting in pragmalinguistic failure, it should not be *assumed* that this is pragmatic failure on the part of the learner; it may well be the case that this is one of those instances where the learner has *intended* to be impolite. It should be borne in mind here that overall, statistically, there is practically no mismatch between the raters' politeness *perceptions* and the learners' politeness *intentions*.
In a related example, the subject responded:
(30) "Okay, what is the matter? How old is she?"
Here, the subject at first seems to have taken the mistaken choice of formula a step further, producing "What is the matter?" where "It doesn't matter!" was perhaps intended. The lack of an apology is impolite. Again, however, it must not be *assumed* that pragmatic failure is involved here, for it may have been the learner's *intention* to be impolite.

Conclusion

Even though L1 English speakers intended to be less polite than L2 English speakers in their production of the speech act of apology, there is no misunderstanding between the two parties within this context. This is contradictory to all previous research that supports miscommunication between L1 and L2 speakers. This may be due to the change in methodology that was followed here. Most previous researchers asked raters from one of the two parties (mostly L1 speakers) to evaluate the politeness or the acceptability of the utterances of the other party (typically L2 speakers), without taking into consideration the intentions of the speakers. This study contends that if the speaker intends to be impolite to the hearer and the hearer perceives him or her as such, there is no linguistic problem.

Analysis of the results of this study leads to the conclusion that there is a one-sided relationship between proficiency level and the degree of politeness of apologies as produced by L2 English speakers, who are L1 Arabic speakers. L1 English speakers consider L2 English speakers more polite than themselves. On the other hand, L2 English speakers perceive L1 English speakers as being as polite as themselves. The degree of offense has no effect on the relationship between L2 English proficiency and the degree of politeness in the production of the speech act of apology by L2 English speakers, who are L1 Arabic speakers.

The results also reveal that there is no relationship between the degree of directness and L2 English proficiency level, but that there is indeed a positive correlation between the degree of politeness and that of directness in the production of the speech act of apology. Finally, it should be noted that the researchers succeeded in designing an objective scale for measuring the directness of apologies, which is something that had not been done before.

Implications for Teaching

The researchers find that there are no further suggestions to be put forward to L2 teachers and curriculum developers other than what already exists, which is enough to prevent miscommunication between L1 and L2 speakers within the context of apologies. L2 English learners (at least AUC ELI students) are already getting what they should get.

Limitations

There were several limitations to the study. The study was limited to three ELI levels only at the American University in Cairo, in addition to the native English speakers. It investigated only one speech act: apology. The effect of intonation, dominance, age, gender, and social distance was not investigated. Moreover, AUC students cannot be considered to be typical Egyptian university students. Besides being more affluent, they are more in contact with Americans, and, as a result, they are closer to second-language learners than the other foreign language learner groups in Egypt. CAC students are also different from typical American students in that they have lived in L2 English speaking communities for a long time. Hence, the results are only generalizable to AUC ELI students and CAC high school students, but could be suggestive for other groups.

Nonetheless, even though the directness raters were all Egyptians, this should not cause any problems since the scale is objective. In addition, even though the directness scale was not validated, it was based on the work of such experts as House and Kasper (1981) and Haverkate (1988) in developing similar scales for other speech acts. This suggests that the scale, probably, has content validity. Finally, the study was not able to explain the interaction between situation, proficiency level, and the degree of politeness intentions, since the moderating variable (the degree of offense) had nothing to do with it.

References

Blum-Kulka, S. 1983. "Interpreting and Performing Speech Acts in a Second Language: A Cross-cultural Study of Hebrew and English," in N. Wolfson, and E. Judd (eds.), *Sociolinguistics and Language Acquisition* (36–55). Rowley, Mass: Newbury House.

Blum-Kulka, S. 1987. "Indirectness and Politeness in Requests: Same or Different?" *Journal of Pragmatics* 11, 131–146.

Cohen, A.D., Olshtain, E., and Rosenstein, D.S. 1986. "Advanced EFL Apologies: What Remains to be Learned?" *International Journal of the Sociology of Language* 62, 51–74.

Haverkate, H. 1988. "Politeness Strategies in Verbal Interaction: An Analysis of Directness and Indirectness in Speech Acts." *Semiotica* 71, 59–71.

House, J., and Kasper, G. 1981. "Politeness Markers in English and German," in F. Coulmas (ed.), *Conversational Routine: Explorations in Standardized Communication Situations and Prepatterned Speech* (157–185). The Hague: Mouton.

Poike, D.A. 1989. "Pragmatic Competence and Adult L2 Acquisition: Speech Acts in Interlanguage." *The Modern Language Journal* 73, 279–289.

Stevens, P.B. 1991. "Conflicting Pragmatic Norms between English and Arabic Speakers in Egypt: A Study of Pragmatic Failures," in H.S. Gindi, A. El Menoufy, and S.A. Kamal (eds.), *Essays in Honour of Saad Gamal El Din: Cairo Studies in English* (97–114). Cairo: Cairo University Press.

Stevens, P.B. 1994. "The Pragmatics of Street Hustlers' English in Egypt." *World Englishes* 13, 61–73.

Thomas, J. 1983. "Cross-cultural Pragmatic Failure." *Applied Linguistics* 4, 91–112.

Trosborg, A. 1987. "Apology Strategies in Natives/Non-natives." *Journal of Pragmatics* 11, 147–167.

Appendix 1

Directness Scale

(1 = least direct; 5= most direct)

1. Acknowledgment that P (the offense) is bad or minimizing P
   (Example: "That's too bad / No one's hurt.")

2. Implicit acknowledgment of responsibility for P by giving explanations
   (Example: "The bus was late.")

3. Explicit acknowledgment of responsibility
   (Example: "It's my fault.")

4. Implicit apology by offering repair or promising forbearance
   (Example: "Let me buy you another one. / I won't do it again, I promise.")

5. Explicit apology
   (Example: "I'm sorry.")

Appendix 2

Apology Scenarios

The "Chairs at a Swimming Pool" scenario:

At a crowded pool, you see two empty chairs and quickly start to carry them away. A stranger calls out:

"Hey! Those are our chairs. Can't you see our clothes on the ground next to them?"

You:

The "It's a She, Not a He" scenario:

Walking along the street, you notice a stranger holding a cute little 9–month old baby.

You: "What a cutie! How old is he?"

The stranger: "It's a she, not a he!"

You:

The "Wrong Bus Direction" scenario:

An acquaintance you have given bus directions to the day before sees you on the street.

The acquaintance: "You know, you gave me the wrong bus number for the movie theater yesterday! By the time we got there we had already missed half the movie."
You:

The "Meeting at the Library" scenario:
A friend of a classmate phoned yesterday and asked to borrow some class notes of yours. You agreed to meet her this afternoon at the library, but then you forgot. This evening, she phones again.
Her: "Hello, this is Ruth. Remember, I called you yesterday and we agreed to meet at the library today. I waited for you for an hour."
You:

The "Bumping into an Older Person" scenario:
At the library, you accidentally bump into an older person about 60 who is holding a stack of books. The person is startled, but unhurt. A few of the books fall on the floor.
You:

The "Bumping into a Car" scenario:
You don't stop in time for a red light and bump into the car in front of you. The other driver and you get out and see that there is considerable damage to the other car. The driver is still very upset.
You:

The "You Forgot the Medicine" scenario:
You promised you would buy your neighbor medicine for her sick child when downtown, but you forgot.
Your neighbor: "Did you get the medicine?"
You:

The "Spilled Coffee" scenario:
In a cafeteria, you accidentally bump into an older person about 60 who is holding a cup of coffee. The coffee spills all over the person, scalding his/her arm and soaking his/her clothing.
The person (screaming, startled): "Oooh! Ouch!"
You:

Hyperbolic Expressions in Egyptian Arabic and British English

Ola Hafez

This paper examines hyperbolic expressions in Egyptian Arabic and British English. In spite of the common negative attitude to their use and their departure from the truth, the paper argues for the universality of hyperbolic language though the exact formulas may differ from one language to another. For this reason, the paper attempts to build a taxonomy of hyperbolic expressions in Egyptian Arabic and British English, analyzing them in terms of semantic fields, pragmatic functions, and genre distribution. The paper concludes with pedagogical implications for approaching hyperbolic expressions in English Language Teaching (ELT).

Definition

Hyperbolic expressions are extravagant exaggerations used deliberately and not meant to be taken literally. In other words, they involve intensification and excess, as opposed to hedges, which mitigate or attenuate the effect of the illocutionary force of the utterance. A requirement for hyperbole is that it be not only counterfactual, which is evident to both S(peaker/s) and H(earer/s), but also literally impossible, as in "the destruction of an entire department" because somebody pressed the wrong computer button, which H corrects into "computer systems without failsafes can cause problems" (McQuarrie and Mick 1996). Hyperboles are often used for certain functions such as emphasis, impressing others, and expressing strong emotion. (See section 9 below for more functions.)

"Hyperbole" is the term for overstatement, or exaggeration, in traditional rhetoric. As early as Aristotle, hyperbole was considered a rhetorical device, or trope, in Greek literature. It has often been used in literature
together with such tropes as "litotes" (i.e., understatement for emphasis,
as in "not bad" for "very good") and "irony" (i.e., saying the opposite of
the intended meaning). Such tropes have often been used traditionally
in religious and literary books alike. Examples from the Bible include the
following: "Ye blind guides, which strain at a *gnat* and swallow a *camel*"
(Matthew 23:24). This verse is hyperbolic, as the term "gnat" stands for
smallness, and "a camel" stands for largeness, and neither is to be taken
literally. Similarly, in the following verse: "Jesus says we must *hate* our
father and mother in comparison to Him" (Luke 14:26). Jesus can only
be understood to have meant that we must love Him more than our parents, rather than "hate" them. Along the same lines, in the Qur'an some
concepts are expressed in absolute terms, as in the verse /faman jaˁmal
miθqaːla ðarratin xajran jarah, wa man jaˁmal miθqaːla ðarratin ʃarran
jarah/" (al-Zalzala, 7–8) ("He who does a *particle's weight* of good shall see
it and he who does a *particle's weight* of evil shall see it").

Hyperbolic language is also used in literature to celebrate ideals of
romanticism, heroism, love, and similar strong emotions, to aggrandize
the deeds of the epic hero, and to maximize interest through unpredict-
ability (Osteen 1995). Hyperbole also helps contribute to the tone of the
text as humorous, amused, shocked, thrilled, etc. According to Cuddon
(1991), hyperbole and similar tropes created the ranting, bombastic quality of speeches in Tudor and Jacobean drama. Examples of literary hyperbole include the following lines from *Henry IV Part I*:

> By heaven, methinks it were an easy leap
> To pluck bright honour from the pale-fac'd moon
> (I, iii, 201–202)

Another example of hyperbole from the poetry of a later period comes
in Alexander Pope's lines about Timon's villa in *Moral Essays*, Epistle IV:

> Greatness, with Timon, dwells in such a draught
> As brings all Brobdingnag before your thought.
> To compass this, his building is a Town,
> His pond an Ocean, his parterre a Down:
> Who but must laugh, the Master when he sees,
> A puny insect, shiv'ring at a breeze!
> Lo, what huge heaps of littleness around!
> (In Cuddon 1991:957)

Obviously counterfactual, such exaggeration reinforces the dramatic effect of the description of the villa. The violation of truth of such hyperbolic expression is engaging, as readers become involved through inferring what is meant from what is said.

Negative Attitude to Hyperbole

In spite of its use in both classical rhetoric and literature, the term "hyperbole" is often associated with lying, deception, and unjustified misrepresentation. It is often used in non-academia as a synonym for bragging in the media and politics, usually leading to skepticism, especially when listening to politicians mentioning "skyrocketing" and "astronomical" production figures that are hard to believe when not substantiated with factual justification. This lay use of the term "hyperbole" misses one aspect of the definition of the term, namely that hyperbole is not meant to be taken literally.

The tendency of the media to overuse hyperbole (where everything is the *best, biggest, grandest, tremendous, terrific, awesome* [i.e., good], *a genius* [i.e., clever], *a tragedy* [i.e., newsworthy], /xaṭiːr/ [literally "dangerous"; i.e., great], /tuħfa/ [literally "antique"; i.e., remarkable], /haːʒil/ [literally "overwhelming" or "terrifying"; i.e., wonderful], /maħaṣalʃ/ [literally "it didn't happen," i.e., unprecedented]) for maximizing interest has led to "verbal gigantism." According to McQuarrie and Mick (1996), "language's ability to convey certain meanings with appropriate force" is progressively deteriorating, as in the use of "terrific," which "once meant the defining characteristic of something truly frightening [while] it now means something 'very good,'" a process intensified by advertising. Such "linguistic inflation" (Osteen 1995), has resulted in a process of diminishing returns and has destroyed credibility. Hence, the need for litotes (i.e., understatement), to regain credit and restore credibility.

In academia, hyperbole is also mistrusted in teaching and pedagogy, as well as in other life domains. According to *The Harper Handbook of College Composition* (1981, cited in Baiyi and Aili 1995:6), exaggerated expressions are misleading and ludicrous, and should therefore be avoided in academic writing. Such avoidance and condemnation result in not only ignoring hyperbole in foreign-language teaching but even advising learners against its use in essay writing and academic discourse, both of which constitute the core of language teaching to the exclusion of the language of everyday conversation as well as other genres. Even in the native language (L1), the use of hyperbole is often regarded negatively, especially when the exaggeration is unjustified and when the difference between the stated and the implied fact is not great enough (Baiyi and Aili 1995). This avoidance leads to learners' non-standard usage of hyperbolic expressions due to interference of L1 forms and distribution.

Truth Conditions and the Role of Context

Grice's Cooperative Principle (1975) was prescriptive in its assumption of communicative cooperation where S is expected to be truthful, abiding by the "Maxim of Quality." According to Leech (1983), hyperbole violates the maxim of quality as S's statement is stronger than warranted and is so much at variance with context that no one could reasonably believe it to be the truth, the whole truth, and nothing but the truth. Hence, conversational implicature results as an indirect illocutionary force of S's remark. However, according to Brown and Levinson, hyperbole violates the "Maxim of Quantity" (1987:219) by exaggerating or choosing a point on a scale which is higher than the actual state of affairs. Although counterfactual, hyperbole is not deceptive because such violation of truth is interpretable. The actual words do not directly reflect S's intentions, as it is obvious to both S and H that the utterance is at variance with truth and stronger than warranted by the state of affairs described. In line with Leech (1969), hyperbolic expressions can be classified into two types in relation to their interpretability, namely context-dependent and context-independent.

Context-independent hyperboles are incredible in any context and under any circumstances. For example, "I haven't seen you for ages!" which indicates an obviously improper length of time, is transparent and formulaic. It is neither illogical nor lying because it is too far from the truth and not within the allowance of common sense. Similar examples are: "She's as old as the hills" and /min ʔajjaːm sajjidna nuːħ/ ("Since the days of Noah"). Similarly, "I'm starving" or /majjit min ig-guːʕ/ ("Dead from hunger"), and /wa law ʔiddituːni: maːl ʔaːruːn/ ("Even if you give me Qarun's wealth") would be hyperbolic in any context; and since their literal interpretation would be inappropriate in any context H will routinely look for another reasonable interpretation for why S has violated truth. Taking hyperbole at face value and failure to recognize the implied meaning or intention of S's apparent lie would reveal H's pragmatic incompetence, an incompetence often demonstrated by children or learners.

On the other hand, some hyperbolic expressions are context-specific. These are usually realistic but at variance with known facts in a particular situation, and are interpreted as hyperbolic due to S–H shared knowledge.

These seem like exaggerations to the onlooker but may be meant seriously by the speaker. They can be misleading when the literal meaning is probable, so that H accepts it as real rather than looking for its implied, hyperbolic meaning (Baiyi and Aili 1995). For this reason, H may accept lies as true but see through hyperbole as untrue and search for the implicature. Thus, what is hyperbolic in one situation may be non-hyperbolic in another. For example, Kreuz et al.'s (1998) "It took X years to find Y" is realistic in "It took me years to find the perfect partner" but hyperbolic in "It took the waiter years to bring me the bill!" bearing in mind our background knowledge of the restaurant situation or "script" (to follow Schank and Abelson [1977]). World knowledge thus allows H to correctly detect utterances that are meant hyperbolically and to have greater certainty about the interpretations. An example of this is the utterance "Tom's got acres and acres of land," said of someone who has one or two acres; in the absence of such information, H would have to learn how many acres Tom has. Similarly, on a hot day someone may say /ħaṭlaʕ min hudu:mi min il-ħarr/ ("I'll burst out of my clothes from the heat"), upon which H has to rely on knowledge of the likely behavior of S as well as the conventions of the location of the utterance. (This utterance would thus be interpreted literally at the swimming pool or at home, but would be heard hyperbolically at the workplace or in the street, for instance.) Also, the usually hyperbolic idiom /ṣo:tu gajib mida:n it-taħri:r/ ("His voice could reach Tahrir Square [in downtown Cairo]") may be meant literally if said of somebody yelling in a microphone or other sound-amplifying device a block from the square.

Some psycholinguists, like Colston and Keller (1998), postulate three degrees of hyperbole: realistically possible (e.g., "It's 40 degrees centigrade," on a warm day in Cairo), possible but improbable (e.g., "It's 50 degrees centigrade!"), and outlandishly impossible (e.g., "It's 100 degrees!"). However, what is at stake here is how the context (i.e., S–H shared knowledge) determines the choice between the hyperbolic and the literal meaning of the utterance.

Literature Review

In both Arabic and English, hyperbolic expressions have been studied extensively by literary scholars and students of rhetoric for centuries. It is only recently that they have received some attention from linguists. This attention is shared by work in psycholinguistics (e.g., Kreuz et al. 1998), theories of communication (e.g., Grice 1975), and politeness (e.g., Holmes 1984, 1990; Brown and Levinson 1987). It has been understudied in comparison to metaphor and irony, and its overlap with simile ("His heart started beating like a drum") and with irony ("I'll never be able to thank you for your help!") has been completely overlooked.

In psycholinguistics, work on hyperbole and exaggeration has focused on language comprehension. Colston and Keller (1998) for instance study how S expresses surprise by noting the contrast between what was expected and what actually happened. After investigating the range of levels of hyperbole by having participants comment upon expressed situations using hyperbole, irony, or both hyperbole and irony, they conclude that the greater the degree of inflation of the discrepancy between expected and ensuing events, the easier it is for interpreters to determine that S is surprised. In a similar study, Kreuz et al. (1998) discuss a continuum of physical ability with application to different degrees of quantitative hyperbole. They made participants read twenty scenarios and do a number of tasks including completion, interpretation, recall, and rating alternatives according to degree of possibility, appropriateness, and likelihood of use. They concluded that H draws on world knowledge to realize that an utterance is unlikely and therefore hyperbolic. They also conclude that after reaching some optimal level of exaggeration, hyperbole may be less effective, a conclusion that they call the "just right" hypothesis, highlighting the correlation between the degree of exaggeration and H's judgment.

Study of exaggeration or overstatement as a communicative strategy has often concentrated on its role in reinforcing the speech act performed. According to Holmes (1984), attenuating and boosting speech acts are strategies that modify the strength of the illocutionary force of speech acts. While boosting negatively affective speech acts increases social distance, as in the criticism "My God, you're such a fool!" or the threat "I'll bloody well kill that dog of yours," boosting positively affective speech acts increases solidarity, as in the compliment "Really, you are amazingly pretty!" The positive or negative politeness effect of a pragmatic particle will depend on the illocutionary force of the speech act it modifies so that boosting an offensive comment will never be perceived as in any way polite (Holmes 1990). Hyperbolic expressions can also benefit from work on modality (e.g., Palmer 1986), as they intensify the degree of S's certainty and commitment to truth (i.e., epistemic modality) and on affective modality by showing how such hyperbolic expressions reinforce S's attitude to H, thus increasing or decreasing solidarity or social distance. Brown and Levinson's work (1987) has investigated the use of overstatement as an off-record strategy, and intensifying interest as a positive politeness strategy. However, their work is limited to the use of strategies that redress face threat but does not cover ones that intensify such a threat for varying communicative purposes.

Language Universality/Specificity

The use of hyperbolic language has usually been considered a language-specific characteristic varying from one language to another, so that different languages have different stances with regard to hyperbole, with some avoiding hyperboles and others preferring them. For instance, in Japanese communication, people fail to understand jokes, sarcasm, irony, understatement, and hyperbole. Japanese conversation tends to be serious and not casual, usually avoiding teasing, joking, hyperbole, and other language games. Similarly, in Yup'ik communication, Eskimos tend to misunderstand non-literal language uses like irony where S intends the opposite of the literary meaning. Newcomers to either place are advised to avoid sarcasm, irony, hyperbole, and understatement (Anonymous 1, n.d.). Similarly, according to Edelmann *et al.* (1989), British speakers tend to understate their embarrassment while Greeks tend to overstate it.

In contrast, Arabic is often stereotypically described as a language characterized by exaggeration and over-assertion (Shouby 1951; Kaplan 1966; Patei 1973). According to Shouby, for instance, Arabic is characterized by preference for exaggeration: "a contrast could be created between Arab assertion and exaggeration and British tact and understatement" so that "meaning is lost in the Arabic version if no devices of assertion and exaggeration are added" (1951:300). Such statements are very strong, as they do not consider the universality of exaggerated language. Along the same lines, Cohen (1987) mentions difficulties in American–Egyptian diplomatic relations due to the "Egyptian propensity for exaggeration" (cited in Kreuz *et al.* 1998). In fact, Arabic may tend to overuse hyperbole without its necessarily being functional, probably because of lessons received in school in the use of hyperbole in poetry and its beauty that fail to address the motivation for its use and treat it simply as an example of highly literate and literary style.

This study postulates the widespread occurrence of hyperbolic expressions cross-linguistically. However, the specific formulae may differ from one language to another, as in, for example, "Thanks a million" as opposed to /ʔalf ʃukr/ "A thousand thanks," rather than either *"Thanks a thousand" or /miljuːn ʃukr/ ("A million thanks"). Similarly, the utterance "I waited *for hours* but there was no sign of them" is hyperbolic as it is exaggerated and most probably counterfactual in most instances of its occurrence. The Egyptian Arabic counterpart /baʔaːli saːʕa mistanniːk/ ("I've been waiting for you for an hour") is not too unrealistic, as in Egyptian culture one person might well wait for another for a whole hour. This study thus shows that although the use of hyperbolic expressions is shared by many languages, there is no one-to-one correspond-

ence between the forms used in various languages, and it requires
learner attention. In the remainder of this study, a qualitative analysis
of hyperbolic idiomatic expressions will attempt to prove their com-
monality to both English and Arabic and formally describe "equivalent"
formulas used.

Corpus

The examples of hyperbolic expressions cited and analyzed in this study
have been collected from authentic as well as elicited data. The authentic
examples come from direct observation of language used in everyday
conversation and the media (the news, plays, films, commercials, etc.)
Additionally, a questionnaire was administered to fifteen Egyptian upper
intermediate undergraduate students of English. They were given eight
scenarios to comment on using hyperbole. These included a sofa too
heavy for two people to move so that they need a third person to help,
hikers who have to walk much longer than expected, and other similar
involving contexts and familiar topics ensuring participants' prior script
knowledge.

A Taxonomy of Hyperbolic Expressions

Idiomatic hyperbolic expressions are usually frozen formulas conven-
tionally used to express hyperbolic meanings, i.e., exaggerations that
are counterfactual and not meant to be taken literally. Although many
creative speakers invent new hyperboles according to the needs of the
situation (as in referring to a scratch as a wound, or to a problem as a tragedy), the focus of this study is on conventionalized idiomatic hyperbolic
expressions. When analyzed in semantic terms, these can be classified
into such categories as quantifiers, modifiers, comparison, idioms, etc.
The following taxonomy identifies some of the major types observed in
hyperbolic expressions, but is far from being exhaustive.

To refine the definition of "hyperbolic expressions" to the exclusion
of non-hyperbolic ones, a test is postulated in this study along the lines
of the "hereby" test on performative speech acts. Expressions that can
be given a hyperbolic reading in some contexts can accept the introduction of the adverb "literally" or /ħaʔiːʔi/ or /fiʕlan/ to block the possible
hyperbolic reading of such utterances. In an utterance such as "we are
starving," two readings are possible: that we are very hungry (hyperbolically), or that we are dying due to hunger (non-hyperbolically). By adding

"literally," S is aware of the possibility of the hyperbolic reading and is blocking it by doing so. Similarly, in saying /ʔana ħaʔiːʔi mistanniːk baʔaːli saːʕa/ ("I've truly been waiting for you for an hour"), S blocks the possible hyperbolic reading of /baʔaːli saːʕa/ and allows only for the literal one. Also, /ʔil-walad fiʕlan ʔadd il-xartiːt/ means either that he is extremely fat or that he is literally as fat as a rhinoceros. The addition of /fiʕlan/ here marks the possibility of a hyperbolic reading and either blocks it or reinforces it even further. Similarly, the use of "literally" in "We literally froze to death" also marks the hyperbolic reading as extremely cold. At any rate, the mere use of "literally" or /ħaʔiːʔi/ or /fiʕlan/ marks the possibility of a hyperbolic reading either by blocking the hyperbolic reading or enhancing it.

Quantifiers

A large set of hyperbolic expressions are quantifying expressions that cite a number, measurement terms (of weight, length, area, etc.), containers, or time units disproportionate to the real facts of the situation. According to Colston and Keller (1998), exaggerating about an event or fact that was of greater quantity than expected can stretch to infinity, while an event of lesser quantity or magnitude than expected can stretch only to zero.

Numerical quantifiers cite a number, usually a round figure, larger than warranted by the facts of the context. Examples of numerical hyperbole in English include "dozens," "hundreds," "thousands," "millions," "billions," "trillions," and "zillions." While a dozen literally means "twelve," it often means "lots of" as in "She's got dozens of boyfriends"; similarly, larger numbers are usually unwarranted by the situation. Examples are "I could give you a hundred reasons for staying here"; "Thanks a million." In the example "She's a zillion times better than he is," the imaginary numeral denotes an indefinite large number. In addition, to describe an object hyperbolically as unique, expressions like "one in a million" are often used, as in "We haven't a chance in a million of winning." Arabic numerals are also used hyperbolically, as in /ʕaʃaraːt is-siniːn/ ("tens of years"), /miːt marra/ ("A hundred times"), /ʔalf ʃukr/ ("a thousand thanks"), /dastit ʕijaːl/ ("a dozen children"), /sittiːn ʔalf marra/ ("sixty thousand times"), /li-l-marra il-miljuːn/ ("for the millionth time"), the ill-formed */ʕushrumiːt marra/ ("ten hundred times"), by analogy with, for example, /subʕumiːt/ ("seven hundred"), and also percentages like /ʕaʃara ʕala ʕaʃara/ (literally "ten out of ten," i.e., very good, perfect), /mijja mijja/ (literally "a hundred percent," i.e., perfect). Notice how some Arabic hyperbolic numeral expressions can take a number of stresses and repetition, as in /ʔalf ʔalf mabruːk/ ("a thousand thousand thanks"), and vowel lengthening, as in "/sittiːn ʔalf marra/" ("sixty thousand times").

Quantitative expressions of measurement (i.e., length, weight, area, etc.) can also be disproportionate to the actual referent. English examples include "tons of," "miles of," "acres of," as in "tons of money," "tons of work," i.e., large amounts of money/work. Similarly, "miles" indicates a very long distance or "by far," as in "You're miles away" (daydreaming), "She's miles better today," "You missed the goal by a mile." Similarly, in Arabic, quantitative measurement is involved in such hyperbolic expressions as /ki:lu/ ("a kilogram"), /ṭinn/ ("a ton"), /ʔinṭaːr/ (approximately a hundredweight), /ʔiraːṭ/ (a square measure equal to 175 square meters), /faddaːn/ (approximately an acre), as in /labsa ki:lu dahab/ ("She's wearing a kilo of gold"), /bijiʃtiru il-manga bi-l-ʔinṭaːr/ ("They buy mangoes by the hundredweight"), /ħaṭṭa ki:lu makjaːʒ/ ("She's wearing a kilo of make-up"), /ʔiraːṭ ħazz wala faddaːn ʃaṭaːra/ ("A little bit of luck is preferable to a feddan of cleverness").

Expressions using container items are often used hyperbolically. The expressions "buckets of" (rain or tears, as in "She wept buckets," "The rain fell in buckets"), "oceans of" (food, drink, or time), "a flood of" (tears, anger, letters, immigrants) are all very familiar, expressing a continuous flow. Arabic uses similar hyperboles with the containers /zaka:jib/ ("sacks"), /baħr/ ("sea"), /biːr/ ("a well"), as in /zaka:jib fulu:s/ ("sacks of money"), /ʕajmi:n ʕala baħr bitruːl/ ("they're floating on a sea of oil"), /iʃ-ʃaːriʕ baʔa baħr/ ("the street became a sea," i.e., after rain).

Abstract as well as concrete items are often exaggerated by describing them in terms of piles, using such expressions as "loads of," "heaps of," "piles of," "stacks of," as in "loads of friends," "stacks of bills to be paid," "Do have a second helping—there's heaps more," "The children eat piles of butter on their bread." Such "pile" terms all mean "plenty of" the item so modified. Notice how such items do not have to be countable (i.e., quantifiable), e.g., "loads of money" or "loads of time." Arabic container items include /ruzam/ ("stacks"), /ʔikwaːm/ ("piles"), and /ʔurṭa/ ("bunch"), as in /ʔurṭit ʕijaːl/ ("a bunch of children").

Hyperbolic time expressions are used to exaggerate either the length of time or the speediness of action. Expressions exaggerating length of duration include "hours," "days," "weeks," "years," "centuries," "ages"; and /saʕaːt/ ("hours"), /ʔajjaːm/ ("days"), /lajaːli/ ("nights"), /siniːn/ ("years"). Familiar examples of time hyperbole are "We've been waiting for hours for this to happen" and "Haven't seen you for ages!" Arabic time expressions sometimes use /ji:gi/ ("around") when used hyperbolically: /baʔaːli ji:gi sana maʃuftakʃ/ ("I haven't seen you in around a year"). Arabic hyperbolic time expressions also sometimes use historical references, as in /min ʔajjaːm sajjidna nuːħ/ ("since the days of Noah"). Similarly, the idioms /min il-ʕaṣr il-gaːhili/ ("since the pre-Islamic age") and /min

ʔajjaːm il-faraʕna/ ("since the days of the pharaohs") reinforce the distant nature of the time reference. In contrast, both languages make use of time expressions denoting immediacy or extreme frequency. The idioms "in a minute" or "just a minute" are all too familiar; they are often used hyperbolically in such utterances as "Just a minute till I'm finished with this meeting" "Her clothes are always up to the minute!" (i.e., very fashionable). Similar are "a second," and its Arabic equivalent /sanja waħda/, "a blink" and the equivalent /fiː ɣamḍit ʕeːn/, and even "femtosecond," as in Nobel prize winner and inventor of the term Ahmed Zewail's humorous comment "I get asked this question every femtosecond!"

Some inclusive quantifiers, such as "all," "every," "everyone," "everywhere," "always," "entire," "whole," are used hyperbolically to extend a scale to its extremities to include all members. Conversely, all members can be excluded through extreme negation using such expressions as "not a soul," "any," "at all," "never." Similarly, in Arabic, among inclusive extremes are to be found /kull in-naːs/ ("all people") and /kull ħaːga/ ("everything"), while among exclusive ones are /mafiːʃ xaːlis/ ("there isn't at all") and /ʕumri/ ("never").

Modifiers

In addition to quantifiers used hyperbolically by using a numerical or quantifying descriptor disproportionate to the item being described in quantity, hyperbolic expressions also use scalar modifiers, expressing unwarranted extremes of a value scale. These usually choose a higher point on a scale to intensify the effect.

Gradable adjectives and verbs are often used hyperbolically by choosing an extreme point on the scale. These include adjectives that describe size such as "vast," "massive," "immense," "gigantic"; and /mahuːl/ ("fantastic"), /muriːʕ/ ("terrifying"), /ḍaxm/ ("huge"). Similarly, expressions of rarity include "unique," "unheard of," "one of a kind"; and the verbal /maħaṣalʃ/ ("unprecedented"), and /mafiːʃ zajju/ ("peerless").

Another semantic domain involving intensification is that of suffering, as evidenced by such hyperbolic expressions as "starving," "freezing," "boiling," "dying," "shocking/-ed"; and /majjit min it-taʕab/ ("dead from fatigue"), /majjit min ig-guːʕ/ ("dead from hunger"), and such verbs as /ʔitsalaʔna/ ("we were boiled"), /ʔitʃaweːna/ ("we were grilled"), /ʔitgammidna/ ("we were frozen"), /ʔitʃalleːt/ ("I was paralyzed," i.e., I was extremely frustrated), /ʔitʕam eːt min il-ʔiraːja/ ("I went blind with reading," i.e., my eyes got tired).

Expressions of approving wonder include "great," "glorious," "divine," "terrific," "awesome," "brilliant," "fantastic," and the idiom "out of this world." In Arabic, approval is expressed hyperbolically through such expressions as /rɑhiːb/ ("terrifying"), /xɑṭiːr/ ("dangerous"), /fɑẓiːʕ/ ("awful"), /rɑːʔiʕ/ ("frightening"), /tuħfɑ/ ("antique," i.e., marvelous), /mɑhuːl/ ("frightening"), /wahmi/ ("illusory") and such verbs as /jigɑnnin/ ("it drives (one) mad"), /jihwis/ ("it drives (one) mad") and the clausal /bɑmuːt fiːh/ (literally "I'm dying over him/it," i.e., I adore him/it). This list of verbal and adjectival intensifying expressions is far from exhaustive.

The superlative form of gradable adjectives expresses the highest point on the scale, as in "the newest," "the largest (ever)," "the most," often used in commercials, in describing a product as, for instance, "the best thing that ever came between two meals." It is also used in emotive narratives as in "It was just the most awful thing." Arabic counterparts usually specify the set of compared items, as in /ʔahsan wɑːhid fi-l-ʕeːla/ ("the best member of the family"), /ʔɑxṭɑr rɑgul fi l-ʕɑːlam/ ("the most dangerous man in the world").

Intensifiers are often used to strengthen or emphasize certain elements of the proposition (House and Kasper 1981), mainly adjectives. These adverbials include "absolutely," "extremely," "terribly," "really," "very," "so," "definitely," as in "absolutely fabulous" and "terribly important." Arabic counterparts include /ʔawi/ ("very"), /xɑːlis/ ("very"), /giddɑn/ ("very") and the slangy /ṭɑhn/ ("extremely"), as in /hilwa ʔawi/ ("very pretty"), /sahl xɑːlis / ("very easy"), and /wihiʃ giddɑn/ ("very bad/ugly").

Swear words like "hell" and "bloody" are often used, according to House and Kasper (1981), as lexical intensifiers to show negative social attitude, as in "You're making a hell of a noise," "That's bloody mean of you", and "They're filthy rich." Arabic "swear words" do not necessarily show negative attitude, as in /fikra guhannamijja/ (literally "a hellish [i.e., brilliant] idea"), or /da rassɑːm ibn kalb ʃuɣlu mumtɑːz/ ("He's a son-of-a-bitch painter; his work is excellent").

The Definite Article
The definite article is often used in English to indicate the uniqueness or genericity of the noun phrase it precedes. It can be used hyperbolically to indicate the uniqueness of the referent of a noun phrase that is not necessarily unique in fact. Examples of this are: "The royal wedding was *the* event of the year!" and "In Egypt, football is *the* sport!" Notice how generic "the" receives extra stress and uses the strong form /ði/. The equivalent in Arabic is the third person pronoun /huwwa/ ("he/it") or /hijja/ ("she/it"), as well as the definite article, as in /kurit il-qɑdɑm hijja ir-rijɑːḍɑ/ (literally, "Football, it is the sport,"i.e., football is *the* sport) and /kukakula hijja il-ʔaṣl/ (literally, "Coca Cola, it is the origin," i.e., Coca-Cola is the real thing).

Comparisons

Comparison, usually implicit in simile and metaphor, enables speakers to speak of one thing in terms of another. They can thus choose an item on a higher scale to exaggerate the meaning. Hyperbolic idioms involving comparison include "as soft as silk," "as strong as an ox," "as light as a feather," "as white as snow," "as dry as a bone," "like a fish out of water." Notice how such similes include the compared-to item as well as the grounds for the comparison. Arabic uses comparison hyperbolically too. Expressions like /zajj il-ʔamar/ ("like the moon," i.e., pretty), /zajj il-fiːl/ ("as the elephant," i.e., fat), /zajj il-ʕigl/ ("like an ox," i.e., fat), /zajj in-nisma/ ("like a breeze," i.e., tender and soft), /baḥibbik ʔadd id-dunja/ ("I love you as much as the world," i.e., very much), /dalma kuḥl/ ("dark as kohl," i.e., very dark). Notice how /zajj il-full/ ("like jasmine," i.e., clean, neat) has extended its meaning and use to "of good quality," as in /ʔakl zajj il-full/, /il-faraḥ zajj il-full/, /iʃ-ʃuɣl zajj il-full/, describing food, a wedding party, and work, respectively.

Improbable/Impossible Conditionals

The second and third conditionals, indicating improbable and impossible conditions respectively, are often used hyperbolically to indicate the impossibility of the result clause by using an absurd condition, as in "If could pigs fly," or "Even if you kneel on all fours, I won't forgive you for what you did." Similarly, "even if" is used emphatically in hypothetical conditionals as in "I wouldn't marry you even if you were the last person on earth" (Celce-Murcia and Larsen-Freeman 1983:352). The first conditional is also used sometimes in sarcastic speech (Celce-Murcia and Larsen-Freeman 1983:349) as in "If he's intelligent, then I'm Albert Einstein." Arabic equivalents include /lamma tinṭabiʔ is-sama ʕala-l-ʔard/ ("if/when the sky is folded onto the earth"), /lamma titnaṭṭat/ ("if/when you keep jumping"), /wa law ʔiddituːni maːl ʔaruːn/ ("even if you give me Qarun's wealth"). These conditions are all used to refuse the result clause beyond negotiation.

Idioms

Idioms, i.e., word groups whose overall meaning cannot be derived from the sum of the parts, are often hyperbolic in meaning. These may have equivalents or near equivalents in English and Arabic, but some are culture- and language-specific. Examples of these can be classified according to their semantic domains. Hyperbolic idioms based on body parts include "head over heels" ("deeply in love"), "mind boggling" ("confusing"), and its Arabic equivalent /ḥaːga tlaxbaṭ il-ʕaʔl/ ("something that confuses the mind), "a walking dictionary" and its equivalent /qamuːs mutaḥarrik/, "working one's fingers to the bone" and its equivalent /biʔidajja wi sna:ni/ (literally "with my hands and teeth", i.e., working very hard and very fast to meet a tight deadline), "It made my blood boil" and its equivalent /ħa:ga tfawwar id-damm/ (literally "Something that boils the blood").

Body-part hyperbolic idioms indicating endearment like /nu:r ʕe:ni/ ("the light of my eyes") and /ru:ħ ʔalbi/ ("the soul of my heart"), and so on seem to be specific to Arabic. Another use of body-part idioms in Arabic indicates a threat of the removal of a body part to intensify an oath as in /ʔaʔṭaʕ dira:ʕi/ ("I'd cut off my arm"), /ʔaħlaʔ ʃanabi/ ("I'd shave off my moustache"). To verify the truth of a statement, S would wish to lose his/ her eyesight if lying by saying /ʔinʃalla ʔanṭaṣṣ fi naẓari/ ("I'd rather lose my eyesight"). Similarly, S might reinforce the impossibility of a request with the idiom "over my dead body" or its Arabic equivalent /ʕala gussiti/. Other English body-part idioms include "to escape by a hair's breadth" (i.e., narrowly), and "an eye for an eye," equivalent to /ʔal-ʕajn bi-l-ʕajn/, both invitations to an equal punishment.

Idioms relating to disease indicate condemnation, as in "epidemic," "virus," /waba:ʔ/ ("epidemic"), /ħuʔna/ (literally "an injection," i.e., a nuisance), /ʃu:ṭa/ ("plague"). Similarly, idioms based on military metaphors include /guju:ʃ naml/ ("armies of ants," i.e., a large number), and /ɣazw it-tata:r/ ("the invasion of the Tartars," i.e., a large crowd occupying a place very fast). Arabic is abundant in religious idioms like /ħara:m ʕale:k/ (literally, "taboo on you" i.e., shame on you), /walla:hi/ (literally "by God," i.e., I swear, please, or in fact, according to the context).

Notice how different languages use different idioms to express the same meaning, as in "over the moon" and /ṭa:jir min il-farħa/ (literally "flying out of happiness"). Similarly, giving the gist in a few words is exaggerated in English in "in a nutshell," while Arabic uses the metaphor of a capsule in /fi kabsu:la/. On the other hand, seemingly similar idioms may have different meanings, as in two idioms related to fingertips: whereas /bi-ṭarf ṣuba:ʕu/ ("with his fingertip") means he did it extremely easily, the English idiom "at your fingertips" means that a thing is easily accessible. Still other hyperbolic idioms are specific to one language, as "raining cats and dogs" (i.e., raining heavily) or "at sea" (i.e., mentally confused).

Whatever their category, hyperbolic expressions can be even further upgraded and intensified through the use of two ploys, repetition and clustering. A hyperbolic expression can be repeated a number of times with the use of conjunctions to imply its repetitive occurrence beyond limits. An example of this is the reference to someone who bought two acres of land as having "acres and acres." Similarly, in storytelling, speakers often repeat conjoined parts to maximize effect, as in "I just cried and cried and cried" (i.e., I cried a lot, or "I cried my heart out"—another hyperbolic idiom), or "I just kept drinking and drinking and drinking." In addition to the upgrading involved in such repetition, the clustering of various hyperbolic expressions in the same utterance maximizes effect. This is evident in the following sentence: "We waited for hours and hours and hours on end but not a single soul passed by!" Compare the latter, for instance, with the non-hyperbolic equivalent "We waited for a long time but no one passed by."

Pragmatic Functions of Hyperbolic Expressions

Having examined the semantic categories of hyperbolic expressions, it is important to consider their pragmatic functions in actual contexts. Hyperbolic expressions are used to fulfill a variety of discourse goals, such as providing information about S's attitude, state of mind, and feelings. It may be argued that they relate to epistemic modality, as they often express S's certainty and confidence. They are also relevant to emotive language, as they convey a strong emotion felt by S that literal, non-hyperbolic expressions are insufficient to convey. S thus goes to extremes, as in the utterance "The day will come when every inch of the earth is populated with human beings," used to convey S's intensity of concern (Baiyi and Aili 1995).

The use of hyperbolic expressions is a pragmatic strategy for reinforcing effect. According to Brown and Levinson (1987:147) "strengtheners," or emphatic hedges like *exactly, precisely, emphatically,* indicate S's commitment toward what he is saying. Similarly, according to Holmes (1990), boosters reinforce and intensify the force of the utterance, increase the strength of illocutionary force, and strengthen S's commitment to the proposition. They boost the extent of S's desire in directives like "I really want you to read this for me," or the strength of S's commitment in commissives, as in "I solemnly promise I won't be late home tonight." Hyperbolic expressions are thus a strategy for achieving S's purposes to modify the force of the illocutionary act by strengthening it in both face-supporting and face-threatening acts. The positive or negative politeness effect of a hyperbolic expression will depend on the illocutionary force of the speech act it performs.

Intensifying Face-supporting Acts
Hyperbolic expressions are often used to intensify interest, dramatize narration, and address politeness by strengthening bonding, sympathy, praise of H, apology, and congratulations. To dramatize narration, S often

resorts to hyperbole, as in "It was just incredible! Those three women sat on a bench chatting for years and years and years!" Similarly, hyperbole can be used to maximize bonding between interlocutors by reinforcing welcoming expressions, as in "I haven't seen you for ages" or its Arabic situational counterpart /nɑwwɑrtuːnɑ/ ("You have enlightened us"), /ʃɑrrɑftuːnɑ/ ("You have honored us"). Hyperbolic expressions are also used to reinforce praise of H, as in "How absolutely marvelous!" or "Brilliant!" or /tuħfɑ!/ or to strengthen the effect of congratulations, as in /ʔalf ʔalf ʔalf mabruːk/ ("A thousand, thousand, thousand congratulations!"). They also help to intensify sympathy for H, as in "What a tragedy it must be to have lost your cat."

In addition to their use in such H-oriented face-supporting acts, hyperbolic expressions are also used in S-oriented ones such as modesty and apology. They can be used to intensify S's modesty implied in self-criticism, as in "I've got such abhorrent wrinkles around my eyes" or "I must have been studying at this university for a million years now." By strengthening self-criticism, S can maximize his/her modesty and place that of H on a higher rank. Another S-oriented face-supporting act that hyperbolic expressions can boost is apologizing. An unwilling S can reinforce an apology by saying "I have millions of reasons for not doing something," and a late-returning husband can apologize to his wife by saying "There were a million people in the shop tonight and I left with the most dreadful headache" (i.e., that's why I'm late). On the other hand, a speaker can minimize the effect of a delay by saying "I'll be done in a second/minute."

Intensifying Face-threatening Acts

Most of the work on politeness addresses S's attempt to redress face-threatening acts and attend to H's face wants. However, hyperbolic expressions are used not only to maximize politeness but also to maximize the face threat of some speech acts. They are often used to intensify criticism, strengthen the urgency of their requests, etc. To start with, S often uses hyperbolic boosters to intensify disapproval of H or a referent, as in "How outrageous! How can you say something so awful?" Hyperbolic expressions can also reinforce criticism of the referent, as in the following dialogue:

X: She's put on weight. She's extremely uh....
Y: Gigantic.
X: Yeah.

S here collaborates in criticizing the referent through the use of the hyperbolic expressions "extremely" and "gigantic." When making a complaint, S often criticizes her/her interlocutors to ask for redress. By intensifying the criticism, a "Face-Threatening Act" (FTA) (Brown and

Levinson 1987), as in "What a huge mess you've made! You've completely ruined my files!" simultaneously implies the need for redress off the record. Similarly, in making a request, S often intensifies the statement of a problem s/he is facing through the use of hyperbolic expressions, as in "This sofa definitely weighs a ton; it's absolutely impossible to lift it on your own," thus implying the need for help, an off-record request. Similarly, intensified complaints such as "You never lock the door after you come in!" and "We've been waiting forever" intensify the relevance of a forthcoming apology and redress on the part of H.

Distribution

Hyperbolic expressions are used in a wide variety of genres. First and foremost, they abound in informal everyday conversation. The more spontaneous, involved, informal, and animated the conversation is, the more it makes use of hyperbolic language. This contrasts with academic writing, which is more formal, polished and detached (Hatch 1992) and therefore completely avoids hyperbolic expressions. Between the two—informal everyday conversation and academic writing—there are a number of genres that make heavy use of hyperbolic expressions.

Another genre that habitually makes use of hyperbolic language is advertising. The role of commercials is to maximize the interest of the product to potential buyers. According to McQuarrie and Mick (1996), advertising routinely uses "words whose original meanings far exceed the properties of the products they are designed to sell." To motivate reading of advertisements in the first place and make them memorable as preconditions to persuasion, hyperbole "informs postmodern television commercials, such as the American Isuzu ad that features a man praising the Isuzu's capacity to deliver 5000 miles to a gallon of gas" (Anonymous 2). Riley (1977) cites the unprovable claims made in ads such as "the newest, largest, friendliest cruise ship on the East Coast" said of a cruise liner, or bath oils that "turn skin into silk." Similar hyperbolic ads include the following.

- "Miraculous soap turns skin into silk,"
- "The best your money can buy."
- "It's as easy as ABC."
- "Superclean sparkling teeth."
- /maʃaklik kullaha ħatintihi maʕa ʔiːva/ ("All your problems will end with Eva.")
- /ʔivaridi saʕaːt wi saʕaːt wi saʕaːt/ ("Eveready [for] hours and hours and hours [of performance].")
- /kulluku kasbaniːn kasbaniːn/ ("All of you are sure to win.")

- /ṭuːl ma fiːh bajukliːna mafiːʃ buʔʕa tistaʕṣɑ ʕaleːna/ ("As long as there is Biocleana, no stain will be too difficult for us."
- /il-ḥaja: min ɣeer firaːx basma matsawiːʃ/ "Life without Basma Chicken is not worth it."

It is easy to see how advertising pictures the advertised commodities as the best using extreme points on the descriptive scale.

In addition to advertising discourse, racist discourse is also notorious for the use of hyperbolic language. It is often characterized by exaggerating negative pictures of the Other (i.e., minorities). Van Dijk discusses how crime, for example, is exaggerated as "extremely high rates of criminal activities," and "most serious pathology," where the hyperbolic superlative "most serious" modifies the hyperbolic metaphor "pathology" to seriously condemn minorities (Van Dijk 1996). He also discusses their role in stereotyping and overgeneralization, so that "all are alike" and "everyone dresses alike."

Additionally, hyperbolic language is quite common in a number of other genres like popular art, literature, and fairy tales. It is also characteristic of cartoons, jokes, and caricature in general, as it relies on exaggeration of certain elements rather than others. The distribution of hyperbolic language is also said to correlate with speaker gender. Female speech is said to be characterized by exaggeration to intensify interest and rapport. Lakoff (1975:56) claims that women "speak in italics" by using emphatic particles to assert their views with certainty and confidence (cited in Holmes 1990). However, such claims have not been proved empirically.

The genre that makes least use of hyperbolic language is academic discourse. According to Holmes (1984), academics are among the greatest attenuators in any speech community. Academic writing usually resorts to "hedges," i.e., rhetorical devices that project modesty, cautiousness, and diffuseness. They are also used for "diplomatically creating research space in areas heavily populated by other researchers" (Swales 1990:174–75).

Pedagogical Implications

It has been shown how certain genres make use of hyperbolic expressions while others avoid them altogether. Rather than being used for deception, hyperbolic language is mainly used in everyday life for face-supporting and face-threatening acts, and therefore should not be avoided in foreign language teaching. What needs to be addressed and taught is how and when to use it. Foreign-language learners face two problems due to pragmatic transfer: learners do not know what expressions to use, and when to use them (e.g., conversation versus essays and reports).

To avoid pragmatic errors speakers of Arabic make when using hyperbolic expressions in English, it is advisable that teachers include the pragmatic aspects of language use in language teaching, one of them being the use of hyperbolic expressions. In other words, teaching should address the appropriate idiomatic hyperbolic expressions in the target language, as the specific formulas have been shown to vary from one language to another in spite of their being a language universal. Students should learn cultural equivalents to the hyperbolic idioms they use in Arabic.

In addition to teaching the language-specific hyperbolic formulas, the distribution of their occurrence should also be addressed so that learners can use them effectively in English. Hyperbolic expressions should be taught in terms of their function and distribution. This seems to contrast with the traditional approach to teaching hyperbolic language in Arabic, which involves looking at its beauty (in studying Arabic literature), hyperbole being regarded as indicative of a highly literate style, without considering other justifications or motivations for its use. Teachers can start teaching recognition of hyperboles by having students read Arabic and English texts and identify hyperboles and their functions or translate them into literal counterparts (i.e., pragmatic paraphrase). Then teachers can proceed to teaching production of hyperbolic language by giving blanket statements for learners to complete with a hyperbole, or asking them to rewrite a short story with a character who uses hyperbole constantly.

Future research can look into frequency of use of hyperbolic expressions in different languages as well as their production by foreign language learners. It could also look into different genres cross-linguistically to point out further areas of similarity and difference in order to avoid stereotyping languages vis-a-vis the use of hyperbolic expressions.

References

Anonymous 1. n.d. http://www.alaskool.org/language/central_yupik/yupik.html

Anonymous 2. n.d. http://www-ditl.unilim.fr/ART/hyperbole.htm

Baiyi, Liu and Xiao Aili. 1995. "On the Causal Mechanism of Hyperbole." *Forum* 33/3, 16–22.

Brown, Penelope and Stephen Levinson. 1987. *Politeness: Some Universals in Language Usage*. Cambridge: Cambridge University Press.

Celce-Murcia, Marianne and Diane Larsen-Freeman. 1983. *The Grammar Book: An ESL/ EFL Teacher's Course*. Rowley, MA: Newbury House.

Chafe, Wallace. 1982. "Integration and Involvement in Speaking, Writing and Oral Literature," in Deborah Tannen (ed.) *Spoken and Written Language*. Norwood, N.J.: Ablex, 35–53.

Coates, Jennifer. 1996. *Women Talk*. Oxford: Blackwell, chapter 7.

Cohen, R. 1987. "Problems of Intercultural Communication in Egyptian-American Diplomatic Relations." *International Journal of Intercultural Relations* 11, 29–47.

Colston, Herbert and Shauna Keller. 1998. "You'll Never Believe This: Irony and Hyperbole in Expressing Surprise." *Journal of Psycholinguistic Research* 27/4, 499–513.

Connor, Ulla. 1996. *Contrastive Rhetoric*. Cambridge: Cambridge University Press.

Cuddon, J.A. 1991. *The Penguin Dictionary of Literary Terms and Literary Theory*. London: Penguin.

Culpeper, Jonathan. 1996. "Towards an Anatomy of Impoliteness." *Journal of Pragmatics* 25, 349–367.

Edelmann, R., J. Asendorpf, A. Contarello, V. Zammuner, J. Georgas, and C. Villanueva. 1989. "Self-reported Expression of Embarrassment in Five European Cultures." *Journal of Cross-Cultural Psychology* 20/4, 357–371.

Grice, H.P. 1975. "Logic and Conversation" in Cole, P. and J.L. Morgan (eds.) *Syntax and Semantics: 3. Speech Acts*. New York: Academic Press, 41–58

Hatch, Evelyn. 1992. *Discourse and Language Education*. Cambridge: Cambridge University Press.

Holmes, Janet. 1984. "Modifying Illocutionary Force." *Journal of Pragmatics* 8, 345–365.

———. 1990. "Hedges and Boosters in Women's and Men's Speech." *Language and Communication* 10/3, 185–205.

House, J. and G. Kasper. 1981. "Politeness Markers in English and German," in Coulmas, F. (ed.) *Conversational Routine*. The Hague: Mouton de Gruyter.

Ibrahim, Zeinab, and Deborah Kennedy. 1996. "Figurative Language in the Speech Patterns of Egyptians and Americans," in Elgibali, Alaa (ed.) *Understanding Arabic*. Cairo: The American University in Cairo Press, 181–209.

Johnstone, Barbara. 1991. "*Repetition in Arabic Discourse*." Amsterdam: John Benjamins.

Kaplan, Robert. 1966. "Cultural Thought Patterns in Inter-cultural Education." *Language Learning* 16/1: 1–20.

Kreuz, R., M. Kassler and L. Coppenrath. 1998. "The Use of Exaggeration in Discourse: Cognitive and Social Facets," in Fussell, S. and R. Kreuz (eds.) 1998. *Social and Cognitive Approaches to Interpersonal Communication*. Mahwah, N.J.: Lawrence Erlbaum Associates, 91–111.

Kreuz, R. and R.M. Roberts. 1995. "Two Cues for Verbal Irony: Hyperbole and the Ironic Tone of Voice." *Metaphor and Symbolic Activity* 10, 21–31. (http://citd. scar.utoronto.ca/Metaphor/10.1.21.html)

Lakoff, Robin. 1975. *Language and Woman's Place*. New York: Harper and Row.

Leech, Geoffrey. 1969. *A Linguistic Guide to English Poetry*. London: Longman.

Leech, Geoffrey. 1983. *Principles of Pragmatics*. London: Longman.

McQuarrie, Edward and David Mick. 1996. *Figures of Rhetoric in Advertising English*. (http://www.ouc.bc.ca/fina/glossary/l_list.html).

Osteen, Mark. 1995. The Economy of Ulysses: Making Ends Meet. Syracuse: Syracuse University Press. Cited in http://www.english.moe.edu.tw/Literary/Local/Conference/sota-cheng.htm

Palmer, F.R. 1986. *Mood and Modality*. Cambridge: Cambridge University Press.

Patei, Raphael. 1973. *The Arab Mind*. New York: Charles Scribner's Sons.

Pope, Alexander. 1951. *Epistles to Several Persons*, ed. F.W. Bateson. London: Methuen.

Prothro, E.T. 1955. "Arab-American Differences in the Judgment of Written Messages." *Journal of Social Psychology* 42, 704–714.

Riley, S. 1977. "Rhetorical Devices Help Ad Students Develop Copy Style." *Journalism Educator* 31/4, 24–26.

Schank, R. and R. Abelson. 1977. *Scripts, Plans, Goals, and Understanding*. Hillsdale, N.J.: Lawrence Erlbaum Associates.

Shakespeare, William. 1965. *Henry IV Part I*. Ed. J. Colmer and D. Colmer. London: Longman.

Shouby, E. 1951. "The Influence of the Arabic Language on the Psychology of the Arabs." *The Middle East Journal* 5/3, 284–302.

Sperber, D. and C. Wilson. 1986. *Relevance: Communication and Cognition*. Oxford: Blackwell.

Swales, John. 1990. *Genre Analysis: English in Academic and Research Settings*. Cambridge: Cambridge University Press.

Van Dijk, Teun. 1996. *Critical Discourse Analysis*. (http://www.hum.uva.ni/~teun/cda.htm).

Hedging in Arabic

A Pragma-syntactic Perspective

Nahwat A. El-Arousy

This study focuses on hedging as a speech strategy in spoken and written Cairene Arabic in contrast with English.* "Hedging" is a general term used to describe the strategy when a speaker or a hearer wishes to avoid coming straight to the point or to avoid speaking directly (Fraser 1975; Carter and McCarthy 1997). For example, "She was *sort of/somewhat* mixed up in her feelings about him." The hedges (in italics) allow speakers to personalize or otherwise soften the force of what they say. In most cases there is sensitivity to "face," either for purposes of self-protection or because the speaker does not want to put the listener or reader in a face-threatening situation (Brown and Levinson 1987).

Hedging includes the use of a wide range of language, such as "vague language," (Channel 1994). Vague expressions are common when factual information is given and approximations are common with times, dates, and figures (e.g., "They're coming in six weeks *or so*"). Vague expressions such as "sort of" and "kind of" also serve to allow the speakers not to commit themselves completely to the truth-value of a proposition.

Hedges and modality in language are closely linked. Many modal verbs contribute to hedging (e.g., may, might, could), and there is an extensive range of adverbs that mitigate the force of what is written or said, for example, "perhaps, probably, generally, slightly," etc.

The two varieties of Arabic under investigation are Modern Standard Arabic (MSA), a high variety that is used for most written and formal spoken purposes, and Egyptian Colloquial Arabic (ECA), a low variety that is used in everyday conversation (Ferguson 1972).

---

*   A shorter version of this paper was presented at the Second International Conference on Contrastive Rhetoric, March, 2001, at the American University in Cairo.

The study attempts to answer the following questions:
- What are the words and expressions that count as hedges in Arabic?
- What are the grammatical and pragmatic functions of hedges in Arabic?
- How do hearers and readers understand and decode hedging?

Literature Review

Hedging and Pragmatics

Tannen (1993:43) claims that there are numerous words and phrases that may be classed as hedges or hedge-like. By qualifying and modifying a word or phrase, hedges measure the word or idea against what is expected. They caution "not so much as you might have expected," and include such expressions as "really," and "anyway." She adds that "to consider all hedges would be a 'mammoth' study in itself." In most cases, it is a strategy that correlates with pragmatics.

Grice's theory of "implicature" (1975) assumes that conversation is a cooperative venture and that speakers adhere to what he calls Cooperative Principles (CP). The CPs involve both parties knowing and using four rules for conversation, which Grice calls maxims. They are as follows:

1. The maxim of Quality [be truthful according to the evidence you have]
2. The maxim of Quantity [be informative but not over informative]
3. The maxim of Relevance [be relevant to the conversation]
4. The maxim of Manner [say things clearly, unambiguously, briefly]

One way in which the maxims are relevant to hedging is that hedging may be used to enable speakers to follow the maxims; for example, in the utterance "As far as I know, they're married," the speaker is not certain about the accuracy of the statement. Cautious notes or hedges of this type can also be used to show that the speaker is conscious of the quantity maxim (Yule 1996:38).

The other way in which the CPs are of interest for the study of hedging may be observed when one of the maxims is flouted. When flouting occurs, specific effects, called "implicatures" (Grice 1975) are created. The flouting of a maxim occurs for example when an individual tries to deflect unwelcome attention by giving an improbable or obviously untrue response. For instance, if someone asks a woman her name and she doesn't want to give it, she might say: "I'm the Queen of Sheba" (Thomas 1995:68).

Another important area of pragmatics is within the theory of scalar implicatures (Yule 1996:41). These are created by the choice of one member from a set of related linguistic items, where the choice implies further meanings than are encoded. For example, consider the set *always, often, sometimes*. "I often get home late" implicates that I do not always get home late (otherwise I would have said so), but entails that I sometimes do, because often is more frequent than sometimes. Scalar implicatures, as Channel (1994:33–34) claims, are important features of hedging. On the lexico-grammatical level, hedging is relevant to the use of vague expressions and modality, as the following sections indicate.

Hedging and Vague Expressions

Vague expressions, as Carter and McCarthy claim (1997:19), are more extensive in all language use than is commonly thought and they are especially prevalent in spoken discourse. When we interact with each other, there are times when it is necessary to give exact and precise information (for example, concerning departure times of trains), but there are occasions where it would not be appropriate to be precise as it can sound unduly authoritative and assertive. In most informal contexts, most speakers prefer to convey information that is softened in some way by vague language, although such vagueness is often wrongly taken as a sign of careless or sloppy thinking (Channel 1994:1; Carter and McCarthy 1997:19).

Examples of vague language in English include phrases such as "or something," "or anything," "whatever," all usually in clause-final position, e.g., "Can you get me a sandwich or something?" "Have they got mineral water or anything like that?" In Arabic, examples of vague expressions include phrases such as: /ʔajj ħaːga/, or /mahma kaːnit izˌ-zˌuruːf/, as in the following examples: /maʕandakʃ ʔajj ħaːga tittaːkil/ ("Don't you have anything to eat?"), or /laːzim tiːgi mahma kaːnit izˌ-zˌuruːf/ ("You should come whatever the circumstances ").

Channel (1994:19–20) gives a working definition of vague language. She states that an expression or a word is vague if:

a) It can be contrasted with another word or expression that appears to render the same proposition;

b) It is purposely and unabashedly vague;

c) Its meaning arises from the "intrinsic uncertainty" referred to by Pierce (1902:748); i.e., uncertain because the speaker's habits of language are indeterminate.

Since the present study is concerned with modality in Arabic and English, it seems appropriate to summarize the main constituents of the verb phrase (VP) in Arabic and at the same time to introduce some terms that might be unfamiliar to some readers.

The Verb Phrase in Arabic

The sentence in Arabic, as in English, consists of a noun phrase and a verb phrase (VP). The principal constituents of the VP as stated in Mitchell and Al-Hassan (1994), Abd-el-Latif (1996), and Benmamoun (2000) are the following:

The only essential constituents of the VP are "verbs proper." So-called "verbless sentences" are regarded as containing a "deleted" copula and are not, therefore, exceptional. The VP may contain more than one verb. In a sentence such as the ECA utterance /bijħa:wil jittiṣil bi:na/ ("He is try-ing to contact us"), the second verb /jittiṣil/ and following elements are regarded as "embedded" sentences and the preceding verb as the matrix. Embedded sentences are often introduced (as complements) by the com-plementizer /ʔinn/ as in the ECA /xa:fit ʔinnu jiktiʃif ʔis-sirr/ ("She was afraid that he might discover the secret").

Second, verbal particles, such as /qad/ are exclusively associated with verbs, as in the MSA sentence /qad nagaħat kull ʔal-ʕamalijja:t/ ("All the operations have been successful"). Verbal particles include the modal and aspectual particles as well as negative particles such as ECA /miʃ/ and MSA /la:/, /lam/, and /lan/. Particles of command and request like /jalla/ as in the ECA /jalla nru:ħ/ ("Let's go") also belong here.

Third, preverbal elements are illustrated by the modal elements /laaz-im/, /ʕa:jiz/, etc. as in /la:zim ʔaru:ħ lil-dukto:r/ ("I must go to see the doctor"). Preverbal elements precede any verbal particles and the most frequent of them are participial or nominal in form.

Fourth are the complements of verbs, which are of several kinds and include, for example, predicative complements in sentences containing copular verbs (so that the predicative adjective /ʕatʃa:n/ is complemen-tary in the ECA /ʔil-kalb ka:n ʕatʃa:n/ ["The dog was thirsty"]) and object complements like the direct object in MSA /ʔal-ba:b/ in /fataħ ʔal-ba:b/ ("He opened the door"). The complement may be an embedded sentence, e.g. MSA /ʔaṭ-ṭaqṣ taɣajjar/ as part of /la:ħaẓtu ʔanna ʔaṭ-ṭaqṣ taɣajjar/ ("I noticed that the weather had changed"). Other sentences of this kind may occur as subjects included in matrix sentences as in the ECA /jisʕidni ʔinni baʃtaɣal maʕa:ki/ ("It pleases me that I am working with you"). With the sensory verb /simiʕ/, /jismaʕ/ ("to hear"), and others of the same type, /ʔinna/ marks "hearsay" in contrast to direct aural perception, but the sentence remainders after /simiʕt/ are both object complements in e.g. /simiʕtu bij mʃi/ ("I heard him walking along") and /simiʕt ʔinnu sa:fir/ ("I heard he had gone away"). Moreover, it is possible to base a classification of verbs (intransitive, copular, mono-transitive, di-transi-tive, catenative, etc.) on the forms of their appropriate complementation, though a classification will not be attempted here.

Fifth are the adjunct complements, which should be distinguished from adjuncts. Adjuncts are an adverbial subclass that can be omitted without prejudice to the completeness of the sentence (Mitchell and Al-Hassan 1994:5). Adjunct complements, on the other hand, cannot be omitted because they have an important function in the clause. The direct object /ʔal-baːb/ in the earlier /fataħ ʔal-baːb/ ("He opened the door") and the reciprocal /baʕd/ in /ʔiʃ-ʃahhatiːn bijikrahu baʕd/ ("Beggars hate one another") are both complements and cannot be omitted, or the sentence will be incomprehensible. Adjuncts, unlike complements, often correspond to the traditional adverbial division of time, place, manner, purpose, and cause, as well as to other modal forms, as the following section indicates.

Hedging and Modality

"Modality," closely linked to hedging, is a term used in grammatical and semantic analysis to refer to contrasts in meaning signaled mainly by verbs, but also by associated forms. The reference is basically to unrealized states or possible conditions of everyday situations. Modality covers verb phrases in English such as "must be," "could be," "ought to be," and "might have"; in ECA /laːzim jikuːn/, /jimkin jikuːn/, /mumkin jikuːn/; or in MSA /laː budda wa ʔan jakuːn/, /rubbamaː jakuːn/, /qad jakuːn/. Modality can also be signaled by modal adverbs in English such as "possibly," "probably, "presumably," "definitely," and "unfortunately." In MSA and ECA modality can also be signaled by modal adverbs such as /ṭabʕan/, /li-l-ʔasaf/, /muṭlaqan/, /muħtamal/ ("of course," "regretfully," "absolutely,"and "probably").

Modal forms are thus interpersonal aspects of grammar and are central to all spoken and written language use. Yet, in conversational discourse, they serve to work out personal relationships and to some extent to frame the nature of the interaction between speakers. In written discourse, on the other hand, they emphasize the writer–reader relationship and mitigate the force of the writer's propositions so that (s)he does not sound authoritative (Carter and McCarthy 1997:18).

According to Halliday (1994:68–99), modal adjuncts are important to "clause as exchange." They can be divided into two kinds, namely "comment adjuncts" and "mood adjuncts." Comment adjuncts (such as "unfortunately" in "Unfortunately, the doctor hasn't left a message") are relatively easy to identify as they are often separated by commas. A list of the different types of comment adjuncts is given in Halliday (1994:49). To this list the researcher has added MSA and ECA forms in Table 1. The researcher agrees with Abbas (1995:97) that there are common features to the two languages with regard to adverbials, which include optionality, mobility, and similarity in function. Therefore, adverbials in English and Arabic can be classified using the same categories.

Table 1: Comment adjuncts in English and Arabic

Types	Meaning	Examples in English	Examples in Arabic
Probability	How likely?	Probably, possibly, certainly, perhaps, may be...etc. (e.g., "Perhaps he went to see the doctor.")	/min ʔal-mustaṭaːʕ/; /ħatmijjan/; /qɑd jakuːn/; /rubbama/ (MSA); /jaguːz/;/jimkin/ (ECA) (e.g. /rubbama ðahaba lizijaːrɑti ʔaṭ-ṭabiːb/ MSA; or /jimkin raːħ lid-duktoːr/ (ECA)
Usuality	How often?	Usually, sometimes, always, (n)ever, often, seldom	/ʕaːdatan/; /ʔaħjaːnan/; /ʔabadan/; /muṭlaqɑn/; /ɣaːliban/; /naːdiran/; /daːʔiman/ (MSA and ECA)
Typicality	How typical?	Occasionally, generally, regularly, for the most part	/min ħiːn/; /waqt liʔaːxar/; /ɣaːliban ma/ (MSA) /ʕaːmmatan/; (MSA and ECA); /ʕumuːman/; /min waʔt litaːniː/ (ECA)
Obviousness	How obvious?	Of course, surely, obviously, clearly	/bil-ṭabʕ/; /bit-taʔkiːd/; /biwuḍuːħ/;/waːḍiħan/ /galijjan/ (MSA and ECA)
Opinion	I think	In my opinion, personally, to my mind	/fiː ʔal-ʔiʕtiqaːdi/; /ʃaxṣijjan/; /fiː raʔjiː/; /min wighati naẓariː/...etc. (MSA and ECA)
Admission	I admit	Frankly, to be honest, to tell you the truth	/biṣaraːħa/; /biʔamaːna/; /ħaqiqatan/; /fil-ħaqiːqa/ (MSA and ECA)
Persuasion	I assure you	Honestly, really, believe me, seriously	/biʔamaːna/; /bigadd/; /ṣaddiqni:/ (MSA and ECA)
Entreaty	I request you	Please, kindly	/biragaːʔ/; /min faḍlika/; /faḍlan/; /law samaħt/; /ragaːʔan/ (MSA and ECA)
Desirability	How desirable?	(Un)Fortunately, to my delight/ distress, regrettably, hopefully	/liħusn, lisuːʔ ʔal-ħaẓẓ/; /lifarṭ saʕaːdati/; /litaʕasaːti/; /lilʔasaf/; /bikul ʔasaf/; /ʕala ʔamal ʔan/; /ʔamalan ʔan/ (MSA and ECA)

Types	Meaning	Examples in English	Examples in Arabic
Reservation	How reliable?	At first, tentatively, provisionally, looking back on it	/liʔawwali wahla/; /ʔawwalan/; /taqri:ban/; /ʔiħtija:ṭijjan/; /maʕa ʔat-taħaffuz/; /biʔiʕa:dati ʔannaẓar fi:/ (MSA and ECA)
Validation	How valid?	Broadly speaking, in general, on the whole, strictly speaking, in principle	/biṣifa ʕa:mma/; /ʕa:mmatan/; /ʕalal-ʕumu:m/; /biʃakl muħaddad/; /mabdaʔijjan/ (MSA and ECA)
Evaluation	How sensible?	(Un)Wisely, understandably, mistakenly, foolishly	/bitaʕaqqul/; /bidu:n taʕaqqul/; /min ʔal-mafhu:m/; /min ʔal-xaṭaʔ/; /min ʔal-bala:ha/; /min ʔal-ʕabaθ/ (MSA and ECA)
Prediction	How expected?	To my surprise, surprisingly, as expected, by chance	/min ʔal-mudhiʃ/; /wa lidahʃati:/; /kama ka:na mutawaqqi:ʕan/; /biṣ-ṣudfa/; /muṣa:dafatan/ (MSA and ECA)

The second group of modal adjuncts are more difficult to identify, because most of them appear to be modifying the verb and may thus look like circumstantial adjuncts (Halliday 1994:83; Thompson 1996:54). However, they are in fact most closely related not to the predicator in the verbal group but to the finite: they express meanings associated with the mood and are called "mood adjuncts." As Halliday states, mood adjuncts are more grammatical than circumstantial adjuncts, although it is sometimes difficult to see the difference. To look at some clear examples, "already" is related to tense (e.g., "He has already left"), "yes" is related to polarity, and "maybe" is related to modality. Examples where the link with mood meanings is perhaps less obvious include "regularly" (related to temporal meanings) and "at all costs" (related to modal meanings of obligation). A list of the main items that function as mood adjuncts is given in Halliday (1994:82–83). In Table 2, forms of MSA and ECA mood adjuncts are added to the list given by Halliday.

Table 2: Mood adjuncts in English and Arabic

Types	Examples in English	Examples in Arabic
Adjuncts of polarity and modality	a - Polarity: not, yes, no, so	(a) /la:/; /lam/; /naʕam/; /wa ha:kaða:/ (MSA) /la/; /miʃ/; /ʔajwa/ ; /kida/ (ECA)
	b - Probability: proba-bly, possibly, certainly, perhaps, maybe	(b) /min ʔal-ga:ʔiz/ (MSA); /jagu:z/ (ECA); /min ʔal-muħtamal/; /ʔiħtima:lan/; /bil-taʔki:d/; /bil-qatʕ/; /qatʕijjan/; /rubbama:/; /qad jaku:n/ (MSA and ECA)
	c - Usuality: usually, sometimes, always, never, ever, seldom, rarely	(c) /ʕa:datan/; /ʔaħja:nan/; /da:ʔiman/; /ʔabadan/ /mutˤlaqan/; /na:diran/ (MSA and ECA); /qallama:/ (MSA)
	d - Readiness: witting-ly, readily, gladly	(d) /biriḍa:ʔ/; /binafs ra:ḍija/; /bikull suru:r/; /bitirħa:b/; /ʕala ʔistiʕda:d/ (MSA and ECA)
	e- Obligation: definitely, absolutely, possibly, at all costs, by all means	(e) /bit-taʔki:d/; /fi: gami:ʕ ʔal-ʔiħtima:la:t/; /biʃatta: ʔatˤ-tˤuruq/; /fi: gami:ʕ ʔal-ʔaħwa:l/ (MSA and ECA)
Adjuncts of tem-porality	f - Time: yet, still, already, once, soon, just	(f) /lajsa baʕd/; /maza:la/; /ða:t marra/; /fi: ʔat-taww/; /baʕd/ (as in /lam jaṣil baʕd/ ("He hasn't arrived yet")) [MSA]); /fi: ʔal-ħa:l/; /ha:lan/; /fiʕlan/; /bil-fiʕl/ (MSA and ECA); /lissa/; /xala:ṣ/ (ECA)
	g - Typicality: occa-sionally, generally, regularly, mainly, for the most part	(g) /min waʔt lit-ta:ni/ (ECA); /min hi:n liʔa:xar/ (MSA); /ʕumu:man/; /ʕalal-ʕumu:m/; /ʕa:datan/; /fil-ʕa:da/; /ʔasa:san/; /ɣa:liban/ (MSA and ECA)
Adjuncts of mood	h - Obviousness: of course, surely, obvi-ously, clearly	(h) /bil-tˤabʕ/; /bit-taʔki:d/; /biwuḍu:ħ/ (MSA and ECA)
	i - Intensity: just, sim-ply, merely, only, even, actually, really, in fact	(i) /faqatˤ/; /bibasa:tˤa/; /ħatta: law/; /fi:l-wa:qiʕ/; /ħaqqan/; / fi:l-ħaqi:qa/ (MSA and ECA)
	j - Degree: quite, almost, nearly, scarce-ly, hardly, absolutely, totally, utterly, entire-ly, completely	(j) /bil-ka:d/ (MSA); /tama:man/; /taqri:ban/; /na:diran/; /ka:milan/ (MSA and ECA); /bit-tama:m wal-kama:l/; /kullu(h)/ (ECA)

With many types of mood adjuncts, however, there is a strong counter-tendency to make them thematic, in which case they occur at the beginning of the clause before the topical theme, e.g., "usually" in ("Usually they don't open before ten"). In addition, they may also be added at the end of the clause as an afterthought. As Halliday claims (1994: 82), there are four possibilities:

- but usually they don't open before ten (thematic).
- but they usually don't open before ten (neutral).
- but they don't usually open before ten (neutral).
- but they don't open before ten usually (afterthought).

In a study that contrasts adverbial positions in English and Arabic, Abbas (1995:213) concludes that the two languages coincide remarkably in specifying normal positions for their adverbials in the sentence sequence. This highlights the distinction between normal usage and emphatic usage. He adds that the two languages view most adverbials as optional elements whose omission leaves no semantic or syntactic loss to the sentence. Yet a notable characteristic of Arabic is to license adverbial movement to sentence-final position by a perceptual preference for shifting "modifiers" to the end. At the same time, his study demonstrates that Arabic word order is, grammatically speaking, flexible enough to place the adverbial almost anywhere in the sentence, even between the two parts of a two-word verb, as in: /ʔiṭṭalaʕtu ʕal -l-kitaːb jawma ʔas-sabti/ ("I read the book on Saturday"), or /ʔiṭṭalaʕtu jawma ʔas-sabti ʕala-l-kitaːb/ (MSA).

Method

To study hedging in Arabic, however, it is necessary not only to draw on linguistic theories but also to follow a well-founded methodology. As it is impossible to study everything to the same depth, let us describe qualitatively some samples of hedging in MSA and CA, as used by educated native speakers of Arabic. In data collection, an attempt is made to minimize the variations arising from intervening elements.

Levels of Data Analysis

In approaching data analysis, the lexico-grammatical structure of the utterances/sentences is described for the purposes of theory-building and following the rules of grammar and lexical choice referred to above. In accounting for the linguistic behavior of the speakers and writers quoted in the study, it has been noted that their lexico-grammatical choices work together with the mechanisms of pragmatic rules. Data analysis, for this reason, will be done on the lexico-grammatical and pragmatic levels.

Data Collection

This study involves accounting for real occurrences of talk or writing, rather than accounting for invented decontextualized sentences. In addition, using authentic data has certain other advantages:

a) All utterances are attested as having been produced in non-experimental linguistic situations.

b) Examples drawn from real data can be seen in their linguistic context.

c) Real data reveal many features of language that do not arise from introspection.

Types of Data Used

Two types of data are found in this study:

a) Attested conversation examples. These are mainly MSA and ECA data. Many of these examples were observed and noted down when the researcher heard them, but were not tape-recorded.

b) Attested written examples. These are also MSA and ECA data that were collected from a random selection of reading matter encountered in newspapers and magazines. The main focus will be, thus, on Arabic data, as English, unlike Arabic, has been extensively studied in the literature. However, in another study by the present researcher (El-Arousy 2003), boosters, the counterparts of hedges, are contrasted in Arabic and English samples. Unlike hedges, boosters intensify rather than soften the force of an utterance.

Discussion

In this section the structure of the hedging adjunct is analyzed and discussed first on the lexico-grammatical then on the pragmatic level.

The Structure of the Hedging Adjunct in Arabic

Data analysis on the syntactic level indicates that hedges could occur as a comment adjunct at the beginning of a sentence/utterance and/or in the context of a complement or a modal adjunct in the verb phrase that is sometimes thematized (i.e., put at the beginning of the sentence) for emphasis.

Table 3: The structure of the hedging adjunct in MSA

Samples of MSA	Type	Structure
1–(a) /bi ʔama:na wa ʔiħqa:qan lil-ħaqq/ (b) /lam jakun huwa/ (c) /ʔas-sabab fi: xalq ʔal-muʃkila/. ("Honestly speaking and to tell the truth, he was not the cause of the problem").	Factive	1–(a) Two comment adjuncts of admission; (b) an adjunct of polarity and modality that consists of a negative particle + a copular; (c) a predicative complement.
2–(a) /ʔaʕtaqid ʔannahu min ʔal-ħikm ti ʔan nuʕa:lig ʔal-muʃkil / (b) /bihudu:ʔ wa taʕaqqul/ ("I think it's wise to deal with the problem quietly and reasonably").	Non-factive	2–a) A comment adjunct of evaluation which includes a catenative mental verb ʔaʕtaqid ʔannahu/ ; (b) adjuncts of mood and degree preceded with a proclitic /bi/ (i.e. "with") which has a prepositional function.
3–(a) /kunt ʔatamanna ʔan tangaħ mufa:waḍa:t ʔas-sala:m/ (b) /lakinnaha li-l-ʔasaf wa kama ka:na mutawaqqaʕa faʃalat/ (c) /li-l-marrati ʔal-milju:n/ ("I hoped for the peace negotiations to succeed, but regrettably, and as was expected, they failed for the millionth time").	Contra-factive	3–(a) A comment adjunct of desirability preceded with a past tense copular form and followed by a catenative verb /ʔan tangaħ/; (b) comment adjuncts of desirability + prediction; (c) a hyperbolic adverbial adjunct.
4–(a) /hayha:ta ʔan jaṣil/ (b) /ʔaħad ʔila: maka:nati nagi:b maħfu:z fi:-l-ʔadab/ ("It's far fetched to suppose that someone could reach Naguib Mahfouz's standard of proficiency in literature").		4–(a) An adjunct of polarity and modality which includes a hyperbolic expression of impossibility and a catenative verb + a preposition /ʔan jaṣil ʔila:/; (b) a predicative complement.

Table 4. The structure of the hedging adjunct in ECA

Samples of ECA	Type	Structure
5-(a) /ʔuʔakkid lak ʔannu/ (b) /hatta law ʔintabʔit is-sama ʕala-l-ʔarḍ/ (c) /miʃ hajwa:fiʔ/ ("I assure you that no matter what happens, he will not accept." [Literally, "If the sky meets the earth, he will never accept"]).	Factive	5-(a) A performative verb in the context of an adjunct of polarity and modality + a catenative verb joined with the pronoun particle /h/ representing /huwa/in Arabic and "he" in English;(b) a hyperbolic expression of impossibility and polarity expressed by the negative particle (miʃ) and the proclitic /ha/, which expresses future tense.
6-(a) /ʔana ʕumri ma ʃuft/ (b) /ʔil-marhu:m bass smiʕt ʕannu kti:r/ ("I never saw the deceased but I have heard a lot about him").	Factive	6-(a) An adjunct of modality and temporality expressed by using the hyperbolic expression /ʔana ʕumri/, which means (I have never in my life) and includes the CA negative particle /ma/; (b) a euphemistic expression which means the dead person + an adjunct of temporality followed by another of degree.

Hedges, as exemplified in Tables 3 and 4, enable the speaker/writer to admit (cf. 1), evaluate (cf. 2), desire, predict (cf. 3) exaggerate (cf. use of hyperbolic expressions in 3, 4, and 5), and soften (cf. use of a euphemistic expression in 5). In addition, hedges enable speakers and writers of MSA and ECA to express different degrees of mood, namely polarity and modality (cf. 1–5). Hedges thus enrich the meaning of propositions by making them multi-functional and multi-layered in contrast with the linear meaning of a proposition such as /sa:fara bi-l-ʔamsi/ ("He traveled yesterday"). The following three samples of written MSA (two extracted from a newspaper, the third from a magazine) indicate the rhetorical function of hedging.

(1) (a) /law ka:na ʕa:m ʔalfajn ʔallaði: juwaddiʕuna ṣa:mitan ʔal-jawm huwa ʕa:m ʔal-ʔahla:m ʔal-ḍa:ʔiʕa fi:-l-rija:ḍati ʔal-miṣrijja wa ʕa:m ʔal-hudu:ʔ wal-ruku:d fi:-l-rija:ḍati ʔal-mayribijja fahuwa/ (b) /bila ʃakk ʕa:m ʔal-ʔahla:m ʔal-saʕi:da fi: haja:t ʔal-rija:ḍa ʔal-xali:gijja ʔallati: ʃa:hadat duxu:l ʔas-saʕu:dijja wa ʔal-kuwajt/ (c) /li-ʔawwali marra fi: ta:ri:xihima: sigill ʔal-midalja:t fi: dawrat ʔal-ʔalʕa:b ʔal-ʔu:lumbijja/ (*al-Ahram*, 31 December

2000) ("If the year 2000, which bids us farewell today, is the year of lost dreams for Egyptian sport and the year of quietness and stillness for Moroccan sport, it is, no doubt, the year of happy dreams in the life of Gulf sport, which witnessed the inclusion of Saudi Arabia and Kuwait for the first time in their history in the Olympic Games' record of medals.")

(2) (a)/ʔallaːhumma ʔigʕalhu ʕaːmin/ (b) /la baʔsa bihi/ (*Rose al-Yusuf*, January 2001) ("Please God make the year not bad! [i.e., better than expected]")

(3) (a)/ʕiːdun/ (b) /biʔajjati haːlin ʕudta/ (c) /ja ʕiːdu/ (*al-Ahram*, 5 March, 2001) ("Eid! In what [sorry] state do you return, Eid?")

Extract 1 begins with a hypothetical proposition (a) that consists of the Arabic particle /law/ plus the past tense copular form /kaːna/ ("if it was"), which is, seemingly, thematized to have the force of probability. The modality expressed in the proposition together with the metaphors of realized and unrealized dreams reflect a rhetorical device manipulated by the writer to express his point of view. In (b), on the other hand, the writer uses an adjunct of presumption that consists of the proclitic /bi/ ("with") and the particle of negation /la/ ("no") preceding the noun /ʃakk/ ("doubt"). This hedge, together with the temporality expressed in (c) /li-ʔawwali marra fi: taːriːxihima:/ ("for the first time in their history") apparently reflect the writer's reaction to the factuality of the proposition; namely, that both Saudi Arabia and Kuwait won medals in the 2000 Olympic games.

The underlined hedges in extracts 2 and 3, on the other hand, are more implicit. The entreaty expressed in 2(a) /ʔallaːhumma/ ("please God") and the vague expression in (b) /la baʔsa bihi/ ("that is not bad") contrast with the traditional expression /ʕaːm saʕiːd/ ("Happy New Year"). The modality used here reflects the writer's psychological stance. It seems that, in the writer's opinion, happiness is too much to hope for, and that all she wishes for is a year that is not bad.

Extract 3, likewise, reflects the writer's point of view. He is quoting a verse from a poem by the well-known Arab poet al-Mutanabbi to comment on the pathetic state of affairs in the Middle East at the present time, and on the occasion of Eid al-Adha. The term /ʕiːd/ in Arabic is usually used to mean a religious feast that is celebrated as a happy occasion. In 3(a) the term /ʕiːd/ is thematized and repeated in 3(c) at the end for further emphasis. By addressing the /ʕiːd/, the poet is thus metaphorically personalizing it. The /ʕiːd/ is reprimanded for returning once again at such a wretched time, for both the poet and the newspaper writer, who is commenting on Middle East affairs.

In the three extracts discussed above, hedges have a rhetorical function. Yet hedges also have a pragmatic function, as the following section illustrates.

The Pragmatic Function of Hedging

When we examine the MSA and ECA samples from the Grician theory perspective (see above), we note the following:

First, that the writers/speakers of these samples have followed the maxims of quality and relevance by being truthful in expressing their points of view, attitudes, and feelings in the context of their propositions.

Second, the maxim of quantity has been violated, because although the use of hedges makes the propositions more meaningful and multifunctional (see Tables 3 and 4), they become over-informative.

Third, on the other hand, the use of vague expressions in some samples (cf. the written samples of MSA in particular) makes the propositions less informative than is required, thus violating the maxim of manner.

Conclusion and Recommendations

The discussion of the findings above responds to the research questions set out at the beginning of this study. These are summarized in the following conclusions and recommendations:

First, hedging as a speech strategy involves the use of linguistic means to influence the attitudes and behaviors of listeners or readers. Readers and listeners, on the other hand, are capable of understanding and decoding hedges because of shared knowledge.

Second, on the grammatical level, hedging includes the speaker's or writer's modal means of indicating his or her own attitude or psychological stance toward a factive, non-factive, or a contra-factive proposition.

Third, by using hedges, speakers and writers of MSA and ECA are capable of expressing different degrees of modality, polarity, and temporality. Propositions enriched with hedges thus become more multifunctional and multilayered in meaning than propositions that are free from hedges and are linear in meaning. (These multifunctional hedges should be distinguished from the expressions used by speakers as fillers when stammering.)

Fourth, hedges are expressed either explicitly through the extensive use of modality, or implicitly and indirectly through the use of vague expressions. In both cases, hedges could have rhetorical functions in the spoken and written forms of the language. Sometimes they are thematized for further emphasis.

Fifth, examining hedging as pragmatic behavior from the Grician theory perspective supports the findings stated in the previous section. This study has focused on the multiple functions of hedges. Further research needs to be done employing other types of data and other genres to uncover other functions not dealt with in here. Further research also needs to be done to contrast the types of hedges dealt with in this research, including sounds that are used as fillers when stammering or searching for the right word.

References

Abbas, A.K. 1995. "Contrastive Analysis: Is It a Living Thing?" in *International Review of Applied Linguistics* XXXIII/3, August, 195–215.

Abd-el-Latif, M.H. 1996. *Bina' al-gumla al-'arabiya* Cairo: Dar al-Shuruq

El-Arousy, N. 1998. "The Structural Markedness of Speech Acts in Affectively Charged Citations," in *Philology* XXX, Literature and Linguistic Series, Ain Shams University. Cairo: Al-Alsun Press, 151–240.

Benmamoun, E. 2000. *The Feature Structure of Functional Categories: A Comparative Study of Arabic Dialects.* Oxford: Oxford University Press.

Brown, P. and Levinson, S.C. 1987. *Politeness: Some Universals in Language Usage.* Cambridge: Cambridge University Press.

Carter, R. and McCarthy, M. 1997. *Exploring Spoken English.* Cambridge: Cambridge University Press.

Channel, J. 1994. *Vague Language.* Oxford: Oxford University Press.

——. 2003. "Boosters in Arabic and English." *Egypt TESOL Journal.*

Ferguson, C.A. 1971. "Diglossia," in *Language Structure and Language Use: Essays by Charles Ferguson.* Stanford: Stanford University Press, 325–40.

Fraser, B. 1975. "Hedged Performative," in Cole P. and Morgan J.L. (eds.) *Syntax and Semantics 3: Speech Acts.* New York: Academic Press.

Grice, H.P. 1975. "Logic and Conversation," in Cole P. and Morgan J.L. (eds.) *Syntax and Semantics 3: Speech Acts.* New York: Academic Press, 113–127.

Halliday, M.K.M. 1994. *An Introduction to Functional Grammar* (2nd edition). London: Edward Arnold.

Lyons, J. 1971. *Semantics 2.* Cambridge: Cambridge University Press.

Mitchell, T.F. and Al-Hassan, S.A. 1994. *Modality, Mood and Aspect in Spoken Arabic, with Special Reference to Egypt and the Levant.* London and New York: Kegan Paul International.

Pierce, C. S. 1902. "Vagueness," in Baldwin, M. (ed.) *Dictionary of Philosophy and Psychology II.* London: Macmillan.

Shalaby, A.I. (ed.) 1996. *Ma'ani al-huruf.* By Abu al-Hasan ibn 'Isa al-Rumani. Cairo: Dar Nahdat Misr

Tannen, D. 1993. *Framing in Discourse*. Oxford: Oxford University Press.

Thomas, J. 1995. *Meaning in Interaction: An Introduction to Pragmatics*. London: Longman.

Thompson, G. 1996. *Introducing Functional Grammar*. London: Arnold.

Yule, G. 1996. *Pragmatics: Introduction to Language Study*. Oxford: Oxford University Press.